FROM ANTIQUITY TO ETERNITY

TO ETERNITY

The Lord God Reigns

by Velda Stearns

PERMISSION TO QUOTE

FOREWORD

For most of her life Velda Stearns has searched for truth. In her latest book, *From Antiquity to Eternity,* she has laid out a path for us to follow that puts the pieces of biblical history together in an intriguing, comprehensive manner, making the past come alive and shining a light on the future.

She chronicles the covenants God made with man, and the men He chose to covenant with. As we follow man's search for meaning and the consequences, good or bad, we see the results by the response to God's direction. We see the strengths and weaknesses of the men God chose to reveal himself to. Flaws and all, God used men and women who sought him—not always the strongest, the bravest, or the smartest, but those who longed to have a relationship with Him.

The pages of her book are laced with hope and encouragement. Even though we are surrounded by wickedness, we can see into the future through God's Word and know that our redemption lies just over the horizon with Jesus' return.

From Genesis to Revelation, Mrs. Stearns shares obscure parts of history that connect events leading us to the glorious culmination at the end of the age. Weaving past events with things making new headlines today, she lets us see the panorama of God's plan from beginning to end for his people on Planet Earth.

You will come away with a sense of hope, and that current events are simply stepping stones in the Hands of a Master Planner.

Jan Brand – Arlington, Texas

VELDA STEARNS' TESTIMONY

I accepted Christ at an early age and developed a love for God's Word, reading the entire Bible at the age of twelve. I graduated from high school at the age of sixteen and college at the age of twenty.

I met Bob Stearns while teaching High School. We fell in love and were married. Bob wanted four children as quickly as we could have them. Keith, our first son was born in the first year of our marriage. David, our second son, was born two years later, followed by Michelle and Angela.

After Bob graduated from Oklahoma City University, he went to work for Shell Oil Company. We were transferred to Denver, Colorado and a year later to Glendive, Montana. What a shock for a southern girl! It got down to 50 degrees below zero that winter.

One night while I was reading my Bible, God's presence came into my room stronger than I had ever felt Him before. He told me two words, "TRUST ME". Instead of trusting Him, I was extremely afraid. I thought something terrible was going to happen.

A few weeks later on spring break we went to see our parents in Oklahoma. I started experiencing numbness in my feet. When the numbness increased and got to my waist. I had a great deal of pain in my head and spine and extreme vertigo. My eyesight and hearing were also affected. I was numb from my waist down.

As I lay in bed at my mother's house, I felt extremely loved that God would tell me in advance to trust Him. I dedicated my life to God anew and told Him, He could use my life in any way He desired. Within a few weeks, my health improved and I was able to care for our children again.

We were transferred back to Denver and lived there for three years and were transferred to New Orleans. God gave me a scripture as we planned to move. *"Those who trust in the Lord are as strong as Mount Zion, unmoved by any circumstance."*

After the transfer, I was extremely fatigued. My feet started getting numb again and I was cold all the time. Three years before this, I had a similar experience. I was referred me to a team of neurologists at Oschner's Clinic in New Orleans, a hospital comparable to the Mayo Clinic. They confirmed that I had every symptom of Multiple Sclerosis. They sent me home with pain pills and valium to help with the muscle spasms. When the doctors informed me of my situation, I was terribly afraid.

Numbness started in my toes and each day the numbness extended a few inches up my body until I was numb from my breast down. At that time my body was racked with pain, headaches were a terrible ordeal. I had difficulty walking. My vision and hearing were greatly affected. Muscle spasms were so bad, I could only sleep for a short period of time and awake with another muscle spasm jerking my body. Daily the symptoms of the disease grew stronger as the numbness increased and extended to a greater part of my body. Fatigue was so great; I spent my days in bed. I was in my early thirties at this time. Our four children were between four and nine years old.

Bob spent much time in prayer, seeking an answer. He felt that God said; "Everything is going to be okay." I was shocked to see his great faith. When people visited our home, Bob kept praising God for His goodness to us.

I lay in bed reading God's Word, hour after hour, too weak to hold the Bible in my hands. I saturated myself in God's Word, daily crying out for strength. The Psalms were a great comfort. *You are my refuge and my shield and your promises are my only source of hope.*

Oh the horror of being told by your doctor, "You have Multiple Sclerosis". Oh the horror of seemingly unceasing pain. Oh the horror of seeing my physical body grows weaker and weaker until I could barely walk. But, oh the joy of knowing my sins are forgiven! Oh, the joy of knowing I am right with God! Oh, the strength that comes from God's promise that all things work together for good to those that love the Lord! While I was sick, I wrote this poem and taped it on my mirror.

All our testing has a purpose; someday we will see the light,
All He asks is that we trust Him, Walk by faith and not by sight.
Do not fear when doubt besets you; Just remember He is near.
He will never, never leave you, He will always, always hear.

For several weeks the attack grew steadily worse. I called my pastor in Denver. While he was praying, it seemed as if a person walked in the room and applied pressure to my spine, once, twice, three times. God's presence filled my heart with joy and peace.

The next morning I was delighted to find that the numbness had started going away. I praised God that He touched my body! Even though God touched me, but there were still other symptoms of MS. Many nights I lay awake with headaches and muscle spasms. One night I was fearful of another attack, because the numbness was extending into my shoulders.

When I opened the Bible, the first verse I read was underlined. It said: *"Christ took upon Himself all our diseases and our illnesses."* I placed my finger in the Bible and changed positions. When I reopened my Bible, I was shocked to see that my Bible was turned to a different page that said, *"Daughter, be of good cheer, your faith has made you whole".*

Trembling with excitement, I believed that God was speaking directly to me. God's presence filled the room. His joy and peace filled my heart to overflowing. That night all fear left! I had great peace--and much more--for God had given me the assurance that He would heal my body.

Daily I thanked God that He was my healer, in spite of the symptoms of the disease. Every morning I said: *"Thank you Lord that you are the God that heals me."* My body was still very weak. I could only get out of bed for a few minutes, just long enough to wash a load of clothes or clean off the table. Then I would go back to bed to rest for several hours. This became my routine. In spite of the weakness and symptoms, I continued to thank God that He was my healer.

Gradually the symptoms of M.S. went away. Six months later, I was able to stay up all day for the first time. The one symptom that remained was fatigue. When we first moved to Texas, I spent a day a week in bed, resting and reading God's Word. This not only refreshed me physically, but spiritually as well. It has been thirty years since I had the last attack of MS.

I pray you are richly blessed as you read *From Antiquity to Eternity*.

Velda Stearns

ACKNOWLEDGEMENTS

From Antiquity to Eternity is dedicated to the Ladies Life Group at Gateway Church in Southlake, Texas who supported me as I taught the significance of prophecies in God's Word. I want to thank my husband, Robert, who allowed me to spend countless hours in research. I also want to give credit to Jan Brand, editor and my son, Keith Stearns who helped edit. I want to thank my son-in-law Russell Pond who self published the book. I pray you will be greatly blessed as you study the prophecies in God Word.

ENDORSEMENTS

I have been attending the Gateway ladies group led by Velda for four years. I have learned much about Israel past, present, and future while sitting at the feet of this gifted teacher. Her book is the story of promises fulfilled and prophecies yet to be fully accomplished. It is such a blessing to follow the thread of God's love and His recorded interventions on behalf of His beloved creation from Antiquity to Eternity. ~ **Deborah Farmer**

I am honored to endorse the book *From Antiquity to Eternity*". Velda is an excellent teacher and writer. Her book is full of knowledge of the prophecies in God's Word. God is still in control in the midst of end time events unfolding around us. So rejoice in her book of golden nuggets, you won't be disappointed. Jesus is coming soon. ~ **Paula Geyer**

I have sat under Velda's teachings for seven years and have been impressed with her research. She has been diligent to find the truth and put it forth in writing. ~ Loiese Bryan

Velda has done an excellent job of detailing proof from God's Word that Jehovah is in control. This is a good read of prophecies that will occur in the future. ~ **June Coburn**

Velda has vision, insight and information that will educate all who are hungry to know about prophecies in God's Word that will be fulfilled before the return of Yeshua, the Jewish Messiah. I consider it a privilege to sit under her teaching as she shares rich insights revealing how all people of the earth will be blessed through Israel (Genesis 12:3) - Honored to be her friend. ~ **Delma S. Hansen**

After years of intense research, Velda reveals in her book From Antiquity to Eternity the significance of the prophetic predictions in God's Word. Velda details how events predicted in the Old Testament, centuries before their appointed time, have been fulfilled in history with amazing accuracy showing Jehovah God has been in control from the beginning. ~**Nancy L.**

TABLE OF CONTENTS

> CHAPTER 1
PROPHECIES IN GENESIS

The Bible is full of breathtaking prophecies, like no other book in the world. Prophetic insights can be found in almost every book of the Bible, but searching the book of Genesis reveals mind-boggling prophecies that are still being fulfilled.

The first nine chapters of Genesis include the creation of the heavens and earth, the creation of Adam and Eve, as well as the animal kingdom. God blessed them and gave them dominion over the earth.

God's Command to Adam

"The Lord God took the man and put him in the Garden of Eden to work it and take care of it. The Lord God commanded the man, 'You are free to eat from any tree in the garden; but you must not eat from the tree of the knowledge of good and evil, for when you eat from it you will certainly die'" (Genesis 2:15–17 NIV).

Adam and Eve sinned when they ate the fruit of the forbidden tree and were banished from Eden. Their disobedience resulted in spiritual death—loss of fellowship with God—and later physical death. This was Satan's plan because his goal has always been to kill, steal and destroy.

God's Word to Adam and Eve

"To the woman he said, "I will greatly multiply your pain in childbirth, in pain you will bring forth children; yet your desire will be for your husband, and he will rule over you. Then to Adam He said, 'Because you have listened to the voice of your wife, and have eaten from the tree from which I commanded you, saying, 'You shall not eat from it'; Curse is the ground because of you; In toil you will eat of it all the days of your life. Both thorns and thistles it shall grow for you; by the sweat of your face you will eat bread, till you return to the ground, because from it you were then; for you are dust, and to dust you shall return"(Genesis 3:16-19 NASB).

God Placed a Curse on Satan

"I will cause hostility (hatred) between you and the woman, and between your offspring and her offspring. He will strike your head, and you will strike his heel" (Genesis 3:15 NLT).

This verse reveals a long, continuing struggle between the seed of the woman and the seed of the serpent. This struggle between good and evil began in the Garden of Eden.

Immediately after the temptation and fall of man, God placed a curse on the serpent, because he seduced Eve into eating the forbidden fruit. This scripture promised that the seed of the woman (Messiah) would someday crush Satan's head. The head represents authority or rule. This shows a picture of a man's heel on the head of a snake, grinding it into the ground.

Everywhere in the scriptures people are referred to as having come from a man. Only Christ is the seed of a woman, and the seed of the woman will "bruise your head, and you shall bruise his heel." This means that Satan was going to bruise the heel of Christ, bringing about His death on the cross. But He (Christ) would rise and totally destroy Satan. This is the first Gospel.[1]

The serpent was told that his seed would bruise the Seed of the woman. The bruised heel implies the long struggle between good and evil. The serpent wounds the heel that crushes his head. A bruised or crushed heel can be healed but a crushed head leads to death.

The serpent of old was identified as Satan, or the Devil (Revelation 12:9), the one who deceives the whole world. God placed a curse on the serpent, because he seduced Eve into eating the forbidden fruit, bringing spiritual death. This prophecy described an enmity (hatred) that has existed between the seed of the woman and the seed of Satan.

Satan knew that his ultimate defeat would come at the hands of the Messiah. He attempted over and over again to prevent the Messiah's birth by destroying His ancestors, the Jews.

Christ Came to Reverse the Curse of Sin

Man lost the right to communion with God through disobedience. A man had to regain that right, but none was able. Man had the authority and title as Prince of this World, but there in the Garden, he gave it to Satan.

So God clothed himself in flesh, becoming the God-man, Jesus, to take back the right to the Tree of Life. The curse of sin was broken by the thorns He wore on His head as He became a curse for us by hanging on a tree (the cross). The Just took the punishment for the unjust. Because He did this for us, God, the Father, gave His only Son a place above all.[2]

This is a picture of the coming Messiah who crushed Satan's authority. Jesus' death on the cross forever crushed the head of the serpent. Jesus, the spotless Lamb of God, took the curse of our sins by hanging on the tree. This provided salvation for all mankind and offered man the privilege of one day eating from the Tree of Life to live eternally.

Jesus Christ came to earth that He might destroy the works of the Devil. The Messiah (seed of the woman) was bruised by the seed of the serpent at the cross. This coming Deliverer saved man from the deceiver and provided salvation to all mankind. For this purpose the Son of God was manifested, that He might destroy the works of the devil.

Beginning of Civilization

Three of Adam and Eve's sons were mentioned in Genesis; Cain, Abel and Seth. After Cain slew his brother Abel, God placed a curse on Cain, saying that Cain would be a homeless wanderer on the earth. Cain replied to the Lord, "My punishment is too great for me to bear! God put a mark on Cain to warn anyone not to kill him.

"Cain left the Lord's presence and settled in the land of Nod, east of Eden. Cain had sexual relations with his wife, and she became pregnant and gave birth to Enoch. Then Cain founded a city, which he named Enoch, after his son" (Genesis 4:16-17 NLT).

Cain's descendants multiplied and became very powerful. Lamech was the first man to marry two wives and the second man to commit murder. Jabal lived in tents and herded cattle. Jubal played the lyre and flute. Zillah gave birth to Tubal-Cain, who was an expert craftsman in bronze and iron. Cain's line ended with the Flood in Noah's day. People who are alive today are all descendants of Noah, who was a descendant of Seth, Adam and Eve's third son.

Length of an Old Testament Year

How long was a biblical year? In the Old Testament a year was 360 days. Noah's flood was on the earth for 150 days (Genesis 8:3). It started on the 17th day of the second month (Genesis 7:11) and the ark rested on the 17th day of the seventh month (Genesis 8:4). Noah's flood was on the earth for five months or 150 days (Genesis 7:24). 150 divided by 5 = 30 days. The ancient Jewish calendar was a 30-day month. When you multiply 30 days x 12 months, it equals 360 days.

The patriarch who lived before the Flood had an average lifespan of about 900 years. The ages of post-Flood patriarchs dropped rapidly and gradually leveled off (Genesis 11). Some suggest that this was due to major environmental changes brought about by the Flood.[3]

Seth's Descendants Carried the Messiah's Seed

Adam and Eve's two sons, Cain and Abel, are mentioned in the fourth chapter of Genesis. Abel was a keeper of sheep and Cain a tiller of the ground. After Cain killed Abel, God gave them another son; named Seth, which means "appointed one."

God had promised that He would send a Deliverer to undo the curse of sin that befell the human race after Adam and Eve sinned. Christ's genealogy came through Seth, the godly seed, establishing the line of the seed of the woman.

Descendants of Adam and Seth

Adam – 930 years (Gen. 5:5)
  Seth - 912 years (Gen. 5:8)
    Enosh - 905 years (Gen. 5:11)
      Cainan – 910 years (Gen. 5:14)
        Mahalalel – 965 years (Gen. 5:17)
          Jared – 962 years (Gen. 5:20)
            Enoch – 365 years (Gen. 5:23, 24) – Translated
              Methuselah – 969 years (Gen. 5:27)
                Lamech – 777 years (Gen. 5:31)
                  Noah – 950 years (Gen. 9:29)
                  GREAT FLOOD
                    Shem – 600 years (Gen. 11:10, 11)
                      Eber – 464 years (Gen. 11:16, 17)
                        Terah – 205 years (Gen. 11:32)
                          Abram – 175 years (Gen. 25:7)

Godly Men Descended From Seth

Seth's descendants did not have the great achievements like Cain's descendants. If you study the genealogy in Genesis five you will discover that Seth's descendants demonstrated faithfulness to God.

Three prominent men of faith descended from Seth. Enosh was the son of Seth and grandson of Adam. His name means mortal. Men began to call on the name of the Lord after his birth. Enosh lived from the time of Adam to the birth of Noah. For seven generations people continued believing in God as master of the universe, but then they fell into sin and depravity.

Enoch, Son of Jared– 7th Generation from Adam

Enoch, the son of Jared, was the 7th generation after Adam. When Enoch was 65 years old, he became the father of Methuselah. In contrast to the other nine descendant of Seth, Enoch lived an outstanding life of dedication to God. He lived and enjoyed an intimate relationship with God in the midst of unspeakable wickedness.

Enoch was the seventh generation from Adam. Enoch was sixty-five years old when his son, Methuselah was born. He lived for another 300 years, and had other sons and daughters. Enoch lived 365 years, walking in close fellowship with God. Then one day he disappeared, because God took him. God spared Enoch from physical death because of his righteousness, affirming God's power over death. Elijah was the only other man who shared this experience (2 Kings 2:11).

Methuselah Lived From Adam to Noah

Adam lived until Methuselah was forty-six years old. They bridged the gap between creation and the Flood. Adam probably told Methuselah about walking with God in the Garden of Eden, the original sin, and being cast out of the Garden of Eden. Methuselah repeated this story to Noah, his grandson.

Methuselah lived 969 years, longer than any other man on earth. I would imagine that he told his great-grandchildren stories that Adam had told him. Methuselah lived 107 years after Shem was born. Shem lived 210 years after Abraham was born. Shem probably told Abraham about the flood, how Noah had worked a hundred years building the ark, saving their lives and about Adam and Eve in the Garden of Eden, and about the one true God.

All of Noah's ancestors, including his father, Lamech, and his grandfather Methuselah died before the flood. God may have allowed him to live to reveal to mankind the goodness and longsuffering God in the midst of a sinful generation.

Noah, a Man Who Walked With God

Later, God chose Noah, a descendent of Seth and a righteous man, to save mankind when God judged the wicked men on the earth in the Great Flood. Through Noah's son Shem, in the ninth generation, God chose another man named Abram (meaning "exalted father") to be in the lineage of the Savior, the Lord Jesus Christ.[4] Noah was God's instrument for saving mankind from extinction.

Genesis vs. Revelation[5]

In Genesis	In Revelation
The earth was created.	The earth passes away.
Satan's first rebellion	Satan's last rebellion
The sun, moon and stars were created.	The heavenly bodies are for earth's judgment.
The sun was to govern the day.	There is no need of a sun.
Darkness is called night.	There is no night.
The waters were called sea.	There is no more sea.
The entrance of sin	The exodus of sin
The curse is pronounced.	The curse is removed.
Death entered.	There is no more death.
The beginning of sorrows	There is no more sorrow.

Let's also look at an interesting timeline Jack Kelly developed to demonstrate the ease with which pre-flood knowledge and experience could have been made available to those who came after. We'll assume Adam was created in Year One and use biblical life spans.

Ten Generation Chart[6]

Name	Born	Died	Name Means
Adam	1	930	Man
Seth	130	1042	Appointed
Enosh	235	1140	Mortal
Kenan	325	1235	Sorrow
Mahalalel	395	1290	The Blessed God
Jared	460	1422	Shall come down
Enoch	622	987	Teaching
Methuselah	687	1656	His death shall bring. The flood came when He died.
Lamech	874	1651	Despairing – Lamech was 56 years old when Adam died.
Noah	1056	2006	Noah means rest. He was alive when Abraham was Born.

These ten names contain the Gospel message. "Man is appointed mortal sorrow, but the blessed God shall come down, teaching that His death shall bring the despairing rest." Seth's descendants focused on spiritual things, rather than the things of this world, even to the extent of naming their sons.[7]

› CHAPTER 2
LIVING IN THE DAYS OF NOAH

Adam and Eve, created in the image of God, formerly walked and talked with God. However Noah's generations degenerated to a race where every thought and imagination was bent on evil. God was grieved that He created mankind.

Adam lived until the seventh generation after him. I imagine he told each generation about living in the Garden of Eden and walking with God in the cool of the day. He lived until his grandson, Methuselah, was 46 years old. Methuselah lived 969 years.

God Saw the Wickedness of Man

"The Lord saw that the wickedness of man was great on the earth, and every intent of the thoughts of his heart was only evil continually. The Lord was sorry that He had made man on the earth, and He was grieved in His heart. The Lord said, "I will blot out man whom I have created from the face of the land, from man to animals to creeping things and to birds of the sky; for I am sorry that I have made them… Now the earth was corrupt in the sight of God, and the earth was filled with violence. God looked on the earth, and behold, it was corrupt; for all flesh had corrupted their way upon the earth. Then God said to Noah, "The end of all flesh has come before Me; for the earth is filled with violence because of them; and behold, I am about to destroy them with the earth" (Genesis 6:5-7, 11-13 NASB).

In the days of Noah immorality was rampant. Every thought and imagination of man's heart was continually evil. The whole world was full of violence and corruption. When God saw the wickedness of man, He told Noah His plans to destroy the world with a flood and instructed Noah to build an ark. It must have taken a great amount of faith to build an ark on dry ground. It had never rained or even drizzled before.

The earth was corrupt in God's sight, and the earth was filled with violence. God saw the earth, and behold, it was corrupt, for all flesh had corrupted their way on the earth. God said to Noah, "I have determined to make an end of all flesh, for the earth is filled with violence through them. Behold, I will destroy them with the earth".[8]

Days of the Giant Nephilim

"The Nephilim were on the earth in those days and also afterward-- when the sons of God went to the daughters of humans and had children by them. They were the heroes of old, the man of renown" (Genesis.6:4 NIV). The wickedness of the human race had long provoked the wrath of God. One cause of their un-righteousness was the intermarriage of the "sons of God" to the "daughters of man."

Giants once inhabited the earth. Moses sent twelve spies into the Promised Land and they reported there were giants in the land. Ten spies gave this report, "So they brought to the people of Israel a bad report of the land that they had spied out, saying, 'The land, through which we have gone to spy it out, is a land that devours its inhabitants, and all the people that we saw in it are of great height. And there we saw the Nephilim (the sons of Anak, who come from the Nephilim), and we seemed to ourselves like grasshoppers, and so we seemed to them'" (Numbers 13:32-33 ESV).

Giants walked the face of the earth and mated with God's creation, thereby corrupting the flesh that God had created. This was the age of the Nephilim, the age of Nimrod, the age of men of renown. We now wonder if this was a time when many of the great ancient monuments were built such as the pyramids of Egypt, the Sphinx, Stonehenge and others. There are a number of ancient wonders that we cannot explain, so we wonder if mighty men constructed these wonders.[9]

Goliath the Philistine giant that David killed was nine feet tall. Og, king of Bashan, had a bed made of iron that was thirteen feet long and six feet wide.

During the late 1950s in Turkey, a construction project in the Euphrates Valley uncovered many tombs and burial grounds containing the bones of giants. At two sites, human femurs (thigh bones) were found that measured nearly 4 feet long. Joe Taylor, Director of the Mt. Blanco Fossil Museum in Crosbyton, Texas, was commissioned to make an anatomically correct sculpture of the human based on the size of the femur. Indications were that the man was 14–16 feet tall.[10]

Noah: A Righteous Man

Noah was the son of Lamech and the tenth generation from Adam. The scriptures tell us little about Noah until he was five hundred years old. Noah has three sons, Shem, Ham, and Japheth.

Noah found grace in the eyes of the Lord. Noah was a just man, perfect in his generations. He was the only blameless person on the face of the earth. He was preacher of righteousness. He walked with God.

Noah was divinely warned of things not yet seen, and prepared an ark for the saving of his household. During this time, Noah warned the ungodly of the approaching doom, but there wasn't a single convert.

God also told Noah, "Seven days from now I will send rain on the earth for forty days and forty nights, and I will wipe from the face of the earth every living creature I had made" (Genesis 7:4).

After the animals had come safely into the ark, Moses recorded that Noah had his family, consisting of his wife and three sons and their wives, also entered the ark. Now the situation was entirely changed. Everything that preceded the Flood was now fulfilled. The door to the ark was shut, and then it began to rain.[11]

God waited patiently while the ark was being built, but people ignored Noah's warnings until the Flood came and destroyed them all. God did not spare the ancient world, but destroyed them all with a flood, except Noah and his family.

Table of Events at the Flood[12]

- Noah was 600 year old when he entered the ark with his family (Genesis 7:1–9).
- The rain began on the 17th day of the second month, and lasted forty days. (Genesis 7:10–17)
- The rain ceased and the water prevailed. (Genesis 7:18–24)
- The ark rested on Mount Ararat on the 17th day of the seventh month. (Genesis 8:1–4)
- The tops of mountains were visible on the first day of the tenth month. (Genesis 8:5)
- The raven and dove are sent out, but returned. (Genesis 8:10–11)
- The dove was sent out seven days later and returned with an olive branch. (Genesis 8:10–11)
- The dove was sent out a third time and no longer returned. (Genesis 8:12)
- The covering of the ark is removed. (Genesis 8:13)

Life Prior to the Flood

In the genealogy from Adam to Noah given in Genesis 5 and 9:29, there were extremely long-life spans. When we exclude Enoch, who was taken by God at the age of 365 years, and Lamech who died at the age of 777 years, we find all of the other eight lived between 895 and 969 years. After the great flood, there was a rapid drop in life span to a little over 400 years. Around the time of the tower of Babel, life spans dropped to a little over 200 years. Then they began to slowly decrease to more modern life spans over a period of hundreds of years.[13] The average life span of the patriarchs averaged about 930 years. After the flood, the life span of the patriarchs decreased from generation to generation.

Most of the patriarchs produced children at about a hundred years of age. However, Noah did not have sons until he was 500 years old. All of Noah's ancestors, including his father, Lamech, and his grandfather Methuselah died before the flood. What does this tell about the goodness of God?

Noah and his family lived on both sides of the flood. Noah was 500 years old when he started building the ark. He was 600 years old when the flood waters covered the earth. He lived 350 years after the flood and was 950 years of age at his death. Noah's son, Shem, was nearly one hundred years when the flood occurred.

God limited man's days on the earth, prior to the flood. "My Spirit will not contend with man forever, for he is mortal; his days will be a one hundred and twenty years" (Genesis 6:3 NIV).

Whatever the result, ultimately there was a judgment upon all of mankind. Previously, God had granted man long life, but He then decided that man's life span should be limited. Consequently, the term of man's existence upon the earth after this would be one-hundred, twenty years. I know it sounds like a long time to us but in comparison to what man had been given, it was a dramatic reduction. Men would now be limited to a lifespan that was one eighth of what it had been.[14]

Life Span Decreased Rapidly After the Great Flood

"A thousand years in your sight are like a day that has just gone by, or like a watch in the night. You sweep men away in the sleep of death; they are like the new grass of the morning- though in the morning it springs up new, by evening it is dry and withered. The length of our days is seventy years—or eighty, if our strength endures. Teach us to number our days aright, that we may gain a heart of wisdom" (Psalm 90:4–6, 10, 12 NIV).

Psalm 90:10 tells us that God limited man's lifespan to 70–80 years. The average life expectancy today is at an all-time record high of 77.6 years. Women are still living longer than men, but the gap is narrowing.

The fountains of the deep were broken up and the windows of heavens were opened at the flood. These catastrophic occurrences, according to some scientific authorities, disrupted a protective environmental shield that had prevented the earth from receiving damaging ultraviolet rays from the sun. With the deterioration of that shield, things upon earth, including human life, began to degenerate and deteriorate at a much faster rate. Life span decreased as a result.

God's Covenant with Noah

The Lord was pleased with Noah's offering and prophesied; "Never again will I curse the ground because of man, even though every inclination of his heart is evil from childhood. Never again will I destroy all living creatures, as I have done. As long as the earth endures, seedtime and harvest, cold and heat, summer and winter, day and night will never cease'" (Genesis 8:21–22 NIV).

"This is the sign of the covenant I am making between me and you and everything living around you and everyone living after you. I'm putting my rainbow in the clouds, a sign of the covenant between me and the Earth. From now on, when I form a cloud over the Earth and the rainbow appears in the cloud, I'll remember my covenant between me and you and everything living, that never again will floodwaters destroy all life. When the rainbow appears in the cloud, I'll see it and remember the eternal covenant between God and everything living, every last living creature on Earth" (Genesis 9:12–16 MSG).

Last Generation Compared With the Days of Noah

"As it was in the days of Noah, so it will be also in the days of the Son of Man: They ate, they drank, they married wives, they were given in marriage, until the day that Noah entered the ark, and the flood came and destroyed them all. Likewise as it was also in the days of Lot; they ate, they drank, they bought, they sold, they planted, they built, but on the day that Lot went out of Sodom it rained fire and brimstone from heaven and destroyed *them* all. Even so will it be in the day when the Son of Man is revealed" (Luke 17:26–30).

The gospel of Luke gives a great deal of information about conditions that will prevail prior to Christ's return. It is compared to the time preceding the Flood. People will be eating, drinking, marrying and giving in marriage, much as they were in the days of Noah. When Lot left Sodom, fire and brimstone fell from heaven and destroyed all of them. The same event will occur when Christ returns at the Second Coming.

People did not believe that judgment was coming in Noah's or Lot's day. They totally ignored the warnings. God did not destroy Sodom until Lot was safely out of the city. The day Lot left Sodom, judgment fell. When Noah and his family entered the ark, the Flood came. These scriptures imply that on the day believers are "raptured" (when they are safely out of this world) God will pour His wrath on the ungodly.

God did not spare the angels who sinned, but cast them into hell and committed them to pits of darkness, reserved for judgment. He did spare the ancient world, but preserved Noah and his family, but destroyed the ungodly with a flood. God condemned the cities of Sodom and Gomorrah with fire and brimstone, but rescued Lot from an ungodly environment. God knows how to rescue the godly from temptation and punish the ungodly on the Day of Judgment.

When Jesus, the Messiah, returns all of His children will be called home, never to suffer again. Keep looking up for your redemption draws nigh. King Jesus will soon return with a shout, with the voice of the archangel and the trumpet of God. Be ready for His return!

❯ CHAPTER 3
GOD'S COVENANT WITH ABRAHAM

The Lord said to Abram, "Go forth from your country, and from your relatives, and from your father's house, to the land that I will show you. I will make you a great nation, and I will bless you, and make your name great; and so you shall be a blessing; and I will bless those who bless you, and the one who curses you I will curse. In you all the families of the earth will be blessed" (Genesis 12:1-4 NASB).

Around 4,000 years ago, God appeared to Abram while he was living in Ur of Chaldeans, a modern and prosperous city in Mesopotamia. He instructed Abram to leave his homeland and travel to a land of promise, a land that God would show him. God later spoke to Abram before he was in Haran. "The God of glory appeared to our father Abraham when he was in Mesopotamia, before he lived in Haran and said to him, 'Leave your country and your relatives, and come into the land that I will show you'" (Acts 7:2–3 NASB).

The covenant with Abram was a major step in divine revelation indicating that God was selecting Abram and his posterity to fulfill His purpose of revealing Himself to the world and bring salvation for all mankind. Though only eleven chapter were used to trace the whole history of the world prior to Abram, including Creation an all the major events which followed, the rest of the Book of Genesis was devoted to Abram and his immediate descendants, indicating the importance of this covenant.[15]

The first eleven chapters in Genesis cover a period of almost two thousand years of human history. Genesis 12–25 covers a period of 100 years, from Abram's call at the age of 75 to his death at the age of 175 years.

Almost one-fourth of Genesis is devoted to this godly, faithful man. God promised to make his name great. Abraham is referred to 180 times in the Old Testament and 70 times in the New Testament. Even the Koran refers to Abraham 188 times.

Three religions consider Abraham their spiritual father; Judaism, Christianity and Islam. This is over half of the world's population. God certainly made Abraham's name great.

Abraham was the twentieth generation from Adam and the tenth from Noah. Terah was Abram's father. His two brothers were Nabor and Haran. Abram was married to Sarai, his half-sister. Lot, the son of Haran, was his nephew.

In Canaan, Abraham entered into a covenant with God in exchange for recognition of Yahweh as his God, God never promised Abraham land for himself, but the land would belong to his descendants.

Circumcision was a Sign of God's Covenant

The rite of circumcision was instituted as a sign of the covenant of Abram. At this time God changed Sarai's name to Sarah which means "princess" and Abram to Abraham, which means "Father of a multitude".

Why God Chose the Jews

"You are a people holy to the Lord your God. He has chosen you to be his people, prized above all others on the face of the earth. It is not because you were more numerous than all the other peoples that the Lord favored and chose you—for in fact you were the least numerous of all peoples. Rather it is because of his love for you and his faithfulness to the promise he solemnly vowed to your ancestors" (Deuteronomy 7:6-8 NET).

God chose the Jewish people to be a blessing to the entire world. Through the Jews we received God's holy Word, the Bible. Isaiah 42:6 said; "I will keep and give you as a covenant to the people, as a light to the Gentiles." The promised Messiah came through the seed of Abraham. Abraham's descendants witnessed to all the earth about the coming Messiah, our Savior, who provided salvation for all mankind. Even though many of the Jews rejected Yeshua as their Messiah, God did not reject them.

Paul, the apostle, asked in Romans 3:3-4 "If some did not believe, does their unbelief nullify the faithfulness of God? Absolutely not! God did not abandon the Jews. He chastened them for their sins, but He never cast them away.

Ur of Chaldeans

A great many people think that Abram left a terrible place in Ur of the Chaldeans and came to a land of corn and wine, a land of milk and honey, where everything was lovely. They think that Abram really bettered his lot by coming to this land. Don't believe it! That is not what the Bible says, and though archaeology we know that Ur of Chaldeans had a very high civilization. In fact, Abram and Sarai might well have had a bathtub in their home! Ur was a great and prosperous city.[16]

Ur was believed to have been founded some five hundred years before the time of Abraham. It could be compared to a modern city, having libraries, schools, and a system of law. It was a rich city and many valuable treasures have been discovered including elaborate jewelry.[17]

Ur of Chaldeans, known today as Iraq, was not far from where Nimrod tried to build the Tower of Babel. It is now known as Tell Mugheir, which lies 140 miles south of ancient Babylon and 150 miles northwest of the Persian Gulf.

Abram's Father Worshipped Idols

The false religion of astrology which began at Babel was practiced in Ur as it was in all Babylonia. Abraham's father, Terah, according to Joshua 24:2, worshiped idols. Jewish tradition refers to Terah as an idol maker. Ur was an idolatrous city worshiping many different gods, such as the god of fire, moon, sun and stars.

Sin, the moon god, was the principal deity of Ur, Abraham's city. Sin's wife was called Ningal, the moon-goddess of Ur. She had many names, and was worshiped in every city as the Mother-Goddess. Nina was one of her names, from which the city of Nineveh was named. Her common name in Babylonia was Ishtar. She was the deification of the sex passion; her worship required licentiousness; sacred prostitution in connection with her sanctuaries was a universal custom among the women of Babylonia. In connection with her temples were charming retreats or chambers where her priestesses entertained male worshipers in disgraceful ceremonies.[18]

Ur was an evil and sinful city as can be seen in the worship practices of the moon-goddess. Every female in the city at some time in her life would have to take her turn serving as a priestess prostitute in the temples.

According to Jewish tradition, Abraham was born under the name Abram in the city of Ur in Babylonia in the year 1948 from Creation (1800 B.C.E.). He was the son of Terah, an idol merchant, but from his early childhood, he questioned the faith of his father and sought the truth. He came to believe that the entire universe was the work of a single Creator, and he began to teach this belief to others.[19]

Abram tried to convince his father, Terah, of the folly of idol worship. One day, when Abram was left alone to mind the store, he took a hammer and smashed all of the idols except the largest one. He placed the hammer in the hand of the largest idol. When his father returned and asked what happened, Abram said, "The idols got into a fight, and the big one smashed all the other ones." His father said, "Don't be ridiculous. These idols have no life or power. They can't do anything." Abram replied, "Then why do you worship them?"[20]

Abram Moved to Haran

Abram obeyed God, left his homeland and crossed over the Euphrates River. His father, Terah, Sarai, his wife and his nephew, Lot traveled with him. It was 600 miles from Ur to Haran. He did not know where he was going. He was called a "Hebrew" which means "stranger" or one who crossed over. His descendants became known as Israelites, and later, Jews.

The moon-god was worshipped at both Ur and Haran and since Terah was an idolater, he probably felt at home in either place. Haran was a flourishing caravan city in the 19ᵗʰ century before Christ. Abram lived in Haran over ten years with his father, Terah and his nephew, Lot.

God spoke to Abram before he left Ur of Chaldeans. He did not speak to him during the time he stayed in Haran. God did not speak to him until he entered the Promised Land and separated from Lot. What does this tell about obedience?

Abram Journeyed to Canaan

Abraham was a descendant of the godly line that descended from Adam. Many scholars believe that Abraham, Isaac, and Jacob became active in Canaan, between 2100–1875 B.C. There he received God's assurance that he would be the ancestor of a mighty people. In Canaan, Abraham entered into a covenant with God in exchange for recognition of Yahweh as his God. God never promised Abraham land for himself, but the land would belong to his descendants.

The Canaanites were a heathen, barbaric race of people. They sacrificed their children in honor of their gods. They practiced sodomy, bestiality, and many other loathsome vices. The Canaanites and other races were put out of the land because of their gross sins. God forbids sexual relations with relatives, sodomy, and offering children to Molech. "Do not defile yourselves with any of these things; for by these things the nations which I am casting out before you have become defiled. For the land has been defiled, therefore I have brought its punishment upon it, so the land has spewed out its inhabitants" (Leviticus 18:24–25).

An ancient Biblical tradition, the Midrash, relates that the Canaanites wrote marriage contracts between man and man and woman and woman, and that this was one reason the land "vomited" them up in favor of the Israelites who took their place.[21]

God's Covenant with Abraham

The twelfth chapter of Genesis contains what has been called the Abrahamic Covenant. Understanding this covenant helps to tie the rest of the Old Testament together. Beginning in Genesis 12, the Bible traced history through the patriarchs, Abraham, Isaac, Jacob, and the twelve sons of Jacob, later known as the Twelve Tribes of Israel. God did not give Abraham any inheritance, not even enough land to set his foot on, but God promised to give the land to his descendants. God repeated this covenant to Abraham, Isaac, and Jacob seven times in Genesis as well as several other times in the Bible.

God made an unconditional covenant with Abram. God did not say, "Abram, if you will do certain things, I will bless you." There were absolutely no conditions on what God promised Abram. Listed below are the six promises God made to Abram in Genesis 12:1-3).

* I will make you a great nation.
* I will bless you.
* I will make your name great and you shall be a blessing.
* I will bless those who bless you.
* I will curse those who curse you.
* In you all the families of the earth shall be blessed.

God Renewed His Covenant with Abraham

"I will establish My covenant between Me and you and your descendants after you throughout their generations for an everlasting covenant, to be God to you and to your descendants after you. I will give to you and to your descendants after you, the land of your sojourning, all the land of Canaan, for an everlasting possession; and I will be their God" (Genesis 17:7–9 NASB).

"The Lord said to Abram after Lot had parted from him, 'Lift up your eyes from where you are and look north and south, east and west. All the land that you see I will give to you and your offspring forever. I will make your offspring like the dust of the earth, so that if anyone could count the dust, then your offspring could be counted. Go, walk through the length and breadth of the land, for I am give it to you" (Genesis 13:14-17 NIV).

> *"God remembers his covenant forever, the word that he commanded, for a thousand generations, the covenant that he made with Abraham, his sworn promise to Isaac, which he confirmed to Jacob as a statue, to Israel as an everlasting covenant, saying, 'To you I will give the land of Canaan as your portion for an inheritance'" (Psalm 105:8-11 ESV).*

Review of God's Covenant to Abram

* Genesis 12:7 – "To your descendant I will give this land."
* Genesis 13:15 – "All the land which you see I give to you and your descendants forever."
* Genesis 15:18 – "To your descendants I have given this land from the river of Egypt to the great River Euphrates."
* Genesis 17:8 – "I give to you and your descendants after you the land in which you are a stranger, all the land of Canaan, as an everlasting possession."
* Genesis 26:3 –"Dwell in the land, and I will be with you and bless you, for to you and your descendants I give all these lands."

- Genesis 28:13 – "The land on which you lie I will give to you and your descendants."
- Genesis 35:12 – "The land which I gave Abraham and Isaac I give to you and to your descendants after you I give this land."
- Deuteronomy 11:24 – "Every place on which the sole of your foot treads shall be yours: from the wilderness and Lebanon, from the river, the River Euphrates, even to the Western Sea, shall be your territory."

God promised them a land which is much larger than anything they ever occupied. It included land from the Euphrates to the Mediterranean and from Lebanon all the way south into the Sinai Desert. This territory included parts of these countries today: Syria, Lebanon, Saudi Arabia, the Sinai, West Bank, Gaza, parts of Egypt all the way to Euphrates River.

Israel has never occupied all the land God gave to them. At the zenith of their power, they occupied 30,000 square miles, but that is not all that God gave them. Actually, He gave them 300,000 square miles. They have a long way to go, but they will have to get it on God's terms, and in God's appointed time.[22]

Abraham's Journey to Egypt

When Abraham left the Promised Land and journeyed to Egypt, he experienced some serious problems while in Egypt. God never promised to bless Abraham in Egypt. The Pharaoh in Egypt heard of Sarah's beauty and took her into his harem. Abram had previously asked Sarah to tell them she was his sister. God struck Pharaoh's house with a great plague because of Sarah. When Pharaoh became aware of the situation, he became angry and escorted Abram out of Egypt. Abram encountered another problem in Egypt, when Sarah acquired a handmaiden named Hagar that gave birth to Ishmael.

God Promised Blessing to Ishmael

God promised to bless Ishmael and to make him a great nation: "As for Ishmael, I will bless him also, just as you have asked. I will make him fruitful and multiply his descendants. He will become the father of twelve princes, and I will make him a great nation" (Genesis 17:20 NLT).

Muslims trace their root back to Abraham, through Ishmael, Isaac's half-brother. Many Arabs consider Ishmael to be their ancestor. Mohammed traced his roots back to Ishmael. They teach that the Holy Land belonged to them through Ishmael.

The descendants of Ishmael have vast lands and oil reserves that reveal evidence of God blessing the sons of Ishmael. These blessings have not been passed on to the people, but have been absorbed through the lavish lifestyles of their leaders.

The Arab people did not obtain the promise to the Holy Land, but they have certainly been blessed. They rule twenty nations surrounding Israel which contain much of the oil reserves in the world.

Abraham's Sons by Keturah

Abraham had six more sons by Keturah, his concubine, after Sarah died. "Now Abraham gave all he had to Isaac; but to the sons of his concubines, Abraham gave gifts while he was still living and sent them away from his son Isaac eastward, to the land of the east" (Genesis 25:5, 6 NASB). Abraham sent all his sons away, but promised the Land of Canaan to Isaac.

The Lord Renewed His Promise to Isaac

The Lord told Isaac: "I am the LORD, the God of Abraham and the God of Isaac. I will give you and your descendants the land on which you are lying. Your descendants will be like the dust of the earth, and you will spread out to the west and to the east, to the north and to the south. All people on earth will be blessed through you and your offspring" (Genesis 28:13-14 NIV).

The birthright to the covenant was established with Abraham, then to Isaac (not Ishmael or the other sons of Abraham), to Jacob (not Esau), and Jacob's twelve sons, who became known as the Twelve Tribes of Israel. "In Isaac your descendants shall be called".

Abraham Looked for an Eternal City

"By faith Abraham, when he was called, obeyed by going out to a place which he was to receive for an inheritance; and he went out, not knowing where he was going. By faith he lived as an alien in the land of promise, as in a foreign *land*, dwelling in tents with Isaac and Jacob, fellow heirs of the same promise; for he was looking for the city which has foundations, whose architect and builder is God" (Hebrews 11:8-10 NASB).

Abraham was the inhabitant of no mere city. He was not, as he is so often represented, some wandering and ignorant nomadic shepherd; he was a man of culture and sophistication, belonging to one of the aristocratic families of Ur, a city with a very high level of civilization. It was while Abraham was living in such a city that the God of glory appeared to him, and in that revelation, Abraham saw the city of God. He saw the city of God in the person of the God of glory. How he saw the Lord, or what he saw, we do not know, but from that moment he was soiled for anything else. From then on He 'looked for the city which had foundations.[23]

He forsook the splendor of his native city, with its high standards of educa-tion and culture, and never returned to it... He saw that it had not foundations; that it was built on the sands of human genius, human resourcefulness and human ability, and that it must, therefore, pass away. Apprehended by the God of glory, he sought 'the city which had foundations, whose builder and make is God'. The city which he sought was the heavenly Jerusalem, of which the earthly Jerusalem is but the symbol.[24]

A New Covenant with Israel

"The days are surely coming, says the Lord, when I will make a new covenant with the house of Israel and the house of Judah. It will not be like the covenant that I made with their ancestors when I took them by the hand to bring them out of the land of Egypt—a covenant that they broke, though I was their husband, says the Lord. But this is the covenant that I will make with the house of Israel after those days, says the Lord: I will put my law within them, and I will write it on their hearts; and I will be their God, and they shall be my people. No longer shall they teach one another, or say to each other, "Know the Lord," for they shall all know me, from the least of them to the greatest, says the Lord; for I will forgive their iniquity, and remember their sin no more. Thus says the Lord, who gives the sun for light by day and the fixed order of the moon and the stars for light by night, who stirs up the sea so that its waves roar— the Lord of hosts is his name: If this fixed order were ever to cease from my presence, says the Lord, then also the offspring of Israel would cease to be a nation before me forever. Thus says the Lord: If the heavens above can be measured, and the foundations of the earth below can be explored, then I will reject all the offspring of Israel because of all they have done, says the Lord" (Jeremiah 31: 31-37 NRSV).

❯ CHAPTER 4
DELIVERANCE FROM EGYPTIAN BONDAGE

"Because the LORD loves you, and because He would keep the oath which He swore to your fathers, the LORD has brought you out with a mighty hand, and redeemed you from the house of bondage, from the hand of Pharaoh king of Egypt" (Deuteronomy 7:8).

The story began around 3,700 years ago when the family of Jacob (later named Israel) moved to Egypt during a time of severe famine. Jacob had twelve sons including Joseph, his favorite, to whom he gave a coat of many colors. Inflamed by jealousy, Joseph's brothers sold him into slavery. Later, Joseph rose to chief advisor to Egypt's Pharaoh through his wisdom and ability to interpret dreams. Jacob's family moved to Egypt after they learned Joseph was still alive.

They were initially well received. While in Egypt they were provided for by God through the obedience of Joseph. They tended flocks for many years in the land of Goshen next door to Egypt. They spoke the Hebrew language and were called Hebrews (which means wanderers). They also became known as Israelites and later as Jews.

The Pharaoh who ruled Egypt allowed the Hebrews to worship as they pleased. After Joseph died another Pharaoh came into power. No longer, honored guests, the Egyptians enslaved the Hebrews. Carrying heavy bricks and mortar to build the Egyptian cities of Pithom and Ramses, and the great temples, the children of Israel toiled under the burning Egyptian sun for many years. But the more they were afflicted, the more they grew and multiplied.

"There arose a new king over Egypt, who did not know Joseph. And he said to his people, 'Look, the people of the children of Israel are more and mightier than we; Come, let us deal shrewdly with them, lest they multiply, and it happen, in the event of war, that they also join our enemies and fight against us, and so go up out of the land.' Therefore they set taskmasters over them to afflict them with their burdens. They built for Pharaoh supply cities, Pithom and Ramses. But the more they afflicted them, the more they multiplied and grew. And they were in dread of the children of Israel. So the Egyptians made the children of Israel serve with rigor. And they made their lives bitter with hard bondage in mortar, in brick, and in all manner of service in the field. All their service in which they made them serve was with rigor" (Exodus 1:8–14).

Moses as a Baby

When Moses was born, his mother saw that there was something special about him, so she placed him in a basket in the Nile River to protect him from Pharaoh ,who has order all the Hebrew baby boys be killed.

Miriam, the older sister watched the baby to see what would happen. When Pharaoh's daughter came to the Nile to bathe, she saw the basket floating in the Nile. She sent her maid to get it. When she opened the basket, she saw a baby crying and her heart went out to him. She realized that this must be one of the Hebrew babies.

Miriam asked the princess if she would like someone to nurse the baby. When Pharaoh's daughter agreed, Miriam got her mother to nurse the baby. Pharaoh's daughter adopted Moses and raised him. She named him Moses, saying "I pulled him out of the water".

"By faith Moses, when he became of age, refused to be called the son of Pharaoh's daughter, choosing rather to suffer affliction with the people of God than to enjoy the passing pleasures of sin, esteeming the reproach of Christ greater riches than the treasures in Egypt; for he looked to the reward" (Hebrews 11:24-26).

God Called Moses to Deliver the Israelites

God said to Moses, "I am Yahweh—'the Lord.' I appeared to Abraham, to Isaac, and to Jacob as El-Shaddai—'God Almighty'—but I did not reveal my name, Yahweh, to them. And I reaffirmed my covenant with them. Under its terms, I promised to give them the land of Canaan, where they were living as foreigners. You can be sure that I have heard the groans of the people of Israel, who are now slaves to the Egyptians. And I am well aware of my covenant with them. "Therefore, say to the people of Israel: 'I am the Lord. I will free you from your oppression and will rescue you from your slavery in Egypt. I will redeem you with a powerful arm and great acts of judgment. [7] I will claim you as my own people, and I will be your God. Then you will know that I am the Lord your God who has freed you from your oppression in Egypt" (Exodus 6:2-7 NLT).

"The Lord said to Moses; 'When you return to Egypt, see that you perform before Pharaoh all wonders I have given you the power to do. But I will harden his heart so that he will not let the people go. Then say to Pharaoh, "This is what the Lord says: Israel is my firstborn son, and I told you, 'Let my son go, so he may worship me.' But you refused to let him go, so I will kill your firstborn son'" (Exodus 4:21–23 NIV).

The Israelites had no feasts to celebrate or any reason to rejoice. They were down-trodden, strangers in a strange land. They cried out to God to deliver them from their cruel bondage. God answered them by sending Moses to deliver His people. Moses, a Hebrew, was adopted by the daughter of Pharaoh and raised in Pharaoh's court. He heard a message from God to deliver his people.

God heard the groaning of the children of Israel and promised to remember His covenant with Abraham. He promised Moses that He would rescue the children of Israel from Egyptian bondage with an outstretched arm. Then they would know that it was the Lord who brought them out from under the burdens of the Egyptians.

"Then the Lord said to Moses, 'Pay close attention to this. I will make you seem like God to Pharaoh, and your brother, Aaron, will be your prophet. Tell Aaron everything I command you, and Aaron must command Pharaoh to let the people of Israel leave his country. But I will make Pharaoh's heart stubborn so I can multiply my miraculous signs and wonders in the land of Egypt. Even then Pharaoh will refuse to listen to you. So I will bring down my fist on Egypt. Then I will rescue my forces—my people, the Israelites—from the land of Egypt with great acts of judgment. When I raise my powerful hand and bring out the Israelites, the Egyptians will know that I am the Lord'" (Exodus 7:1–5 NLT).

Moses had one message - "Let My People Go". Pharaoh had stepped on God's chosen people. Anyone who steps on God's chosen people are hurting the Apple of God's Eye.

Egyptians Worshipped Many Gods

The Hebrew people worshipped Jehovah, the Creator of the universe, while the Egyptians worshipped hundreds and hundreds of gods. Instead of worshipping the one true Creator God, they worshipped created things.

The Egyptian religion was involved in witchcraft. Pharaoh, who himself claimed to be god, had a coiled snake as his crown. As High Priest of his religion, Pharaoh also had many magicians. These magicians carried sticks that they turned into snakes. The whole symbolism surrounding Egypt was a snake—a snake that had its coils around Israel, the people of God.

So the first sign God chose to perform involved a snake, as the symbol of the Egyptian religion. Aaron, in faith, threw down his rod, and it turned into a serpent. All of Pharaoh's wise men and sorcerers knew how to do this. They threw down their rods, and they turned into serpents as well.

Idolatry dominated Egypt

Many of the gods the Egyptians worshipped were animals. They worshipped cows, bulls, calves, birds, frogs, goats, apes, crocodiles, vultures, hawks, and serpents. Some of the creatures they worshipped were considered sacred by the Egyptians. No one was permitted to kill them.

In the various temples, the sacred animals were fed, groomed and cared for in the most luxurious ways by a great college of priests. Of all the animals, the bull was the most sacred. The animal, upon its death, was embalmed with the pomp and ceremony befitting a king. The crocodile was also greatly honored in his temple at Tanis, by 50 or more priests. This was the religion of the people among whom the Hebrew nation was nurtured for 430 years.[25]

The Egyptians worshipped the earth, the sky, and the Nile River. If the Nile was god, then everything in the Nile was also god. Frogs were sacred because they came out of the Nile. They worshipped frogs, so God gave them frogs to worship. Frogs, Frogs, Frogs. Everywhere they turned there were more frogs. Every time they saw a frog, they had to worship it. Can you imagine worshipping a frog?

Plagues of Egypt

"I know that the king of Egypt will not let you go unless a mighty hand forces him. So I will raise my hand and strike the Egyptians, performing all kinds of miracles among them. Then at last he will he will let you go. I will cause the Egyptians to look favorably on you. They will give you gifts when you go so you will not leave empty-handed" (Exodus 3:19–21 NLT).

Pharaoh, the high priest, also worshipped the Nile River as the god of life. One of the plagues God sent turned the life-giving and sustaining water of the river into blood. God was revealing that He is the one true God. This again showed that the Israeli God was stronger than the Egyptian god.

Many of the plagues God sent to Egypt were intended to show the Egyptians that the gods they worshipped were powerless. In each plague God revealed that the gods they worshipped were not really gods at all. Over and over, by each plague or miracle, God wanted them to know that only the Lord is God.

The Egyptians worshipped Ra, the god of light. The word Pharaoh has Ra in it. Ra was the sun god of the Egyptians. Pharaoh was thought to be the incarnation of light. The ninth plague was the plague of darkness over the land. The god of light, their most powerful god, was rendered powerless. Darkness hovered over Egypt for three days, but in Goshen where the Israelites lived, there was light.

The ten plagues were aimed at the gods of Egypt and were designed to give proof of the power of the God of Israel over the gods of Egypt. Over and over it is repeated by these miracles that both Israel and Egyptians would come to know that the Lord is God.[26] The plagues were an attack against the religious system of the Egyptian people.

The Ten Plagues of Egypt

| Exodus 7:24-25 | The water of the Nile was turned to blood. |
| Exodus 8:1-15 | The frogs were spread throughout the land of Egypt. |

Exodus 8:16–19	Lice infested the land of Egypt.
Exodus 8:20–32	Flies swarmed throughout the land of Egypt.
Exodus 9:1–7	Animals were struck with disease.
Exodus 9:8–12	The Egyptians were struck with boils.
Exodus 9:13–35	A hail storm destroyed the fields of the Egyptians.
Exodus 10:1–20	Hordes of locusts infested the land.
Exodus 10:21–29	Darkness covered the land of Egypt.
Exodus 12:29–30	Every firstborn in Egypt died.

God predicted that the time would come when every idol would disappear from Egypt. Today Egypt is a Muslim country that does not permit idols at all. Every idol has disappeared as God said they would.

Pharaoh first agreed to let the Hebrews go, but then changed his mind and refused. Miracle after miracle was performed by God through Moses. Each plague removed a coil of the snake that held the Israelites in bondage.

Possibly a year had passed since Moses requested Pharaoh to release God's people. But the final blow came with the death of the first born in Egypt, both man and animal (Exodus 12:12). In sorrow, Pharaoh finally agreed to release the Israelites, grieving the loss of his own son.

God Provided Deliverance

The Moses and the people of Israel sang this song to the Lord: "I will sing to the Lord for he has triumphed gloriously; and he has hurled both horse and rider into the sea. The Lord is my strength and my song; he has given me victory. This is my God, and I will bless him—my father's God, and I will exalt him! The Lord is a warrior; Yahweh is his name! Pharaoh's chariots and army he has hurled into the sea. The finest of Pharaoh's officers are drowned in the Red Sea" (Exodus 15:1-4 NLT).

God was getting ready to free the Hebrew people with a mighty deliverance and punish the Egyptians for their sins and stubbornness. The Israelites were by no means guiltless, but God protected them by means of the Passover Lamb.

Finally, the Israelites were ready to leave Egypt. They were just waiting for the word from Moses. The death of the firstborn of each family in Egypt was the final stroke. Pharaoh now asks the Israelites to leave.

While Egypt was embalming their dead, the Israelites made their escape. Egypt was left in shambles. Their crops were destroyed; their flocks and herds were killed; every first born was dead. The gods they worshipped had been shown to be powerless.

God brought the Hebrew people (possibly as many as two or three million people) out of Egyptian bondage under the leadership of Moses, and from the persecution they were suffering under the Pharaoh of Egypt. There were 600,000 men on foot besides women and children. After 430 years in Egypt, God delivered the children of Israel on the same day they had previously entered Egypt.

"Now the time that the sons of Israel lived in Egypt was four hundred and thirty years. And at the end of four hundred and thirty years, to the very day, all the hosts of the Lord went out from the land of Egypt. It is a night to be observed for the Lord for having brought them out from the land of Egypt; this night is for the Lord, to be observed by all the sons of Israel throughout their generations" (Exodus 12:40–42 NASB).

God gave the Israelites favor in the sight of the Egyptians giving them gold and silver. When the Israelites left Egypt, the Egyptians were glad they were leaving for the fear of the Israelites had fallen on them. It was estimated that the gifts given to the Children of Israel by the Egyptians the night of their departure from Egypt was over $1,250,000. This was sort of a recompense for their years of slavery.[27]

God Delivered Israel from Egyptian Bondage

As the Hebrews made their way back to Canaan, back to the land God had promised Abraham and his descendants by blood covenant, Pharaoh changed his mind and set out in hot pursuit with six hundred choice chariots. At the Red Sea he caught up with the multitude of Israelites, and gasped in awe to see them walking across a dry seabed. Emboldened by his arrogance, he tried to follow, but the walls of the Red Sea came crashing down upon him. In the end, Pharaoh's mighty army was consumed by God's wrath.[28]

After the Hebrews left Egypt, Pharaoh changed his mind and took six hundred chariots after them. The Egyptians caught up with them at the Red Sea. The Israelites gasped in fear when they saw Pharaoh and his army pursuing them.

Moses said to the people, "Do not fear! Stand still and see the salvation of the Lord. The Egyptians you see today, you will never see again. The Lord will fight for you. When Moses lifted up his staff, the sea divided. The Children of Israel walked through the sea on dry ground.

God told Moses to "Stretch out your hand over the sea, so the waters will come back on the Egyptians. When Moses stretched out his hand the sea came crashing down on Pharaoh's mighty army. When Israel saw the great power which the Lord used against the Egyptians, they believed in the Lord and his servant Moses.

After their miraculous deliverance from Pharaoh's chariots, Miriam, Moses' sister, led the Children of Israel in worship and praise. When God delivered Israel out of bondage, He adopted them as His own people. He not only wanted to outwardly deliver them from Egypt, but wanted to inwardly sever them from any heathen influence. He wanted them to be a separate people who worshiped only Jehovah.

Ninety different references in the Old Testament tell of God bringing the Israelites out of bondage in Egypt. They left the continent of Africa and went into freedom in Asia. They left Egypt a group of slaves and entered the Promised Land a mighty nation. This is the first recorded time of a national deliverance brought about entirely by the mighty hand of God.

❯ CHAPTER 5
BATTLE FOR JERUSALEM AND TEMPLE MOUNT

"I am going to make Jerusalem a cup that sends all the surrounding peoples reeling. Judah will be besieged as well as Jerusalem. On that day, when all the nations of the earth are gathered against her, I will make Jerusalem an immovable rock for all the nations. All who try to move it will injure themselves" (Zechariah 12:2-3 NIV).

This amazing prophecy said that Jerusalem would be an immovable rock to all the surrounding nations. For over sixty years, Israel's neighbors, including Syria, Jordan, Egypt, Lebanon and Palestinians have launched surprise attacks against her. She has proved to be stronger militarily, even through greatly outnumbered.

Jerusalem, known as the City of Peace, has known more battles and sieges than any other city in the world. How ironic that the one city God chose for His own has seen little but war and violence for the past sixty years. Jerusalem became an even greater source of contention when the Jews renamed Jerusalem as its capital.

The city of Jerusalem has changed hands over twenty different times and been leveled to the ground five times. But God has always brought his people back, just as it was prophesied. We can be confident, that any Bible prophecies, which remain to be fulfilled, will come to pass.[29]

It was been almost fifty years since the city of Jerusalem was united under Israeli rule following the 1967 Six-Day War. During that war, the Israeli Defense Forces captured Jerusalem. Jerusalem came back under Israeli control during the Six-Day War, when Israel captured Judea, Samaria and East Jerusalem from Jordan's King Hussein.

Jerusalem: Important to Three Religions

To illustrate her great spiritual importance, Jerusalem is claimed jointly by the religions of Judaism, Christianity and Islam. These claims apply not only to Jerusalem but also to most other parts of the land. Since these religions include almost three billion people, we can see that Jerusalem and Israel are extremely important to almost half the world's population.[30]

Israel is the home to three world religions: Judaism, Christianity, and Islam. 79% of the people in Israel are Jewish, 15% are Muslims and 6% are others, including Christians. The Muslims consider Friday their holy day, Jews worship on Saturday, and Christians worship on Sunday, the day Christ was resurrected.

Why can't the Jews and Arabs get together in their disputing over the city of Jerusalem? The most important reason Jews and Arabs cannot get together is not land…it is not money or history. The reason for the continual conflict over the city of Jerusalem is theology.[31]

Muslim's Claim to Jerusalem

What special place does Jerusalem hold for the Muslims? Jerusalem was never an Arab capital in contrast to Baghdad, Cairo or Damascus. It has not played any major role in the religious or political lives of the Moslem Arabs. It has never been a national or political center in the Muslim world, nor has it been the capital of any other country other than Israel since biblical times. The passion for Jerusalem was only discovered by the Moslem Arabs in recent years.

Many Muslims think of Jerusalem only by the name Al Quads that means "the farthest Mosque." Mecca and Medina are Muslim's two most holy cities. Thousand of pious Muslims make the pilgrimage to Mecca each year, but Jerusalem is not a place of such pilgrimage. The Qur'an doesn't even mention Jerusalem, but the Bible refers to Jerusalem over 800 times. Mohammad never visited Jerusalem, not even once!

Oddly, though, the Muslims did not use Jerusalem as their district capital, but ruled from various other locations. In order to attract pilgrims to Jerusalem and the story going, to erect a structure that would rival churches in the city, Abd al-Malik built the dome. Begun in 687 A.D., the Dome of the Rock required four years to complete. History would show that he succeeded in producing a building that would outshine the city's churches. He failed to draw Muslims away from their principal devotion of Mecca and Medina.[32]

The Dome of Rock is a mosque, but it serves primarily as a shrine for the sacred rock beneath. It is an octagon of a square base reached by six stairways. But any standard it is magnificently beautiful. In the intervening years, time and earthquakes have taken their tolls and made repairs necessary. What stands today is still very much like what stood there in 691 A.D.[33]

Muslims believe that Ishmael was the son that Abraham offered to God on Mount Moriah, and that the Jews just made up the story that it was Isaac. They claim rights to the Holy Land because God promised it to Abraham and his descendants. They refuse to accept the teaching in the Bible where God gave the Holy Land to the Jewish People. They refuse to accept Roman history that Jerusalem was the home of the Jewish Temple.

Prior to the 1967 Six-Day War, claims to Jerusalem being a Moslem holy city were rare. After Jerusalem was back in the hands of the Jews, the Muslims declared "holy war" to bring the city under Arab control. Jerusalem is the ultimate prize in the modern-day struggle between Israel and the Palestinians with both sides claiming it as their capital.

Call to Divide Jerusalem

Jerusalem was divided for nearly twenty years, but is now under Israeli rule. But Jerusalem has not been recognized as the capital of Israel by the nations of the world. Nearly half of the resolutions of the General Assembly of the United Nations concern Israel. Even the United States does not recognize Jerusalem as Israel's capital by refusing to place the United States Embassy in Jerusalem.

Former Senator Sam Brownback of Kansas said, "This point is essential; Jerusalem has been the capital of the Jewish people for three thousand years. Jerusalem has never been the capital for any other state other than for the Jewish people. The United States must have a more explicit position regarding the status of Jerusalem. Our Embassy cannot remain in Tel Aviv while we claim to support and defend Israel's right to exist."

Many people still insist that the solution to peace in the Middle East is for Israel to divide Jerusalem and give the eastern section to the Moslem Arabs. How unthinkable that that this special city could ever be surrendered to the PLO, or to an enemy of Israel. Yet the nations, and certainly Satan, would love to see such a thing happen.

Jerusalem, God's Advil

God is real serious about the land and covenant. Israel will literally be used as an anvil to destroy the nations that come against Jerusalem. The nations will be drawn to Jerusalem like a moth to a light. Multitudes of people have rejected God and the Bible or just do not believe His word. This rebellion will cause the nations to come against God's anvil. God has warned beforehand what will happen when armies try to destroy Israel and take Jerusalem.[34]

The entire world will see the mighty power of God, as He uses Israel as His anvil. This is all laid out in the Bible. God is using the rebirth of Israel like an anvil to expose false prophets, doctrines and to have a literal witness on the earth to the authority of His word. It is important that one's faith be in accord with the truth of the Bible. God's word has been tested in the furnace of the earth. The word has proven itself to be like pure gold and silver. [35]

Support for Jerusalem

Prime Minister Benyamin Netanyahu said, "Jerusalem has always and will always be ours. It will never be divided or cut in half. Jerusalem will remain under Israel's sovereignty. In united Jerusalem the freedom of worship and freedom of access for the three religions to the holy city will be guaranteed".

Jerusalem has been the only capital of Israel down through the generations. In 1996, Jerusalem celebrated 3,000 years since King David made it the capital of Israel. Since Jerusalem has never been the capital of any other country, many Israelis agree that Jerusalem must remain the Israeli capital. The unification of Jerusalem by Jews in 1967 has been viewed by Jews around the world as the fulfillment of God's ancient promise to their ancestors.

Gentiles in Jerusalem

Christ said that the Gentiles would trample Jerusalem down until the times of the Gentiles are fulfilled. (Luke 21:24b). Gentiles controlled Israel from the destruction of Jerusalem in AD 70 until Israel became a nation in 1948. Gentiles had treaded down Jerusalem from the Romans to the Moslems. It was even controlled by the European Crusaders for 100 years. For most of nineteen centuries the Holy Land has been under some type of Moslem control. The time of the Gentiles will end when Yeshua, the Jewish Messiah, returns at the Second Advent. It is back in the hands of the Jewish people, which is one sign that Messiah will soon come to Zion.

Conflict over the Temple Mount

You can be sure that the struggle in the Middle East will at last center on the tiny 35 acre plot that we call the Temple Mount. All nations will come to Jerusalem and God will judge them there. When all the smoke clear, Jerusalem will remain in this place and God's great redemptive program will continue.[36]

Jerusalem, City of Conflict

It is clear that the insane demonic rage of nations will ultimately bring them to Israel and Jerusalem. In ancient times the Temple Mount was a threshing floor and it seems that God is about to thresh all the nations there. We can be sure that the struggle in the Middle East will at last center on the tiny 35 acre plot that we call the Temple Mount. We can be sure that all nations will come to the Valley of Jehoshaphat in Jerusalem and God will judge them there. The very name of this valley means "God judges." When all the smoke clear, Jerusalem will remain in this place and God's great redemptive program will continue.

With the whole world turning against this tiny land, about the size of the state of New Jersey, who will stand in the gap to intercede on her behalf? As Christians we must be united in support of the Jewish people. It is very clear to me that God is looking for Christians who will pray for her jealously so that her inhabitants may turn to their Messiah.[37]

Pray for the Peace of Jerusalem

"Because I love Zion, I will not keep still. Because my heart yearns for Jerusalem, I cannot remain silent. I will not stop praying for her until her righteousness shines like the dawn and her salvation blazes like a burning torch" (Isaiah 62:1 NLT).

Jerusalem may have seen more war and violence that any other city on the face of this earth. Is it any wonder that God's Word instructs us to pray for the peace of Jerusalem? Pray for the safety of the Jewish people. Pray for the leaders of Israel.

Jerusalem is the focus of the world as many resolutions in the United Nations concern Israel and Jerusalem. It is also the focus of the news on an almost daily basis. Jerusalem will again be the focus of the world when the Jewish Messiah resigns from Jerusalem for one thousand years.

God promised to set watchmen on the wall, who will not rest until Jerusalem is a joy in the earth. When you consider all the conflicts that Jerusalem has faced down through the centuries and the battles for Jerusalem today, we are reminded of a biblical challenge to Pray for the peace of Jerusalem. "O Jerusalem, I have set intercessors on your wall who shall cry to God all day and all night for the fulfillment of his promises. Take no rest, all you who pray, and give God no rest until he establishes Jerusalem and makes her respected and admired throughout the earth" (Isaiah 62:6-7 TLB).

Jerusalem, Future Home of the Messiah

"Arise, Jerusalem! Let your light shine for all the nations to see! For the glory of the Lord is shining upon you. Darkness as black as night will cover all the nations of the earth, but the glory of the Lord will shine over you. All nations will come to your light. Mighty kings will come to see your radiance" (Isaiah 60:1-3 NLT).

Someday soon, the status of Jerusalem will be settled forever. Yeshua, the Jewish Messiah, will place his feet on the Mount of Olives, east of Jerusalem (Zechariah 14:4) and He will be rule the world from Jerusalem, as King of kings and Lord of lords. Jerusalem, the city of the great King, will be center of world government. The nations will see its righteousness and be astounded by its glory. Mighty nations and powerful kings of the earth will bring their wealth to Jerusalem. In that day people from every nation will come and worship His Name in this Holy City. Jerusalem will become the praise center of the entire earth.

❯ CHAPTER 6
JEWISH TEMPLE

The LORD has chosen Zion; He has desired it for His dwelling place: This is My resting place forever; here I will dwell, for I have desired it… My house shall be called a house of prayer for all nations (Psalm 132:13-14; Isaiah 56:7).

In 1004 B.C., David conquered the city of Jebus from the Jebusites and purchased land for the Temple from Oman, the Jebusite, with silver and gold. He built the altar of the Lord and placed the Ark of the Covenant there. He built his fortress there and called it the City of David. He renamed it Jerusalem and built a palace there. David became more and more powerful, because the Lord of Heaven's Armies was with him.

God gave directions and details for the construction of the temple to King David, who desired to build the temple and had gathered much of the material for the temple together, but was permitted to build it because he was a man of war.

Solomon's Temple

"Solomon began to build the house of the Lord in Jerusalem on Mount Moriah, where *the* Lord had appeared to his father David, at the place that David had prepared on the threshing floor of Ornan the Jebusite" (2 Chronicles 3:1-2 NASB).

The Temple Mount was chosen by God and purchased by King David with silver and gold over three thousand years ago. King Solomon made plans to build the temple as soon as he became king. He began to build the Jewish Temple almost 3,000 years ago in 967 B.C. He built it on Mount Moriah in Jerusalem on the very spot that God instructed David to build an altar. Many people believe this is the large rock where Abraham offered Isaac as a sacrifice. Jews consider this to be the most Holy Place on earth.

Solomon's Temple was built by 30,000 Israelites and with the help of 150,000 Phoenicians (Canaanites). It took seven years to build the temple. It was built with stone at the quarry. No hammer or chisel or any iron tool was heard in the temple while it was being built.

"King Solomon finished all his work on the Temple of the Lord. Then he brought all the gifts his father, David, had dedicated—the silver, the gold, and the various articles—and he stored them in the treasuries of the Lord's Temple" (1 Kings 7:51 NLT).

The grandeur of the temple seemed to be the envy of other kings. It was built twice the size of the tabernacle. Surrounding the temple were two courts, an inner court and a great court. It was built of cedar beams, great stones and boards overlaid with gold. The cost of the temple was estimated to be between two and five billion dollars, probably the most extravagant building on the earth at that time.

God's Promise to Solomon

"Concerning this house which you are building; if you will walk in My statues and execute My ordinances and keep all My commandments by walking in them, then I will carry   out My word with you which I spoke to David your father. I will dwell among the sons of Israel, and will not forsake My people Israel" (1 Kings 6:12-13 NASB).

Babylon's Destruction of Jerusalem and Solomon's Temple

Years before the Jewish Temple was built, the Psalmist saw the day of its destruction. "O God, pagan nations have conquered your land, your special possession. They have defiled your holy Temple and made Jerusalem a heap of ruins. They have left the bodies of your servants as food for the birds of heaven. The flesh of your godly ones has become food for the wild animals. Blood flowed like water all around Jerusalem; no one is left to bury the dead. We are mocked by our neighbors, an object of scorn and derision to those around us." (Psalm 79:1-4 NLT). This Psalm accurately foretold of the siege of Nebuchadnezzar and the subsequent Babylonian captivity.

The destruction of the Jewish Temple was understood as God's punishment for violating the covenant God made with Israel. This day was declared a day of mourning in remembrance of the anniversary of the temple's destruction. Nebuchadnezzar's army invaded the tiny nation of Israel destroying Jerusalem. He burned Solomon's Temple on the 9th day of Av in 586 B.C. and carried thousands of Jews to Babylon.

Nebuchadnezzar, King of Babylon, devastated Jerusalem in three assaults and finally destroyed Jerusalem in 586 B.C. The Jewish Temple was burned and the Ark of the Covenant disappeared at this time.

The 2nd Book of Maccabees records that Jeremiah, the prophet, took the Ark of the Covenant and hid it in a cave where Moses had seen the inheritance of God. "Jeremiah came and found a cave, and he brought there the tent and the ark and the altar of incense, and he sealed up the entrance. Some of those who followed him came up to mark the way, but could not find it. When Jeremiah learned of it, he rebuked them and declared: 'The place shall be unknown until God gathers his people together again and shows his mercy. Then the Lord will disclose these things, and the glory of the Lord and the cloud will appear, as they were shown in the case of Moses, and as Solomon asked that the place should be specially consecrated'" (2 Maccabees 2:5-8).

King Nebuchadnezzar took ten thousand captives from Jerusalem, including all the princes and the best of the soldiers, craftsmen, and smiths. So only the poorest people were left in the land. The Southern Kingdom, better known as

Judah, was taken into captivity. Babylon captured King Zedekiah, from the line of David, and dragged him off in chains.

Over a million Jews died when Nebuchadnezzar destroyed Jerusalem and the Jewish Temple. Many died of starvation, some were crucified and others were given over to the gladiatorial arenas. So many Jews were sold into slavery that the price of slaves dropped drastically. The destruction was so devastating that they read like scenes out of the Holocaust.

Period of Restoration

For almost seven decades the Jewish captives were away from their homeland. Many of them became entrenched in the Babylonian society and remained in Babylon. People of royal origin were treated with the most indignity.

The exiles increased in numbers and wealth as they followed Jeremiah's advice to build homes. Their genealogically records were kept intact. They were able to tell who was the rightful heir to David's throne though which the long awaited Messiah would come.

God used Babylon to bring judgment on the Southern Tribe of Judah for seventy years. Many of the Jews lost all hope of returning to Israel, even though Ezekiel and Daniel ministered to the Jews during their captivity.

Persian Empire Conquered the Babylonian Empire

The Babylonian Empire was conquered by the Persians, who had a reputation of allowing exiles to maintain their status and later encouraged them to return to their homeland. Darius, King of Persia, was kindly disposed towards the Jews, as well as Cyrus the Great, who agreed to return the temple articles to Jerusalem.

Cyrus, God's Instrument

God said of Cyrus, 'He is my shepherd, he will certainly do was I say; and Jerusalem will be rebuilt and the Temple restored, for I have spoken it" (Isaiah 44:28 TLB).

This is what King Cyrus of Persia says: "The Lord, the God of heaven, has given me all the kingdoms of the earth. He has appointed me to build him a Temple at Jerusalem. Any of you who are his people may go to Jerusalem in Judah to rebuild this Temple of the Lord, the God of Israel, who lives in Jerusalem!" (Ezra 1:2-3 NLT).

Cyrus felt he had a mandate from God to restore the temple at Jerusalem because Isaiah had prophesied that a man named Cyrus would rebuild the temple. He allowed the Jewish people to return to their homeland and rebuild the Jewish

Temple. An entire generation of Jews was allowed to return to Palestine, a place they had never seen. It required an extremely pioneering spirit and great faith to return to their desolate homeland. Over 42,000 Israelites returned to their ancient homeland after seventy years of bondage.

Second Temple (Zerubbabel's Temple)

Zerubbabel was a descendant of King David in the direct lineage of Jesus Christ. He was the head of the Tribe of Judah during the time of the return from Babylonian exile. He led the first group of captives back to Jerusalem and began rebuilding the Temple on the old site.

He was the prime builder of the second Temple, which was later re-constructed by King Herod. For some 20 years he was closely associated with prophets, priests, and kings until the new temple was dedicated and the Jewish sacrificial system was re-established. The Second Temple was built under the leadership of Zerubbabel during the years 520-516 B.C. It was consecrated about seventy years after the destruction of Solomon's Temple.

Herod's Temple

In the eighteenth year of his reign, Herod started to enlarge and reconstruct the temple at his own expense, which he knew would be his greatest enterprise. After removing the old foundations, he laid new ones, and raised the structure of hard, white stone.[38]

Herod, the Great began rebuilding Solomon's temple in 20 B.C. and the project occupied the rest of his administration. The fifteen-story high temple was constructed during Herod's reign, but the outer counts and walls were not fully completed until A.D. 64, some sixty-eight years after his death.[39]

The Second Temple, better known as Herod's Temple, was one of the wonders of the ancient world. The temple was in existence during the time Christ walked on the earth. The temple built by Herod the Great was magnificent beyond description with much gold and marble. It was destroyed by fire in A.D. 70.[40]

According to the Talmud, Herod's temple lacked five things that were in Solomon's Temple.[41]

1. The Ark of the Covenant
2. The Sacred Fire
3. The Shekinah Glory of God
4. The Urim and Thummin
5. The empty Holy of Holies

Jesus foretold the Destruction of the Temple

"Days will come upon you when your enemies will build an embankment around you, surround you and close you in on every side, and level you, and your children within you, to the ground; and they will not leave in you one stone upon another, because you did not know the time of your visitation" (Luke 19:43-44).

This prophecy was fulfilled in A.D. 70 when Titus, the Roman General, burned Herod's Temple, leaving only the western portion of the retaining wall. Perhaps this was done to remind them of the magnificence of the Temple and its destruction.

Unger's Bible Dictionary states that the temple was destroyed on August 10th, the Jewish Sabbath in the year A.D. 70. The temple was burned when Jerusalem was captured and the Jewish people expatriated. The Romans destroyed the city and massacred many of the inhabitants. There has never been sacrifice offered up to God on Jewish altars since that time.[42]

Josephus, the ancient historian, born shortly after the birth of Christ, witnessed this event and recorded that the Romans set the temple on fire on the exact same day the temple was previously destroyed. He said, "It is God Himself who is using the Romans to purge His temple with fire and exterminate a city so choked with pollution".

Josephus reported that 1,100,000 Jews died during the siege of Jerusalem, many by starvation. 100,000 others were taken prisoners and sent to slave camps in Babylon. This horrible event occurred at the time of the annual Jewish Feast when hundreds of thousands of Jews were in Jerusalem.

C.H. Spurgeon said, "The destruction of Jerusalem was more terrible than anything that the world has ever witnessed, either before or since. Even Titus seemed to see in his cruel work, the hand of an avenging God".

Sadly, both temple were destroyed on the same day—the ninth of Av--about 656 years apart. The Hebrew month of Av usually coincides with late July or mid-August on the secular calendar.

The ninth of Av also happens to be the day that the Jews were expelled from England in 1290, as well as the day that King Ferdinand and Queen Isabella expelled the Jews from Spain in 1492. Any you look at it, the ninth of *Av* has not been a good day for the Jewish people.[43]

Austerities that occurred on the 9th of Av in History[44]

• God promised that the Children of Israel could not enter the Promised Land in 1200 B.C.
• The Babylonian Army destroyed the Jewish Temple in 586 B.C.

- Titus destroyed Herod's Temple in A.D. 70.
- The Jews lost their independence in A.D. 137.

Other Grave Misfortunes on the 9ᵗʰ of Av

- World War I broke out on the eve of Tisha B'Av in 1914 when Germany declared war on Russia. Resentment from the war set the stage for the Holocaust.
- King Edward I of England ordered the expulsion of English Jewry in 1290.
- In the eve of Tisha B'Av 1942, mass deportation began of Jews from Warsaw Ghetto began.
- The Spanish Inquisition culminated with the expulsion of Jews from Spain in 1492.

Jews Mourn the Destruction of the Temple

Millions of Jews prayed each day facing Jerusalem, from every country on earth, during their 2,000-year dispersion. Hundreds of inspired songs and scripture verses have been written about Jerusalem. God's presence dwelled in Jerusalem at this site for over a thousand years.

The Jewish People have mourned the destruction of the Jerusalem Temple since A.D. 70. Even today, Orthodox Jews recite a petition three times daily for the Temple's restoration. Each year at Passover, dispersed Jews remember Jerusalem by saying "Next year in Jerusalem."

Considered a day of national mourning, Jews fast and remove anything that might change their saddened spirits. In the past they were not permitted to read the Old Testament during this time, since it brought gladness. No music or laughter was allowed. Many people wear sackcloth and sprinkle themselves with ashes for times of extreme sorrow.

Even during happy occasions such as marriage, a serious reminder of the temple destruction is included. At the ceremony's conclusion, the groom breaks a glass goblet the couple has shared. The rabbis believe this is a sign of solidarity with the Jewish community in mourning for the Temple.[45]

There is a story told of Napoleon that he passed a crowded synagogue on the 9ᵗʰ of Av and heard the noise of obvious weeping and sorrow, he asked what it meant. He was told that they were weeping in the synagogue for their country and their sanctuary which had been destroyed some 1800 years before. Napoleon, deeply moved observed that a people which weeps and mourns for the loss of its homeland 1800 years ago and does not forget- such a people will never be destroyed. Such a people can rest assured that its homeland will be returned to it.[46]

Changes in Judaism

With the Second Temple, the central focus of Judaism, destroyed, the Sanhedrin needed to interpret how Judaism would be practiced. The priests were replaced by community rabbis and, in the absence of a central place of worship; the synagogue became the hub of each community. Judaism had to be reinterpreted so that it could survive without the Temple in Jerusalem. The beginnings of rabbinical Judaism were established here.[47]

Israel captured the Temple Mount

During the 1956 Six Day War, Israel achieved a stunning victory. Israeli planes destroyed the entire Egyptian air force on the ground. In six days, Israel tripled its territory, gaining the Sinai Peninsula, the Golan Heights, the West Bank, and -- most precious of all -- the Old City and the Temple Mount.[48]

General Moshe Dayan placed the Israeli flag on the Temple Mount where the ancient Jewish Temple once stood. This made the soldiers very happy – but shortly after that he removed the flag to placate the Muslim Arabs.

Since Israel began a nation in 1948, Jews have returned to their ancient homeland by the millions. Their dream is to again worship God in their own temple. At this time, they can only worship at the Wailing Wall, which merely supports the temple wall. Jews and Christians are not allowed to pray at this site. If they attempt to pray there, they will be removed by the Moslem authorities.

Temple Mount Controlled by Muslims

The Temple Mount is a thirty-five acre tract of land called the Noble Sanctuary by Moslems. Today it is a landscaped park, home to the Islamic shrine called the Dome of the Rock and the Al-Aksa Mosque which was completed in A.D. 691 over thirteen centuries ago.

Security experts now believe that the Temple Mount is the most dangerous square mile on the planet. Israeli police and intelligence forces maintain tight security around the site to prevent Jewish or other extremists from trying to blow up the Dome of the Rock and the Al-Aksa Mosque. If the dome and the mosque were somehow destroyed by a terrorist attack, this could unleash a war of horrific proportions as the wrath of a billion Muslims turned against Israel.[49]

Muslims consider this to be where Abraham's great sacrifice occurred, but they believe that Ishmael was offered to God as a sacrifice rather than Isaac. Jews and Christians are not allowed to pray at this site

Many Jewish scholars and archaeologists believe that the Ark of the Covenant and other sacred vessel of the Temple may be in secret tunnels hidden between the Temple Mount and Qumran, where the Dead Sea Scrolls were discovered. These tunnels are not assessable to archaeologists today because Muslims control the temple mount. It certainly would not be in their best interest for these holy articles to be discovered.

Temple Institute in Jerusalem

The Temple Institute's ultimate goal is to see Israel rebuild the Holy Temple in Jerusalem, in accord with the Biblical commandments. The Institute's activities include education, research, and development. They hope to rebuild the Holy Temple on Mount Moriah in Jerusalem.

Over the last thirty years, the Temple Institute in Jerusalem has reconstructed every utensil and every piece of furniture needed for the resumption of temple administration. They recently have even built a new Ark of the Covenant according to the exact specifications given in scripture. Only one thing stands between Israel and the building of her Third Temple. They need the ashes of a red heifer so that worshippers can be purified from contact with a dead body in order to them to construction the new temple.[50]

Importance of the Red Heifer

A red heifer, as described in Number 19, is the only way under Jewish law a person can be purified from contact with a dead body. Consequently, Jews believe a qualified red heifer must be produced before Israel's Third Temple can be built.[51]

In our own times, the commandment of the red heifer takes on more and more significance. For without it, the Divine service of the Holy Temple cannot be resumed. There is a spiritual renaissance today in Israel; after almost 2,000 year, Israel is clearly moving toward the time when the Holy temple on Mount Mount—the prophesied Third Temple –will be rebuilt.[52]

What does a red heifer have to do with any of them? Perhaps it would be difficult for some to believe that a cow could be so important. God has ordained that its ashes alone are the single missing ingredient for the reinstatement of Biblical purity – and therefore, the rebuilding of the Holy Temple.[53]

DNA Test Determines Priestly Tribe

Just recently a gene has been discovered that can determine if you have Jewish blood with a simple blood test. Cohen (Kohanim) is the name of the priestly tribe in Israel. With a DNA test they can tell who is in the priestly line. The Jewish priests in Israel have already been trained to offer sacrifices when the Jewish Temple will be rebuilt. The Priestly Garments have already been prepared.

We are pleased to announce that the weaving of the sacred Ephod garment for the uniform of the High Priest has been completed. The Temple Institute has also completed the complicated task of joining the ephod to the remembrance stones, and affixing the breastplate. This complex project has been based on extensive research by the Institute. This task has been completed and the results have been made public.[54]

Building the Third Temple

"In the last days the mountains of the LORD's temple will be established as chief among the mountains; it will be raised above the hills, and all nations will stream to it. Many people will come and say, 'Come, let us go up to the mountain of the Lord, to the house of the God of Jacob. He will teach us his ways, so that we walk in his paths. The law will go out from Zion, the word of the Lord from Jerusalem'" (Isaiah 2:2-3 NIV).

Israel has not had a temple on the Temple Mount in Jerusalem since the Romans destroyed the Second Temple in A.D. 70. Yet the Bible clearly prophesies that a new Jewish Temple will be standing three and one-half years before the Second Coming of Jesus. Over the last thirty years the Temple Institute in Jerusalem has reconstructed very utensil and every piece of furniture needed to resumption of temple administration. They recently have even built a new Ark of the Covenant according to the exact specifications given in scripture.[55]

The greatest desire shared by Jews worldwide is to rebuild a Jewish Temple on the same site where the original Jewish temple stood. Only the Western (Wailing) Wall is accessible to Jews today. Will they be willing to sacrifice their national security to achieve this goal?

Jewish Temple to be Rebuilt

- John, the apostle, was instructed in Revelation to measure the temple, many years after the temple was destroyed (Revelation 11:1-2).
- Isaiah tells us that in the latter day the Jewish Temple will be established on the top of the mountain and that all nations will flow to it (Isaiah 2:2).
- Many Jews and Christians believe that before the Messiah returns, the temple will be rebuilt.

Gershon Salomon, head of the Temple Mount Faithful, has been making plans for some time to rebuild the Jewish Temple. He said, I don't believe that Jewish life can continue to exist without the Temple Mount. The moment such as an agreement is signed, I am sure that tens of thousands or hundreds of thousands of Israelis and Jews from around the world will go the Temple Mount.

There must be a Third Temple built on the Temple Mount in Jerusalem, on the same spot where the previous two temples stood, in order to fulfill biblical prophecy. Daniel, the Old Testament prophet, spoke of a prince that will make a covenant with the Jewish people and allow them to make sacrifices. This can only be done in the Jewish Temple. The Temple will be desecrated when Antichrist invades the Temple and proclaim that he is God.

Jesus confirmed that a Jewish Temple will be standing in the Last Days when He said, "Therefore when you see the abomination of desolation which was spoken of through Daniel the prophet, standing in the holy place (let the reader understand), then those who are in Judea must flee to the mountains. Whoever is on the housetop must not go down to get the things out that are in his house. Whoever is in the field must not turn back to get his cloak. But woe to those who are pregnant and to those who are nursing babies in those days! But pray that your flight will not be in the winter, or on a Sabbath. For then there will be a great tribulation, such as has not occurred since the beginning of the world until now, nor ever will. Unless those days had been cut short, no life would have been saved; but for the sake of the elect those days will be cut short" (Matthew 24:15-22 NASB).

The apostle John was told to "Go and measure the Temple of God and the altar, and count the number of worshipers. But do not measure the outer court-yard, for it has been turned over to the nations. They will trample the holy city for 42 months" (Revelation 11:1-2 NLT).

Temples in the Bible[56]

The Temple	Description
Solomon's Temple 966-586 B.C.	Planned by David - 2 Samuel 7-1-29 Constructed by Solomon - 1 Kings 8:1-66 Destroyed by Nebuchadnezzar – Jeremiah 32:28-44
Zebubbabel's Temple 516-169 B.C.	Constructed by Zerubbabel & Jews – Ezra 3:1-8; 4:1-14Desecrated by Antiochus Epiphanes Maccabees
Herod's Temple 19 B.C. to A.D. 70	Zebubbabel's Temple restored by Herod – Mark 13:1-2Destroyed by the Romans – Acts 21:27-33

Present Temple	Found in the hearts of the believers. The body of the believers is the Lord's only temple until the Messiah returns.
Temple of Revelation 11 Tribulation Period	To be constructed during the Tribulation - Revelation 11:1-2 To be desecrated by the Antichrist- Matthew 24:15; 2 Thessalonians 2: 3-4
Ezekiel's Millennial Temple	Envisioned by the prophet Ezekiel - Ezekiel 40:1- 42:20 To be built by the Messiah during His millennial reign. Zechariah 6:12, 13
The Eternal Temple of His Presence	The greatest temple of all. "The Lord God Almighty and the Lamb are its temple" (Revelation 21:22; 22:1-21).

The Messiah Will return Though the Golden Gate

In 1517 the Turks conquered Jerusalem under the leadership of Suleiman the Magnificent. He consulted some Jewish rabbis and asked them about the Messiah. They described the Messiah as a great military leader who would return to Jerusalem by means of the Eastern Gate and liberate the city from foreign control. Suleiman decided to put an end to Jewish hope by sealing up the Eastern Gate. It has been sealed ever since.

Someday soon Jesus Christ will return in triumph. Many people believe that He will enter through the Eastern Gate, the gate that has been closed for hundreds of years. He will set up His Millennial Kingdom and rule and reign in Jerusalem for 1,000 years.

Millennial Temple

Thus says the Lord of hosts, "We have a man here whose name is Branch. He will branch out from where he is and build the Temple of God. Yes, he's the one. He'll build the Temple of God. Then he'll assume the role of royalty, take his place on the throne and rule—a priest sitting on the throne!—showing that king and priest can coexist in harmony" (Zechariah 6:12-13 MSG).

The Jewish Temple will be rebuilt and its glory will radiate the whole world. The Shekinah Glory of God departed from Solomon's Temple because of Israel's sin and rebellion (Ezekiel 11:22-23), but the Shekinah glory of God will someday fill the rebuilt Millennial Temple.

Ezekiel describes when the Glory of God will return to the Jewish Temple. "The glory of the LORD came into the Temple through the east gateway. Then the Spirit took me and brought me into the inner courtyard, and the glory of the LORD filled the Temple" (Ezekiel 43:4-5 NLT).

When the Divine Presence dwells once again in Jerusalem, Israel will take its true position as God's Promised Land that will bless all of the nations throughout the world. God's promise was given through the words of Ezekiel: "Then will I sprinkle clean water upon you, and you will be clean; I will cleanse you from all your filthiness and from all your idols" (Ezekiel 36:25 NASB).

The prophecies reveal that it will not be long until the Messiah will return to fulfill all of the great prophecies of the redemption of Israel and the Promised Land. What a glorious day that will be!

❯ CHAPTER 7
MIRACLES IN THE HOLY LAND

The hand of God has been on Israel since she became a nation over 3,000 years ago and especially since she became a nation again in 1948. How Israel has survived relentless terrorist attacks and four major wars is truly a modern day miracle. In this chapter, we will explore how divine intervention from God created the nation of Israel and delivered Israel from four major military conflicts. In this chapter, we will explore how divine intervention from God created the nation of Israel and delivered Israel from four major military conflicts.

Revival swept through England in the nineteenth century bringing about a love for the Jewish people. One English boy was taught to pray that Israel would again be restored to their ancient homeland.

British Gains Control of the Holy Land

England was involved into a war in the early twentieth century that involved the Ottoman Turkish Empire, the power that controlled Israel. The Ottoman Empire crumbled, and in 1917 the British forces led by General Edmund Allenby entered the Holy Land. Allenby was the boy who had prayed every night for God to restore the Jewish people to their ancient homeland.

Allenby prayed that he could take the city without damaging the Holy Land. He wired London for instructions and received a simple reply—a scripture verse! [57]"As birds flying so will the LORD of hosts defend Jerusalem; defending also he will deliver it; and passing over He will preserve it" (Isaiah 31:5).

General Allenby read this scripture verse to his troops. He commanded every available aircraft to fly over Jerusalem. The Turks had never seen an airplane and were frightened. One of the pilots dropped a note demanding surrender – signed by General Allenby.

According to reports, the name of Allenby further frighten them, for the word "Allah" in Arabic means "God" and "beh" is Arabic for "son". The Turks were looking at a demand for surrender signed by Allah-beh, the son of God. In response, they hoisted a white flag and surrendered the city without firing a single shot.[58]

Psalm 17:8 seems to describe that historic event of 1917. "Hide me under the shadow of thy wings" could be another reference to the wings of those British planes.

The sacred city, which had been under the Gentile yoke, was freed on December 9, 1917. This was the first day of the feast Chanukah (Hanukkah), on the 24th day of Chislev. About 2,000 years before, according to the Jewish calendar, Judas Maccabeus, having taken possession of Jerusalem, re-dedicated the Temple and celebrated this remarkable victory. Is it not remarkable that, upon the anniversary of this great victory, this same city should be freed again?[59]

Miraculous Rebirth of Israel

"Who hath heard such a thing? Who hath seen such things? Shall the land be born in one day? Can a nation be brought forth all at once? As soon as Zion travailed, she brought forth her sons" (Isaiah 66:8 NASB).

On May 14, 1948, against all odds, having been dispersed all over the world for two millenniums, Israel was re-birthed as a nation fulfilling prophecies in the Old Testament Books of Ezekiel, Jeremiah, and Isaiah. This rebirth astounded the world. Never before had an entire race of people, widely scattered around the world, without a homeland, re-establish itself as a nation and in one single day, as well! Israel is the only nation with this unique, historical experience.[60]

This is truly a modern day miracle. This prophecy was fulfilled on May 14, 1948, when Israel became a nation in "one day". On that day, the flag of Israel was hoisted over the land for the first time in over 1,800 years. British rule ended and Israel became an independent state. Israel's dream of a homeland came to pass. What a day for rejoicing for Jews all over the world!

This was no surprise to those who believed in biblical prophecy. Jeremiah told of that event many years ago. "Therefore, behold, the days are coming, declares the Lord, when it shall no longer be said, 'As the Lord lives who brought up the people of Israel out of the land of Egypt, but "As the Lord lives who brought up the people of Israel out of the north country and out of all the counties where he had driven them. I will bring them back to their own land that I gave to their fathers" (Jeremiah 16:14-15 ESV).

Israel's Four Major Wars

The United Nations divided the Holy Land into two states, one Jewish and the other Palestinian. The Jews accepted the plan, but the Arab governments refused to recognize Israel. Israel has been in constant danger from their Arab nations since its inception in 1948. The day following Israel's declaration as a nation, she was invaded by five Arab nations. Since Israel began a nation, she has fought four major wars.

1. 1948 - War of Independence with Egypt, Lebanon & Jordan: Restoration of Israel
2. 1956 - Suez Canal War: Assertion of National Sovereignty
3. 1967 - Six-day War: Recapture of the Temple Mount and Golan Heights
4. 1973 - Yom Kippur War: Solidified West Bank Occupation

Israel's War of Independence – 1948

No sooner had Israel proclaimed its independence on May 14, 1948, than five Arab nations, Egypt, Syria, Trans-Jordan, Lebanon and Iraq launched an attack against the newly re-born and tiny nation, on the same day! They were out to destroy the new state, and reclaim the land for the setting up another Arab state. The Arab states far outnumbered and out-gunned the Jews. They had troops, artillery and other military hardware that the Jews did not have.[61]

Israel was ill-equipped to withstand the combined Arab armies. They possessed less than 1,000 rifles and about the same amount of machine guns with only enough ammunition to last a few days. The infant nation was facing a modern-day version of David and Goliath.

Why didn't the United Nations offer a rebuke to the Arab armies who mercilessly attacked Israel on May 16, 1948, on the second day of her rebirth?

With a total Jewish population of only about 650,000, and with limited armaments and resources, the ragtag army of Israel defeated the combined might of the aggressors and established itself firmly within its boundaries. Transjordan (now renamed Jordan) stayed in possession of Judea/Samaria (now known as the West Bank) and the eastern part of Jerusalem. Egypt occupied the Gaza Strip. The price was very high. In this bloodiest of wars imposed on Israel, over 6,000 citizens died—nearly 1% of the population.[62]

Miracles in the War of Independence – 1948

During this conflict, a number or miracles occurred to shift the tide of the war. When an Israeli tank commander found himself and his men in the middle of a mine field, how was the prayer of one of his men suddenly followed by an unprecedented wind that blew away nearly a foot of topsoil and then just as suddenly stop, revealing the hiding places of thousands of mines so the soldiers could escape unharmed?[63]

Why, during the War for Independence, did a battalion of Jordanian soldiers approaching the position of a handful of Israeli soldiers defending Mt. Zion without ammunition, suddenly shout "Abraham" and turn and flee? How could three dozen teenagers, survivors of the Holocaust, walk right past a company of Egyptian soldiers in the Negev without being seen? The fact that these and scores of other unexplainable occurrences fill the pages of every war in Israel.[64]

The Six-Day War – 1967

All of the Arab nations surrounding Israel joined together and formed a united front to annihilate the Jewish state. In the days preceding the Six Day War things looked bleak for the tiny Jewish state. Every military analyst in the world predicted the quick destruction of Israel. The world expected to witness the jubilant Arab armies parading through the streets of Tel Aviv. The atmosphere was tense and rabbis around the world were already preparing their eulogy speeches for the state of Israel and the millions of Jews who were expected to be slaughtered in the Arab onslaught.[65]

During the June 1967 Six-Day War, Israel once again prevailed. In just six days she smashed the armed forces of Egypt, Jordan and Syria. She captured Judea, Samaria and East Jerusalem from King Hussein of Jordan. The Golan Heights was captured from Syria and Gaza from Egypt. Over one million Arabs living in the Judea/Samaria (the West Bank), Gaza Strip and East Jerusalem came under Israeli rule.

Miracles in the 1967 Six Day War

Israeli soldiers told of divine intervention in the Six-Day War. Gershon Salomon lay badly wounded and saw Syrian soldiers moving into their area shooting wounded Israeli soldiers. They were about to shoot him, when all of a sudden they fled the area leaving their weapons behind. The Syrian soldiers later reported to UN officers that they saw "thousands of angels" surrounding the wounded soldier and that was why they ran away. Gershon Salomon went on to found the Temple Mount Faithful, who is trying to restore the Jewish Temple in Jerusalem.[66]

A story is told of a small Jewish community under siege by Arabs who were determined to wipe them out. However, the Arabs encountered huge strange beings with flaming swords, and they ran away in great fear as the astonished village rabbi watched them.[67]

Many miracles occurred in the Six Day War that resembles the Biblical narratives of ancient days when God fought for ancient Israel. These miraculous events were circulated all over Israel and even in secular newspapers. Life Magazine devoted most of one issue to this miraculous war.

Miracles during the 1973 Yom Kippur War

Yom Kippur is the most holy day in the Jewish Nation. This day began with a silent serenity reserved for only this day. The streets were silent and empty. By law, no one works. No buses, no taxes, no shops opened their doors. There was no television or radio. For Israel was at rest and at prayer. Almost all Israeli soldiers were at home or in the synagogue. Israel faced almost total annihilation. The weeks before Prime Minister Golda Meir had dismissed the signs of an invasion as meaningless.

Prime Minister Golda Meir made the wrenching decision, in the few hours before the war actually began, not to strike the Arabs in any preemptive attack, as they had in 1967. The Israeli Government understood that if they attacked first, even to defend themselves, no one would help them, not even the United States. Henry Kissinger said later, if Israel attacked first, the United States would not have supplied Israel with "so much as a nail." Israel absorbed the first blows. It did not have much choice, they were simply not ready. Israel had no powerful friends except the United States, and that friendship might be tenuous.[68]

This is no ordinary Yom Kipper. This was October 6, 1973. At 2:00 pm on that day 100,000 Egyptian Soldiers invaded Israel's southern border. An armada of 1,400 Syrian tanks raced across the Golan Heights toward Tel Aviv. They seemed unstoppable. If they reach Tel Aviv, the entire industrial and economic machinery of Israel would be destroyed. As Golda Meir watched their country face almost total destruction, she contemplated suicide. The cabinet drew up plans for a government in exile. Few generals believed Israel would survive.[69]

Israel was attacked by the combined armies of Egypt and Syria. It was the High Holiday, the single most important day on the Jewish religious calendar. Israeli High Command traditionally has given the vast majority of the Defense Forces the holiday off to return to their homes, to synagogue if they chose. This Yom Kippur was no different. Israeli intelligence was comfortable that, though Arab preparations for some sort of action were easily visible across the Canal, nothing was expected to happen. Political, military leadership cockily expected they would be able to beat back any Arab attack.[70]

Meir is desperate. Without help, Israel would not survive the assault from all sides, despite all the brave soldiers who are fighting for Israel. She picks up the phone and calls the private line of President Richard Nixon. It is 3:00 a.m. in the morning. As he put his robe on, President Nixon sat on the edge of the presidential bed and heard Golda Meir pleading with him. "Please Mr. President, help us". The Jewish People will never survive." He said he could almost hear his mother's voice as she told him stories and read to him from the Old Testament about the heroes of the Bible. He said, one afternoon, she said to me, "Richard, someday you are going to be in a position where you can help save the Jewish people. When that day comes, you must do everything in your power."[71]

He said at that moment he realized, maybe for the first time in his presidency, why he became President for the United States. He said to Golda, "What do you want?" She had her list. The president sent the largest armament since World War II. He kept his word. Everything Golda requested, she got. Every weapon, every vehicle, every piece of equipment and all the ammunition to operate them, were air lifted overnight to Israel's front line. There was a virtual arsenal airlifted to Israel overnight. Many military experts credit that decision, as the essential element that saved Israel from destruction.[72]

Miracle in the Yom Kippur War

An Israeli military historian recorded that during the 1973 Yom Kippur War an Israeli soldier in the Sinai took captive an Egyptian column and led them to where the Israeli troops were. The Egyptian commander was asked why he and his men gave themselves up to the lone Israeli soldier. He responded with surprise; "One soldier? There were thousands of them." He said that as they neared the Israeli lines, the "soldiers" began disappearing. The Israeli soldier reported that he was by himself when the Egyptian commander and his men surrendered to him. He was totally unaware of the "thousands of soldiers" the Egyptian soldiers saw with him, since he himself did not see them. Psalm 91:10-11 promises that "No evil shall befall you, nor shall any plague come near your dwelling, For He shall give his angels charge over you, to keep you in all your ways."[73]

Miracles in the Gulf War – United States against Saddam Hussein

The Gulf War lasted from January 17, 1991, to February 28, 1991, about six weeks. While it was a terrifying experience for all Israelis, resulting in trauma which took some years to overcome, there were also stories about amazing deliverances and curious coincidences. You can decide whether these were indeed miracles or not, but most Israelis made up their minds long ago. One secular woman said if you live in Israel and don't believe in miracles, you're just not being realistic.[74]

Israel came to within a hair of entering the war directly, but at the last second was pressured by the US to stay out of the conflict – no easy task for a country being shot at! (The reason was that several Arab allies with the US vowed they would never fight on the same side as Israel, and it was feared that Israel's involvement would break up the coalition.)[75]

No missiles landed in the city of Jerusalem. Any hits in that area, besides threatening life, would have destroyed ancient archeological sites which could never be replaced. It was reported afterward that the Iraqis had argued about this, and finally decided not to target Jerusalem for fear of hitting the Dome of the Rock.[76]

The first night of the missile strikes against Israel, 27 missiles were fired at once. Patriot missiles knocked out all of them except two. During missile strikes in the West Bank, only injuries were suffered; no lives were lost. A missile landed in a garbage dump but didn't explode. Another missile landed a few feet away from a gas station, but didn't explode. One missile landed between two buildings, completely destroying them but not killing any people.[77]

Several missiles aimed at Israel fell into Mediterranean Sea to the west. Another missile was blown off course by a strong wind. Two missiles aimed at the

IDF base in the Negev desert landed without causing damage. One missile that fell was discovered to have concrete in place of an explosive warhead. Two missiles fired from Iraq suddenly disappeared. A missile hit a bank, but only one person was in the building at the time. A missile went down an airshaft of a 9-story apartment building with 20-30 apartments; it did not explode. [78]

Palestinians stood on their rooftops cheering for Iraq as a barrage of missiles hit Israel. They were following the lead of Yasser Arafat, who openly supported Saddam's war. The next day, some missiles landed in their own villages. Israeli media filmed their panicked race to the nearest security station to demand gas masks for themselves. There were no more rooftop celebrations.[79]

Missiles & Miracles in 1991

The failed attempts of the SCUD missiles to destroy Jewish life were nothing less than miraculous. As the missiles—each loaded with 600 pounds of explosives—rained down upon Tel Aviv, the terrified citizens, huddled in shelters and sealed rooms, listened in disbelief to the news flashes. Buildings crowded with people were hit, yet virtually not a soul was harmed. "G-d threw down mattresses to cushion our falls, pushed walls out of our way," declared one survivor. On the day of Purim, traditionally a day of merry-making for the Jewish people, the war was officially declared over. "Adequate attention is not being paid to these miracles," The popular media throughout the world took note of the miraculous occurrences, yet there is a tendency to offer rationales and explanations. These are miracles that were performed by God! [80]

Israel Surrounded by Arab Nations

Arabs own and occupy more than 99% of the land across northern Africa and the Middle East. By contrast, the state of Israel owns and occupies less than one tenth of one percent of the land area.[81]

Israel is now surrounded by Arab nations who would like to see a world without Zionism. God moved supernaturally in the past and will continue to protect His chosen people. How has she survived four major wars and relentless terrorist attacks, except for the fact that the God of Israel never slumbers or sleeps? Israel has been miraculously delivered from her enemies by the wonderful intervening hand of the Almighty who delivered her repeatedly in time past, and WHO still promises as follows:

"Hear the word of the LORD, O you nations, and declare it in the coastlands afar off, and say, 'He that scattered Israel will gather him, and keep him, as a shepherd keeps his flock. For the LORD hath ransomed Jacob, and redeemed him from the hand of him who was stronger than he. They shall come and shout for joy on the height of Zion, and they will be radiant over the bounty of the Lord—over the grain and the new wine and the oil, and over the young of the flock and the herd; and their life will be like a watered garden, and they will never languish again. Then the virgin will rejoice in the dance, and the young men and the old, together, for I will turn their mourning into joy and will comfort them and give them joy for their sorrow" (Jeremiah 31:10-13 NASB).

❯ CHAPTER 8
GLORY OF THE LORD

"Let the Glory of the Lord cover the earth as the waters cover the sea" (Isaiah 11:9).

God manifested His presence in a number of ways to His people. His presence was sometimes referred to as the glory of God or the "Shekinah glory of God." He often chose to reveal Himself to His people with a visible manifestation of His presence.

God's Glory in the Old Testament

- By the Pillar of Cloud – Exodus 13:21-22
- By the Pillar of Fire – Exodus 13:21-22
- By the Thunderstorm – Exodus 19:16
- By the Brilliant Light – Exodus 33:22

When the Israelites left Egypt, they were led by the cloud in the day and the pillar of fire at night. The presence of the cloud went before them, leading them, giving them shade from the heat. The pillar of fire gave them light and warmth. The presence of the cloud by day and the fire by night must have been a great comfort to Moses and the people. However, the glory of God was not in the cloud or the pillar, but rather the manifest presence of God dwelling in them.

God's Glory Led the Israelites

As they left Egypt, the Egyptian chariots pursued them and drew near to them. The Children of Israel were afraid and cried out to God. Moses told them, "Do not be afraid, stand still and see the salvation of the Lord." God moved the cloud behind the Israelites, between them and the Egyptians. The Pillar of Cloud gave light to the Israelites, but darkness to the Egyptians, so the Egyptians did not come near the Children of Israel. The cloud of glory led the Israelites through the Red Sea. It led them as they traveled in the wilderness.

The priests blew the trumpet and alerted the people. They lead the procession, and the Israelites followed the cloud. When the cloud moved, they moved. When the cloud remained in one place, the people remained there.

Cloud of Glory at Mt. Sinai

The presence of God eventually led them to Mt. Sinai and settled on the top of the mountain. Moses ascended up to Mt. Sinai and stayed there forty day in the presence of the cloud of glory. The voice of God spoke to him out of the cloud at the giving of the law. In God's presence, Moses received the Ten Commandments and directions for the construction of the Tabernacle.

The brilliant light of God's glory left its glow on Moses' face. When Moses came down from the mountain, his face was so aglow from the presence of God that the people could not look upon his face. Moses covered his face with a veil to shield the people's eyes from the bright glow of the Holy Spirit.

God instructed Moses to stand on the rock, and God's glory would pass by. God put Moses in the cleft of the rock and covered him with His hand while He passed by. When God took His hand away, Moses was allowed to see God's glory. The brilliant light of God's glory left its glow on Moses' face.

"Behold the Lord our God has shown us His glory and His greatness, and we have heard His voice out of the midst of the fire; we have this day seen that God speaking with man, yet he still lives" (Deuteronomy 5:24 AMP).

Unusual Events at Mt. Sinai

- Terrible lightning and thunder storm
- Long, loud blast of the trumpet
- Jehovah descended in the form of fire
- Great earthquake

God Revealed Himself to Israel in a Cloud

Clouds were often symbolic of God's presence in the Old Testament. When God wanted to reveal Himself to the Israelites, He often used a pillar of cloud to do so. Before the children of Israel ever reached Mount Sinai, the Lord God led them through the wilderness. "The Lord went before them by day in a pillar of cloud to lead them along the way, and by night in a pillar of fire to give them light, that they might travel by day and by night. The pillar of cloud by day and the pillar of fire by night did not depart from before the people" (Exodus 13:21-22 ESV).

Cloud of Glory at Dedication of the Tabernacle

In God's presence, Moses received the Ten Commandments and directions for the construction of the Tabernacles. At the dedication of the tabernacles in the wilderness, the cloud of glory covered the newly erected tabernacle and the glory of the Lord filled the whole place. It covered the tabernacle and the glory of the Lord filled the whole place. Moses was unable to enter the tabernacle because the cloud rested about it and the glory of the Lord filled the newly erected tabernacle. The mention of this cloud was extremely significant because the people heard the Voice of God speaking.

This was the same cloud that led the Children of Israel through the wilderness.

"The cloud covered the tent of meeting, and the glory of the Lord filled the tabernacle. Moses was not able to enter the tent of meeting because the cloud settled on it, and the glory of the Lord filled the tabernacle. Through all their journeys, whenever the cloud was taken up from over the tabernacle, the people of Israel would set out. If the cloud was not taken up, then they did not set out till the day that it was taken up. The cloud of the Lord was on the tabernacle by day, and fire was in it by night, in sight of all the house of Israel throughout all their journeys" (Exodus 40:34-38 ESV).

The Shekinah glory of God's visible presence covered the Tabernacle and the glory of the Lord filled the whole place. The Cloud of Glory led the people through forty years in the wilderness. It finally led them into the land of Canaan.

God's Glory in Solomon's Temple

When Solomon's Temple was built, the Ark of the Covenant was taken out of the Tabernacle of Moses and moved into the Holy of Holies. The cloud of glory filled the Holy Place so that priests could not stand to minister, because the Glory of God filled the house.

"As soon as Solomon finished his prayer, fire came down from heaven and consumed the burnt offering and the sacrifices, and the glory of the Lord filled the temple. The priests could not enter the house of the Lord, because the glory of the Lord filled the Lord's house. When all the people of Israel say the fire come down and the glory of the Lord on the temple, they bowed down with their faces to the ground on the pavement and worshiped and gave thanks to the Lord, saying, 'For he is good, for his steadfast love endures forever"(2 Chronicles 7:1-3 ESV).

This was the "Cloud" in which Jehovah appeared in the Holy of Holies upon the mercy-seat. This was the "Cloud" which filled the Temple of Solomon. Little wonder that the priests "fell on their faces and they were sore afraid"!

The Glory of God Leaves

The Glory of the Lord departed when the Jewish Temple was destroyed. Ezekiel, saw in a vision, the Glory of God leave the desecrated temple. He later saw the Glory of God leaving Jerusalem on the evening of the destruction of Jerusalem. The Glory of God assumed a shining human form.

This is a warning to us today, to live pure, holy lives before the Lord. God cannot look upon sin, and His presence cannot flow through an unholy vessel.

God's Message came to me: "Son of man, when the people of Israel lived in their land, they polluted it by the way they lived. I poured out my anger on them because of the polluted blood they poured out on the ground. And so I got thoroughly angry with them polluting the country with their wanton murders and dirty gods. I kicked them out, exiled them to other countries. I sentenced them according to how they had lived. Wherever they went, they gave me a bad name. People said, 'These are God's people, but they got kicked off his land.' I suffered much pain over my holy reputation, which the people of Israel blackened in every country they entered'" (Ezekiel 36:16-21 MSG).

Empty Holy of Holies

The Holy of Holies in the second temple was empty. The Ark of the Covenant, along with the cherubim, the tables of the law, Aaron's rod that budded, and the pot of manna were no longer in the sanctuary. The fire that had descended from heaven upon the altar was extinct. What was even more solemn, the visible presence of God in the Shekinah was wanting. How could the will of God be now ascertained through the urim and thummin, nor ever the high priest could be anointed with the holy oil, since its very composition was unknown.[82]

The Tabernacle in Captivity

On his arrival in Babylon, Jeremiah found a cave-dwelling, into which he brought the tabernacle, the ark, and the altar of incense, afterwards blocking up the entrance. Some of his companions came up to mark out the way but were unable to find it. When Jeremiah learned this, he reproached them. He said the place was to remain unknown until God gathered his people together again and showed them His mercy. Then the Lord will bring these things once more to light and the Glory of the Lord will be seen, and so will the cloud as it was revealed in the time of Moses and when Solomon in his wisdom offered the sacrifice of the dedication and completion of the sanctuary. Moses prayed to the Lord and fire came down from heaven and burned up the sacrifice, so Solomon also prayed and fire from above burned up the offering.[83]

Glory of God at Messiah's Birth

At the birth of Jesus the Glory of the Lord was revealed to the shepherds in the fields. Suddenly there was with the angel a multitude of the heavenly host praising God and saying: "Glory to God in the highest heaven, and on earth peace among those whom he favors!"

    "When the angels had left, the shepherds said to one another, "Let us go now to Bethlehem and see this thing that has taken place, which the Lord has made known to us. So they went with haste and found Mary and

Joseph, and the child lying in the manger. When they saw this, they made known what had been told them about this child; and all who heard it were amazed at what the shepherds told them. But Mary treasured all these words and pondered them in her heart. The shepherds returned, glorifying and praising God for all they had heard and seen, as it had been told them" (Luke 2:15-20 NRSV).

God's Glory at the Transfiguration

"Jesus took with him Peter, James and John the brother of James, and led them up a high mountain by themselves. There he was transfigured before them. His face shone like the sun, and his clothes became as white as the light. Just then there appeared before them Moses and Elijah, talking with Jesus. Peter said to Jesus, 'Lord, it is good for us to be here. If you wish, I will put up three shelters—one for you, one for Moses and one for Elijah.' While he was still speaking, a bright cloud covered them, and a voice from the cloud said, 'This is my Son, whom I love; with him I am well pleased. Listen to him!" When the disciples heard this, they fell facedown to the ground, terrified'" (Matthew 17:1-6 NIV).

Crucifixion of Christ Revealed God's Glory

"Then, behold, the veil of the temple was torn in two from top to bottom; and the earth quaked, and the rocks were split, and the graves were opened; and many bodies of the saints who had fallen asleep were raised; and coming out of the graves after His resurrection, they went into the holy city and appeared to many. So when the centurion and those with him, who were guarding Jesus, saw the earthquake and the things that had happened, they feared greatly, saying, "Truly this was the Son of God! (Matthew 27:51-54).

Eyewitnesses to the Resurrection

- An angel met the women at the tomb and told them Christ was alive (Matthew 28:5-7).
- Jesus appeared to the disciples on the day of His resurrection (John 20:19-21).
- Jesus appeared to the disciples for a period of 40 day (Acts 1:3).
- Paul said that Jesus appeared to 500 people at the same time (1 Corinthians 15:6-8).

Jesus Ascends to Heaven

As the disciples watched, Christ was taken up and disappeared in a cloud. As they stood staring into the empty sky, suddenly two men appeared in white robes, saying "Men of Galilee, why do you just stand here looking up at an empty sky? The same Jesus who was taken from among you to heaven will certainly return in the same manner.

After He had said these things, He was lifted up while they were looking on, and a cloud received Him out of their sight. And as they were gazing intently into the sky while He was going, behold, two men in white clothing stood beside them. They also said, "Men of Galilee, why do you stand looking into the sky? This Jesus, who has been taken up from you into heaven, will come in just the same way as you have watched Him go into heaven."

Glory of God at Pentecost

There appeared to them tongues resembling fire that settled on each one of them. Fire, like wind, is symbolic of the Divine Presence. The people present at this tremendous event were made acutely aware that something supernatural was transpiring. Here we see God manifesting Himself in a similar manner that He did when He gave the Ten Commandments to Moses.

What was the purpose of the supernatural joining of sound and sight, of wind and fire? It was essential that the people realize the supreme importance of the moment. When they saw the light and heard the voice, they became keenly aware of the Divine authority of the Law that God gave Moses.

On the Day of Pentecost when the people heard the sound of the violet wind the disciples speaking in other tongues, they knew something supernatural was happening. When the Holy Spirit was poured out, the power of God was manifested in the lives of the disciples and others. A revival spread through the entire region and thousands came to the Lord as the church age began.

God's Glory Revealed Today

God's glory is revealed as the Holy Spirit flows through yielded vessels to make His power known. His glory is revealed through spiritual gifts God has so freely bestowed upon the church. As Christians mature in the Lord, it brings great glory to God.

Just as the cloud gave directions to the Israelites, so the Holy Spirit gives directions to Christians today. Just as the pillar of fire gave light, so Christ is the light of the world. Just as the cloud comforted them, so the Holy Spirit comforts Christians today.

We are beginning to see God's promise fulfilled as He pours out His Spirit in these last days. "It shall come to pass afterward that I will pour out My Spirit on all flesh. Your sons and your daughters shall prophesy. Your old men shall dream dreams. Your young men shall see vision. On My menservants and on My maidservants I will pour out My Spirit in those days. I will show wonders in the heavens and in the earth, blood and fire and pillars of smoke" (Joel 2:18-30).

"Consequently, you are no longer foreigners and strangers, but fellow citizens with God's people and also members of his household, built on the foundation of the apostles and prophets, with Christ Jesus himself as the chief cornerstone. In him the whole building is joined together and rises to become a holy temple in the Lord. And in him you too are being built together to become a dwelling in which God lives by his Spirit (Ephesians 2:19-22 NIV).

Believers are living stones to God. "You are coming to Christ, who is the living cornerstone of God's temple. He was rejected by people, but he was chosen by God for great honor. You are living stones that God is building into his spiritual temple. What's more, you are his holy priests through the mediation of Jesus Christ, you offer spiritual sacrifices that please God" (1 Peter 2:4-5 NLT).

God is revealing His glory in the church today as we see men and women accept Christ as their personal Savior. His glory is revealed when people are saved, restored, and healed. I believe we will see more and more miracles in the day ahead.

"But God, being rich in mercy, because of the great love with which he loved us, even when we were dead in our trespasses, made us alive together with Christ—by grace you have been saved—and raised us up with him and seated us with him in the heavenly places in Christ Jesus, so that in the coming ages he might show the immeasurable riches of his grace in kindness toward us in Christ Jesus" (Ephesians 2:4-7 ESV).

Ezekiel's Vision of a New Temple

The Cloud of Glory that left the defiled temple appeared in a vision to Ezekiel when the outward manifestation of God's glory was revealed to him. This vision is detailed in the forty-third chapter of Ezekiel. Ezekiel's vision may refer to the Millennial Temple, but certainly includes a future temple, not made with human hands, in which God will dwell forever.

"Behold, the glory of the God of Israel came from the way of the east. His voice was like the sound of many waters; and the earth shone with His glory. It was like the appearance of the vision which I saw—like the vision which I saw when I came to destroy the city. The visions were like the vision which I saw by the River Chebar; and I fell on my face. And the glory of the Lord came into the temple by way of the gate which faces toward the east. The Spirit lifted me up and brought me into the inner court; and behold, the glory of the Lord filled the temple. Then I heard Him speaking to me from the temple, while a man stood beside me. He said to me, 'Son of man, this is the place of My throne and the place of the soles of My feet, where I will dwell in the midst of the children of Israel forever'" (Ezekiel 43:2-7).

Cloud of Glory in the Millennium

The Jewish Temple will be rebuilt, and its glory will radiate to the whole world. The Shekinah Glory of God departed from Solomon's Temple because of Israel's sin and rebellion (Ezekiel 11:22-23), but the Shekinah glory of God will someday fill the rebuilt Messianic Temple.

Ezekiel describes when the Glory of God will return to the Jewish Temple. "The glory of the LORD came into the Temple through the east gateway. Then the Spirit took me and brought me into the inner courtyard, and the glory of the LORD filled the Temple" (Ezekiel 43:4-5 NLT). Scriptures reveal that the Divine Presence of God will again dwell in Jerusalem. What a glorious day that will be!

The glory of the Millennial Temple will be manifested in the eternal presence of the Shekinah Glory of God who will dwell there. Ezekiel witnessed in his vision the tragic departure of the Shekinah Glory from Solomon's Temple because of Israel's rebellion in the past. God's plan of redemption for Israel and the Gentiles promises that Jesus the coming Messiah will return in glory to inhabit the Temple of God forever.

⟩ CHAPTER 9
BATTLE OF GOG AND MAGOG

"This is what the sovereign Lord says: 'Prophecy against Gog and say, 'Thus says the Lord God, Behold I am against you, O Gog, prince of Rosh, Meshech and Tubal; and I will turn you around, drive you on, take you up from the remotest parts of the north and bring you against the mountains of Israel'" (Ezekiel 39:1-2 NASB).

Ezekiel said that in the latter years after Israel has returned home from the nations of the world and is finally living in peace that Gog and Magog will come from the far north and attack Israel. Since Israel has not had peace for the past fifty years, it seem likely that this will occur after the Antichrist and Israel sign a covenant of peace. Most commentators believe this war will occur before the Battle of Armageddon.

Twenty-five hundred years ago, Ezekiel prophesied about a coming invasion led by Gog and Magog. Gog is the prince of Rosh. Rosh simply means first as in Rosh Hashanah, the first month of the Hebrew year. Many Bible Scholars believe that Gog is the ruler of Russia and Magog is Russia, the former Soviet Union. Others have taught that Gog is Turkey. While Turkey lies directly north of Israel, it is not in the remotest part of the north.

Look at a globe of the world and you will find that Russia lies directly north of Israel and Moscow lies directly north of Jerusalem. This gigantic outburst of Anti-Semitism is an attempt to destroy Israel and annihilate the Jews.

Russia still commands the largest arsenal of nuclear arms and other weapons of mass destruction in history, inherited from the old USSR. Russia still maintains a vast arsenal of biological and chemical arms and there are reports of secret high-tech super weapons in its stockpile.[84]

Russia is an atheistic, Anti-Semitic nation that has now solidified economically and militarily with other nations in the Gog-Magog coalition. They helped build a nuclear reactor in Iran.

In 1971 Governor Ronald Reagan said "Ezekiel tells us that Gog, the nation that will lead all of the other powers of darkness against Israel, will come out of the north. Biblical Scholars have been saying for generations that Gog must be Russia. What other powerful nation is to the north of Israel? None, but it didn't seem to make sense before the Russian revolution, when Russia was a Christian country. Now it does, now that Russia has become communistic and atheistic, now that Russia has set itself against God. Now it fits the description of Gog perfectly."[85]

When Russia put a rocket past the moon, called the Sputnik, and when it was nearing the sun, the following was heard on the radio in Russia: "Our rocket has bypassed the moon. It is nearing sun. We have not discovered God. We have turned out lights in heaven that no man will be able to put on again. We are breaking the yoke of the gospel, the opiate of the masses. Let us go forth and Christ shall be relegated to mythology."[86]

Ezekiel 38-39 teaches that the nation of Israel will have serious problems with Egypt, Syria, Iran, Sudan, Libya, Turkey and Russia in the future. All of these nations except Russia entered the 21st century overwhelmingly Islamic in their worldview, and Russia could become Islamic within several decades. If these nations continue to be Islamic to the time that Ezekiel 38-39 are fulfilled, then (1) Israel will continue to have serious problems with Islamic nations into the extended future and (2) these Islamic nations will suffer serious judgment from God.[87]

Gog and Magog are identified in Jewish rabbinical writings as Russia. Grant Jeffrey stated in his book *Armageddon, Appointment with Destiny* that Arab writers confirm that in the Arabic language their name for the Great Wall of China is 'the wall of Al Magog' because the Great Wall was built to keep out the invading armies from Magog (Russia).

The word Gog is a reference not to an invading nation, but rather to the individual who leads this invasion. How do we know he is an individual? We know this because Gog is referred to as the "prince of Rosh, Meshech and Tubal" (Ezekiel 38:2). He is the leader of these nations. He's the one in charge. These nations follow his lead in moving against Israel. The name Gog appears eleven times in Ezekiel 38 and 39, thereby indicating that he plays a significant role in this end-time invasion.[88]

Israel was not in desolation when this prophecy was written, but Ezekiel foresaw the terrible desolation that would happen after Israel was returned from the nations of the world. Since Israel hasn't had peace for the past sixty years, it seem likely that this will occur after the Antichrist signs a seven year covenant of peace with Israel. Biblical Scholars believe this war is not the final war with Israel and will occur before the Battle of Armageddon.

Prophecy against Gog

"Thus says the Lord God; I am against you, O Gog, chief prince of Meshech and Tubal; I will turn you around and put hooks into your jaws, and I will lead you out with all your army, horses and horsemen, all of them clothed in full armor, a great company, all of them with shield and buckler, wielding swords. Persia, Ethiopia, and Put are with them, all of them with buckler and helmet; Gomer and all its troops; Beth-Togarmah from the remotest part of the north, with all its troops—many people are with you" (Ezekiel 38:3-6 NRSV).

Ezekiel's prophecy in Ezekiel 38:3-6 indicated that this invasion will occur almost against Russia's own will. God Almighty will put a hook in his jaws. What is the hook in Russia's jaw? Russia needs access to the Middle East Oil. They need a warm-water entrance into the oceans of the world. Israel offers this along the Mediterranean Sea.

All the nations in Ezekiel 38 are listed in the Table of Nations in Genesis 10:2-7, except for Rosh. Magog, Meshech, Tubal were sons of Japheth and grandsons of Moses. Many of the ancient nations have different names today.

While traveling in Turkey, Jimmy DeYoung found an ancient map showing that Turkey was divided into four regions; Meshech, Tubal, Gomer and Togarmah.[89] Ethiopia refers to the geographical territory to the south of Egypt on the Nile River—what is today known as Sudan.

Allies of Gog and Magog- Ezekiel 38:1-6

Ancient Nations	Modern Nations
Rosh	Russia - north of Caspian and Black Sea
The Land of Magog	Former Soviet Union
Meshech, Tubal, Gomer & Togarmah	Turkey
Persia	Iran
Cush and Ethiopia Cush was the son of Ham (Genesis 10:6).	Ethiopia, Sudan
Put	Libya
Many people with you	Various other nations allied to Russia

Gog and Magog Will Invade Israel

"After many days you (Gog) will be called to arms. In future years you will invade a land that has recovered from war, whose people were gathered from many nations to the mountains of Israel, which had long been desolate. They had been brought out from the nations, and now all of them live in safety. You and all your troops and the many nations with you will go up, advancing like a storm; you will be like a cloud covering the land. God gives another message to Gog and Magog. "On that day thoughts will come into your mind and you will devise an evil scheme. You will say, "I will invade a land of unwalled villages; I will attack a peaceful and unsuspecting people—all of them living without walls and without gates and bars. I will plunder and loot and turn my hand against the resettled ruins and the people gathered from the nations, rich in livestock and goods, living at the center of the land" (Ezekiel 38:8-12 NIV).

Daniel 11:40-45 and Ezekiel 38-39 teach that the nation of Israel will have serious problems with Egypt, Syria, Iran, Sudan, Libya, Turkey and Russia in the future. All of these nations except Russia entered the 21st century overwhelmingly Islamic in their worldview, and Russia could become Islamic within several decades. If these nations continue to be Islamic to the time that the prophecies of Daniel 11:40-45 and Ezekiel 38-39 are fulfilled, then (1) Israel will continue to have serious problems with Islamic nations into the extended future and (2) these Islamic nations will suffer serious judgment from God.[90]

Persia, Russia's chief partner in this invasion, was just coming to prominence at the time of Ezekiel. Persia is modern-day Iran. Iran became a nation in 1935 and the Islamic Republic of Iran in 1979. Iran has been ruled by an Islamic fundamentalist government since the overthrow of the Shah of Iran.

Intelligence experts are now calling the Moscow-Tehran alliance one of the most important fixtures of the Post-Cold War Era. No one is more aware of this threat than the leaders of Russia. They were forced to sign a pact with Iran out of fear of this potentially disastrous development. The pact guarantees Iran use of their top nuclear and missile scientists, access to every weapon in their arsenal and a commitment to fight alongside Iran against the West in the event of any future armed interference against them.[91]

According to Paul Goble a specialist on ethnic minorities has predicted that within the next several decades, Russia will become a Muslim majority state. There is another bad news with fast decline in the country's population. This has already become a headache for Russian politicians and policy makers. President Vladimir Putin has already called for Russian women to have more children. He has offered 1,500 rubles for the first child and 3,000 rubles for the second child.[92]

Mr. Vladimir Putin, President of Russia, has solidified control over the country since returning for his third term in May of 2012. Russia needs to get a foot-hold to obtain vast oil reserves in the Middle East. How better to do this than invade Ukraine and Crimea? This invasion will give Putin access to the Water Ways; the Suez Canal, the Gulf of Suez and the Red Sea. Whoever controls this narrow land bridge can control the flow of oil through the three continents of Asia, Europe and Africa.

This land bridge, known as the Levant, includes countries bordering the eastern Mediterranean Sea; modern day Turkey, Syria, Lebanon, Israel, Jordan, and Egypt. Israel is right in the center of this region.

Gas and oil have recently been discovered in Israel. The three to five trillion cubic feet of proven gas reserves beneath Israel's soil could be worth up to $6 billion. Moreover, an Israeli oil company has recently made the largest oil find in the history of the country. One news agency in Israel reports, "Israel may have struck gold—black gold, that is.[93] The recent discovery of oil and gas in Israel could be the motivation for the next war in the Middle East.

A number of wealthy people live in Israel—more than 6,600 millionaires with total assets exceeding $24 billion.[94] Moreover, the mineral resources of the Dead Sea—including 45 billion tons of sodium, chlorine, sulfur, potassium, calcium, magnesium, and bromide-are worth virtually trillions of dollars.[95]

Nations Sitting on the Sidelines

"Sheba and Dedan and the merchants of Tarshish with all its villages will say to you, 'Have you come to capture spoil? Have you assembled your company to seize plunder, to carry away silver and gold, to take away cattle and goods, to capture great spoil?'" (Ezekiel 38:13 NASB)

Sheba and Dedan were cities in what is now Saudi Arabia. They are not involved in the invasion, but rather sitting on the sidelines watching. Lebanon and Syria, extremely anti–Semitic countries, are not included in this battle.

God's Anger against Gog

"This is what will happen in that day: When Gog attacks the land of Israel, my hot anger will be aroused, declares the Sovereign Lord. In my zeal and fiery wrath I declare that at that time there shall be a great earthquake in the land of Israel. The fish in the sea, the birds in the sky, the beasts of the field, every creature that moves along the ground, and all the people on the face of the earth will tremble at my presence. The mountains will be overturned, the cliffs will crumble and every wall will fall to the ground. I will summon a sword against Gog on all my mountains, declares the Sovereign Lord. Every man's sword will be against his brother. I will execute judgment on him with plague and blood-shed; I will pour down torrents of rain, hailstones and burning sulfur on him and on his troops and on the many nations with him. And so I will show my greatness and my holiness, and I will make myself known in the sight of many nations. Then they will know that I am the Lord' (Ezekiel 38:18-23 NIV).

God's patience will be exhausted against the enemies who attempt to annihilate Israel. A great earthquake will occur in the land of Israel causing great panic to the invading armies. They will turn their weapons against each other. All of Gog's army will die before they have a chance to use their weapons. God will pour out pestilence, bloodshed, floods, great hailstones, fire and brimstone on those who attack Israel. Gog and all his troops will fall on the mountains of Israel.

Birds of prey and the beasts of the field will devour the fallen. Search parties will go through the land and put a marker on any bones. It will take seven months to bury the dead. Gog and all his allies will be buried in the Valley of Hamon Gog, east of the Dead Sea (Ezekiel 39:14).

Restoration of God's People

God will demonstrate His power to the nations when they see the punishment inflicted on His enemies. The nations will know that the Lord is the Holy One of Israel. His holy name will be longer be profaned. From that time on, Israel will know that the Lord is God. The scales will be removed from their eyes as they turn to God in repentance.

The Lord God said; "I will demonstrate my glory to the nations. Everyone will see the punishment I have inflicted on them and the power of my fist when I strike. From that time on the people of Israel will know that I am the Lord their God. The nations will then know why Israel was sent away to exile—it was punishment for sin, for they were unfaithful to their God. Therefore, I turned away from them and let their enemies destroy them. I turned my face away and punished them because of their defilement and their sins. So now, this is what the Sovereign Lord says: I will end the captivity of my people; I will have mercy on all Israel, for I jealously guard my holy reputation! They will accept responsibility for their past shame and unfaithfulness after they come home to live in peace in their own land, with no one to bother them. When I bring them home from the lands of their enemies, I will display my holiness among them for all the nations to see. Then my people will know that I am the Lord their God, because I sent them away to exile and brought them home again. I will leave none of my people behind. I will never again turn my face from them, for I will pour out my Spirit upon the people of Israel. I, the Sovereign Lord, have spoken!" (Ezekiel 39:21-29 NLT).

This is first generation in history that can view events over global satellite television in every country in the world. People will be able to watch the prophecies of the Bible being fulfilled before their very eyes. All the nations will be able to see God's glory and judgment via television. Many people, including Jews and Muslims will turn to God and accept Yeshua as Lord and Savior.

Could this event be the end of radical Islam? Many Muslims will abandon Islam and become Christians. Even today, scores of Muslims are turning to Christianity as they see ISIS martyring Christians.

Compare Invasions in Ezekiel and Revelation

In Ezekiel, the nations that attack Israel are primarily from the north and are called by name. In Revelation, Gog and Magog have no geographic location, but rather represent the nations of the world that attack the saints and Jerusalem, the Beloved City.

There is no mention of burying the dead in Revelation. The White Throne Judgment for the wicked dead immediately follows the Battle of Armageddon. The next event on God's agenda will be the destruction of heaven and earth, to be replaced with a new heaven and new earth.

Gog is not another name for the Antichrist. Trying to make this identification leads to prophetic chaos. The Antichrist heads up a revived Roman Empire (Daniel 2:7), but Gog heads up an invasion force made up of Russia and a number of Muslim nations. Gog's moment in the limelight is short-lived. It's all over when God destroys the invading force, whereas the Antichrist is in power during much of the Great Tribulation.[96]

Compare Gog–Magog Invasions

Invasion in Ezekiel – Ezekiel 38 & 39	Invasion in Revelation – Revelation 19-20
Six-nation Coalition from the north – (Ezek. 38:6, 14). Gog will head the armies from the north (vs. 7, 12).	All nations in every corner of the earth attack Israel (Rev. 20:8). Satan will lead the armies, but no geographical is mentioned (Rev. 19:19). Call for the birds and beasts to eat the dead bodies (Rev. 19:17).
God will attack with pestilence, hailstones, and brimstone. The nations fight each other (Ezekiel 39:17-23). It takes seven months to bury the dead (Ezek. 39:12).	Fire will come down from heaven and consume Gog's armies (Revelation 20:8-9).

God Purpose for the Battle of Gog and Magog

What is God's purpose for the Battle of Gog and Magog (Ezekiel 38: 16, 23)? God will make His holy name known in the midst of Israel and they will not profane God's holy name any more. Then the nations will know that I am the Lord, the Holy One of Israel.

The house of Israel will know that I am the Lord their God from that day forward… I will not hide My face from the any longer, for I will pour out My Spirit on the House of Israel, declares the Lord God (Ezekiel 39:22, 29 NASB).

"I will cleanse them from all their iniquity by which they have sinned against Me, and I will pardon all their iniquities by which they have sinned against Me and by which they have transgressed against Me. It will be to Me a name of joy, praise and glory before all the nations of the earth which will hear of all the good that I do for them, and they will fear and tremble because of all the good and all the peace that I make for it" (Jeremiah 33:8-9 NASB).

› CHAPTER 10
BLESSINGS OR CURSES

"He loved to pronounce a curse—may it come back on him. He found no pleasure in blessing— may it be far from him" (Psalm 119:17 NIV).

The Jews have done more to civilize men than any other Nation. They are the most glorious Nation that ever inhabited the earth. The Romans and their Empire were but a bauble in comparison to the Jews. They have given religion to three-quarters of the globe and have influenced the affairs of mankind more, and more happily than any other nation, ancient or modern. John Adams, America's second president.

The LORD said to Abram: "I will make you a great nation; I will bless you and make your name great; and you shall be a blessing. I will bless those who bless you, and I will curse him who curses you; and in you all the families of the earth shall be blessed" (Genesis 12:3).

God Promised Abram a Sevenfold Blessing

1. I will make you a great nation.
2. I will bless you.
3. I will make your name great.
4. You shall be a blessing.
5. I will bless those who bless you.
6. I will curse those who curse you.
7. In you all the families of the earth shall be blessed.

"God remembers his covenant forever, the word that he commanded, for a thousand generations, the covenant that he made with Abraham, his sworn promise to Isaac, which he confirmed to Jacob as a statue, to Israel as an everlasting covenant, saying, 'To you I will give the land of Canaan as your portion for an inheritance'" (Psalm 105:8-11 ESV).

God chose Israel as His covenant people. His covenant with Israel is non-negotiable. God made an oath to Abram and repeated it six more times to Abraham, to his son Isaac and to his grandson Jacob. His covenant with Israel was given through Moses, spoken by the psalmist and prophets. The Apostle Paul repeated it and Jesus affirmed it.

The Apostle Paul said, "My heart is filled with bitter sorrow and unending grief for my people, my Jewish brothers and sisters…They are the people of Israel, chosen to be God's adopted children. God revealed his glory to them. He made covenants with them and gave them his law. He gave them the privilege of worshipping him and receiving his wonderful promises. Abraham, Isaac, and Jacob are their ancestors, and Christ himself was an Israelite as far as his human nature is concerned. He is God, the one who rules over everything and is worthy of eternal praise! Amen" (Romans 2:2-5 NLT).

God Promised to Bless Those Who Bless Israel

Historically, wherever the Jews were welcomed, that nation flourished and prospered. Where the Jews were persecuted, those nations floundered. It is more than just coincidence; it is an identifiable historical pattern that has continued, without deviation, since the days of the Babylonian captivity.[97]

Israel is a special race of people through whom God wanted to bless the whole world. "You are a holy people, who belong to the Lord your God. Of all the people on earth, The LORD your God has chosen you to be his own special treasure" (Deuteronomy 7:6 NLT).

Jewish influence has permeated all corners of the globe and every page of history, including American history. Jews were very involved in Columbus's expedition to find the New World. Levi Ben Gershon, a Jew, invented the sea quadrant, used for navigation, Jewish cartographers drew most of the sea charts of the age. Centuries before Columbus, Jews had disproved the notion that the world was flat. 2000 years before Columbus, Moses do Leon, a Jew, stated that earth revolves like a ball and is covered by daylight on one side and darkness on the other.[98]

Christianity- Both Pro and Anti-Israel

Christianity has, because of its differing theological views about the future of Israel, had a divided attitude about Zionism and the revived State of Israel. For years many mainline protestant denominations have embraced the Replacement Theology that God is finished with the Jews. Since Israel sinned and was displaced from the Holy Land in A.D. 70, she lost her right to the everlasting covenant and annulled God's promises to Israel. This heresy teaches that the Jews are no longer God's chosen people. They believe that God is finished with Israel and the Church will receive the blessings promised to Israel. Israel's enemies are many, but her friends are few.

Many church organizations no longer believe in the literal interpretation of God's word and the importance of God's redemptive plan for Israel. They have little understanding of the importance of God's future plans for Israel as recorded in His Holy Word.

In Psalm 89:30-37, we read: "If his sons forsake My law, and do not walk in My judgments, if they violate My statues, and do not keep My commandments, then I will visit their transgression with the rod, and their iniquity with stripes. But I will not break off My loving kindness from him, nor deal falsely in My faithfulness. My covenant I will not violate, nor will I alter the utterance of My lips.

Once I have sworn by My holiness; I will not lie to David. His descendants shall endure forever like the moon, and the witness in the sky is faithful."

Jeremiah said: "It is the Lord who provides the sun to light the day and the moon and stars to light the night, and who stirs the sea into roaring waves. His name is the Lord of Heaven's Armies, and this is what he says: "I am as likely to reject my people Israel as I am to abolish the laws of nature" (Jeremiah 31:35-36 NLT).

It is totally unbiblical that God is finished with His chosen people. God said that the Jewish people will continue to be a nation for Him forever. In Isaiah 49:14-16 God said: Israel is inscribed on the palms of My hands, your walls are continually before Me.

If God rejected Israel, and there is no special future for the Jewish nation, how do we account for the supernatural survival of the Jewish people among the nations for 2500 years, Israel's rebirth among the nations, a flourishing modern democratic Jewish state, these amazing victories in major wars with the surrounding Egyptian and Arab nations, who have a vastly larger population, supported by great oil wealth? How about the Spirit of God being given to more and more Jewish people, so that the Messianic Jewish community is growing and growing?[99]

BDS Movement – Boycott, Divestment and Sanctions

The BDS movement is the "Boycott, Divestment, and Sanctions" campaign taking root on college campuses and in churches around the country. The goal of the campaign is to economically strangle the Jewish state to force concessions to the Palestinians.[100]

The Vatican, the World Council of Churches and the National Council of Churches are once again embracing the same biblical error regarding the Jewish people and today's Israel. These church organizations have mistakenly and grossly misinterpreted the role of the church in the Bible, thinking erroneously that since the Jews rejected Christ that today's church supplants Israel as God's chosen people. Nothing could be further from the truth (Read Romans 9 -11).[101]

Such organizations as the Roman Catholic Church and the World Council of Churches have, for the last half-century, taken positions favoring the Arab and Moslem enemies of Israel. They have defended this bias partly by claiming representation in the various countries involved. But a vital part of this bias is based on the theological convictions that cannot abide the resurrection of Israel from the ashes of the Dispersion. Part of Christianity has expressed delight with the modern Israel, while part has been very negative toward Israel's very existence.[102]

Pope Francis praised Palestinian President Mahmoud Abbas as an "angel of peace" during a meeting Saturday – May 17, 2015 at the Vatican that underscored the Holy See's warm relations with the Palestinians.[103]

On September 16, 2015, President Mahmoud Abbas, the so called *angel of peace* said, "We welcome every drop of blood spilled in Jerusalem. They (Israelis) have no right to desecrate the Ali-Aqsa Mosque with their filthy feet".

The Palestinian Authority's inflammatory anti-Israel rhetoric has led to a wave of terrorism that threatens to devolve into a third intifada. Although President Abbas claims he wants peace, his words and actions prove he wants to provoke another explosion of violence to win international sympathy and bring pressure on Israel.[104]

The U.S. can pressure Mr. Abbas and the Palestinian Authority diplomatically to cease its lying about the Temple Mount, anti-Semitic slanders and other incitements to violence. In addition, if such incitement does not stop immediately, the U.S. Congress should take steps to reduce the $500 million in aid we currently spend to prop up the Palestinian Authority, millions of which provides "salaries" to convicted Palestinian terrorists in Israeli jails.[105]

America Blessed By God

God has promised to bless the man or nation that blesses his chosen people. History has proven beyond reasonable doubt that the nations that have blessed the Jewish people have had the blessing of God; the nations that have cursed the Jewish people have experienced the curses of God.[106]

The United States was the first country to recognize the new nation of Israel. President Truman issued this statement: "This government has been informed that a Jewish state has been proclaimed in Palestine and that recognition has been requested by the provisional government thereof, the United States recognized the provisional government as the authority of the State of Israel."[107] The United States continued to support Israel throughout the 1950s and 1960s. As America blessed Israel, God blessed America.

Ronald Reagan's Commitment to defend Israel

Israel exists; it has a right to exist in peace behind secure and defensible borders; and it has a right to demand of its neighbors that they recognize those facts. I have personally followed and supported Israel's heroic struggle for survival, ever since the founding of the State of Israel. The pre-1967 borders Israel was barely ten miles wide at its narrowest point. The bulk of Israel's population lived within artillery range of hostile Arab armies. I am not about to ask Israel to live that way again.

Consequences of Dividing Israel

Although America continues to be Israel's principle protector, and continues to enjoy the concomitant blessings that come with it, America's good fortunes began to wane about the same time the White House forced Israel into the Oslo Agreement. The "land for peace" formula called for Israel to give up some of the land of Promise in exchange for peace. In other words, it was a form of blackmail whose terms were drawn up in Washington and forced upon Israel for the express purpose of undoing what God had already done, including dividing Jerusalem and taking part of it from the Jews.[108]

The "land for peace" formula called for Israel to give up some of the Land of Promise in exchange for peace. In other words, it was a form of blackmail whose terms were drawn up in Washington and forced upon Israel for the express purpose of undoing what God had already done, including dividing Jerusalem and taking part of it from the Jews.[109]

World Net Daily reported that President Obama promised Mahmud Abbas, the Palestinian president, that Jerusalem would be his new capital and that he would not let Benjamin Netanyahu 'get in the way' of normalizing US relations with the greater Muslim world. Obama's plan calls for the division of Israel into two states, with one only for Muslims and the other for both Jews and Muslims.

Now it seems like the United States is learning a similar lesson. In the years since the Madrid Conference was held in 1991, a series of "natural" disasters have struck the US, each on the heels of something we did or helped do that runs contrary to God's declaration concerning the real ownership of the Land of Israel.[110]

Nations Who Curse Israel will be Cursed

History has shown many nations that did not bless Israel. God poured out His wrath on ancient Egypt after the Hebrew children were enslaved there for 400 years. Egypt took the lives of baby boys to keep the Jews from reproducing so rapidly. God took the first born of Egypt in the last plague. All the Egyptian soldiers, who followed the Israelites, drown in the Red Sea.

Russia Cursed the Jews

Russia has a long and well-established history of hating Jews. America has a long and well-established history of accepting and blessing Jewish people. The comparison of these two nations is astonishing. It shows the authority of God's word regard the blessing or cursing of the Jews.[111]

Jews lived in terror under communism. The Tsar hindered Jewish worship. The Jews were forced to relocate and nearly starved. While Russia was driving Jews out, America was taking them in. Ten of thousands of Jews began pouring into the United States. Half of the Jews in the world have lived in America for the past sixty years.

According to Paul Goble, a specialist on ethnic minorities in the Russian Federation has predicted that within the next several decades, Russia will become a Muslim majority state. Today Russia has about 8,000 mosques while 15 years ago there were only 300 mosques. According to statistics, by the end of 2015, the number of mosques in Russia will cross 25,000.[112]

Life in Spain Today

A Spanish writer, Sebastian Vilar Rodrigez, described conditions in Europe today. "I walked down the street in Barcelona and suddenly discovered a terrible truth - Europe died in Auschwitz. We killed six million Jews and replaced them with 20 million Muslims. In Auschwitz we burned a culture, thought, creativity and talent. We destroyed the chosen people, truly chosen, because they produced great and wonderful people who changed the world. We have exchanged the pursuit of peace of the Jews of Europe and their talent for a better future for their children, their determined clinging to life because life is holy, for those who pursue death, for people consumed by the desire for death for themselves and others, for our children and theirs. What a terrible mistake was made by miserable Europe. The Global Islamic population is approximately 1,200,000,000; that is one billion two hundred million or 20% of the world's population.[113]

Great Britain's Treatment of the Jews

In modern times Great Britain was Israel's first benefactor. In 1917 the British Crown offered the Jews a homeland via the Balfour Declaration. They promised Israel land from the Mediterranean Sea to Iraq. Later Great Britain changed their minds, in order to please the Arabs, and gave 35,000 square miles of that land to a new Arab state, called Transjordan (modern day Jordan).

After the war, the British broke most of their promises to the Jews, restricted Jewish immigration to the Holy Land, and in the years since have increasingly turned their backs on the Jews that brought them such great blessings for more than 300 years. The British Empire upon which "the sun never set" in 1900, had, by 1948, lost its last colony when Burma declared independence, and the British Empire was no more.[114] By the time Israel declared independence in 1948, the British Empire essentially no longer existed.

Warning to Those Who Persecute Israel

The third chapter of Joel gives us a bird's eye view of the judgment that God will pour out on those who oppose Israel. After God brings back his people to Jerusalem,

He will gather all nations in the Valley of Jehoshaphat at the final battle in order to bring judgment upon them. They will be judged because they have scattered Israel and divided the land. God promises to repay all the evil they had done to Israel.

"I will gather all nations and bring them down to the Valley of Jehoshaphat. There I will put them on trial for what they did to my inheritance, my people Israel, because they scattered my people among the nations and divided up my land" (Joel 3:1-3 NIV).

The Lord gave a warning to those who have set their hearts to destroy and capture Jerusalem. He said, "On that day I will set out to destroy all the nations that attack Jerusalem" (Zechariah 12:9 NIV).

The Nation of Israel Will Never be Destroyed

Thus says the LORD, Who gives the sun for a light by day, The ordinances of the moon and the stars for a light by night, Who disturbs the sea, and its waves roar (The LORD of hosts *is* His name): If those ordinances depart from before Me, says the LORD, *Then* the seed of Israel shall also cease from being a nation before Me forever. Thus says the LORD: If heaven above can be measured, and the foundations of the earth searched out beneath, I will also cast off all the seed of Israel for all that they have done, says the LORD (Jeremiah 31:35-37).

The Apostle Paul said, "Did they (Israel) stumble so as to fall beyond recovery? Not at all! Rather, because of their transgression, salvation has come to the Gentiles to make Israel envious. If their transgression means riches for the world, and their loss means riches for the Gentiles, how much greater riches will their fullness bring!" (Romans 11:11-12 NIV).

This scripture completely contradicts Replacement Theology. If you believe that God has replaced Israel with the Church, then you believe that God did not keep His covenant with them.

"All the covenants were made with Israel as a whole. No one can deny that. At Mount Sinai, God spoke to the entire nation. But only God's children, the faithful within Israel, enjoy the covenant blessings. What does God say to the rest of his people? Does he say, "You are no longer my natural children? No! Instead He says, "Return, you backsliding children and I will heal your backsliding" (Jeremiah 3:22).

Throughout history many nations that lifted their hand against Israel have ceased to exist. But the people of the Book live on. God promised that the Jews would never be destroyed.

Dennis Lindsay said, "Where are those who have persecuted Israel through the ages? They are all historic footnotes buried in the bone yard of human history. Where is Israel – where are the Jewish people? They are alive and well and at the forefront of the cosmic battle of the ages. They will still be around long after Hezbollah and Hamas have been buried in the bone yard. The Israeli flag will still be flying over the ancient walls of the city of Jerusalem and the nation of Israel"!

⟩CHAPTER 11
TWELVE REASONS TO SUPPORT ISRAEL

This chapter discusses why the nation of Israel has a right to exist and is entitled to the land they possess. Israel was the first nation created in the twentieth century with the approval of the United Nations. It is only one quarter of the size of Maine and one quarter of one percent of the land occupied by the Arab Nations. Israel should not receive pressure from other nations to exist and give up land in order to have peace.

Israel and American have much in common. We're both young countries born of struggle and sacrifice. We're both founded by immigrants escaping religious persecution. We have both established vibrant democracies built on the law and open markets. We've both founded on certain basic beliefs, that God watches over the affairs of men, and that freedom is the Almighty God's gift to every man and woman on the face of this earth. These ties have made us natural allies, and these ties will never be broken. America's commitment to Israel's security is strong, enduring and unshakeable.[115]

Biblical Mandate

The Jewish people have a biblical promise to the land of Israel. The Lord said to Abram, "Lift up now your eyes, and look from the place where you are northward, southward, eastward and westward: for all the land which you see, to you will I give it, and to your seed forever" (Genesis 13:14-17).

Israel is the Biblical and historic homeland of the Jewish people. They trace their right to the Holy Land in the Torah, which records Israel's original settlement in the land around 1500 B.C. God promised this land to Israel through an unconditional, eternal blood covenant with Abraham, Isaac and Jacob.

The Lord made a covenant with Abram, saying, "To your descendants I have given this land, from the river of Egypt as far as the great river, the river Euphrates" (Genesis 15:18 NASB).

"Wherever you set your foot, that land will be yours. Your frontiers will stretch from the wilderness in the south to Lebanon in the north, and from the Euphrates River in the east to the Mediterranean Sea in the west. No one will be able to stand against you, for the Lord your God will cause the people to fear and dread you, as he promised, wherever you go in the whole land" (Deuteronomy 11:24-25 NLT). This included land that is now called the West Bank and the Gaza Strip. It also included much of Jordan, Syria, Saudi Arabia, and part of Iraq.

The Jewish people have remained one people in spite of centuries of persecution. Their uniqueness and their race have not disappeared in spite of the Anti-Semitism they have endured. Their survival through centuries of abusive is truly a miracle of God. Their return to the Jewish homeland promised to Abraham, Isaac and Jacob are seen by many as a miracle after centuries of exile.

It has been through the Jewish people that the revelation of the one true and living God has come to the rest of the world. They created no vast empire; they left us no pyramids or sphinx; they are not famous for their architecture, and they have built no great metropolis. They gave us the knowledge of God. Through them has come the word of God to the world, the promise of God and the revelation of his eternal purpose. In them alone of all the nations of the earth, the saving grace and power of God was made known. Above all it was through them that the Savior, the Lord Jesus, the Messiah, come, born of the royal line of King David. Nor was the divine promise to Abraham only fulfilled through the rising and faithfulness of the Jewish people. By the grace of God it was also fulfilled thorough their fall.[116]

Israel's Historic Claim to the Holy Land

Israel became a nation, with Jerusalem as its capital, two thousand years before the rise of Islam. Israel existed as a nation until A.D. 70 when Titus, the Romans General, conquered destroyed Jerusalem and the Jewish Temple. From then, until 1948 the Jewish people had no homeland, but there has always been a Jewish presence in the land. The Jewish people continued to long for their ancient homeland in spite of countless persecutions.

Israel has had a presence in the Holy Land for over 3,000 years. Anytime there is a dig in Israel, it supports Israel's claim that the Jews have been in that land for centuries. The coins, the pottery, the cities, the culture and the scrolls —all support Israel's claim. All the archeological evidence supports the fact that the Israelis have been present in that land before many other nations existed.

The Turks controlled the land for about 400 years until World War I when the British General Edmund Allenby conquered Israel on December, 11, 1917. The British rule, known as the British Mandate of Palestine, listed from 1917-1948, when Israel became a sovereign nation.

Israel is the only state created in the last century whose legitimacy was recognized by both the League of Nations and the United Nations. The League of Nations Mandate did not create the rights of the Jewish people to a national home in Palestine, but rather recognized a pre-existing right - for the links of the Jewish people to their historic land were well-known and accepted by world leaders in the previous century.[117]

Did you know that Saudi Arabia was not created until 1913, Lebanon until 1920? Iraq did not exist as a nation until 1932, Syria until 1941; the borders of Jordan were established in 1946 and Kuwait in 1961. Any of these nations that would say Israel is only a recent arrival would have to deny their own rights as recent arrivals as well. They did not exist as countries. They were all under the control of the Turks.[118]

Humanitarian Concerns

Six million Jews were slaughtered in Europe during World War II. The Jewish people realized that they needed a homeland in order to survive. The land that was given to the Jews is an extremely small area. This land was not claimed by anyone prior to the time Israel became a nation. It was a virtual wasteland. For humanitarian reasons, Israel has a right to exist and live in peace in their ancient homeland.

The Holocaust began when Adolf Hitler came to power in 1933 and ended when the Nazis were defeated by the Allied powers. It was estimated that 11 million people were killed in the Holocaust. Six million of those were Jews. The Nazis killed approximately two-thirds of all Jews living in Europe. An estimated 1.1 million children were murdered in the Holocaust.[119]

The Jewish people realized that they needed a homeland in order to survive. The land that was given to the Jews is an extremely small area. This land was not claimed by anyone prior to the time Israel became a nation. It was a virtual wasteland. For humanitarian reasons, Israel has a right to exist and live in peace in her ancient homeland.

Israeli Accomplishments

Jewish influence has permeated all corners of the globe and every page of history, including American history. Jews were very involved in Columbus's expedition to find the New World. Levi Ben Gershon, a Jew, invented the sea quadrant, used for navigation. Jewish cartographers drew most of the sea charts of the age. Centuries before Columbus, Jews had disproved the notion that the world was flat. Two hundred years before Columbus, Moses de Leon, a Jew, stated that the earth revolves like a ball and is covered by daylight on one side and darkness on the other.[120]

Israel today is a modern marvel of agriculture. Israel is able to bring more food out of a desert environment than any other country in the world. The Arab nations ought to make Israel their friend and import technology from Israel that would allow all the Middle East, not just Israel, to become an exporter of food. Israel has tremendous success in its agriculture.[121]

The technological marvels of Israeli industry, the military prowess, the bounty of Israeli agriculture, the fruits and flowers and abundance of the land are a testimony to God's watchful care over Israel and the genius of this people.

Israel leads the world in the number of scientists and technicians in the workforce. In the field of medicine, Israeli scientists developed the first fully computerized, no-radiation diagnostic instrumentation for breast cancer. The cell phone was developed in Israel by Israelis working in the Israeli branch of Motorola, which has its largest development center in Israel. Most of the Windows NT and XP operating systems were developed by Microsoft-Israel. Voice mail technology was developed in Israel.[122]

Israel's $100 billion economy is larger than all of its immediate neighbors combined. Israel has the highest percentage in the world of home computers per capita. Israel has the highest ratio of university degrees to the population in the world. Twenty-four percent of Israel's workforce holds university degrees — ranking it third in the industrialized world, after the United States and Holland — and 12% hold advanced degrees.[123]

It is said that approximately one third of all scientific Nobel Prize winners are Jewish. The ratio is mind boggling. One third comes from a universe of 15 million Jews and the remainder two-thirds from the much larger pool of 7 billion-plus people.[124]

Of the 660 Nobel Peace prizes from 1901 to 1990, 160 have been won by Jews. Jews have won more Nobel Peace Prizes than any other ethnicity. They have won 40 times more than should be expected of them based upon population statistics.[125]

The global Islamic population is approximately 1,200,000,000, or 20% of the world population. Only twelve Muslims have won a Nobel Peace Prize.

Jewish Support in American Revolution

America owes a huge debt to the Jewish people for their support during the American Revolution. If it were not for financial backing from the Jews, our tiny nation would not have survived.

During a particularly dark time during the American Revolution, George Washington and the Continental Army were freezing and starving in the snows of Valley Forge. Without food, arms, or ammunition, it seemed that the fledging nation was doomed to die.[126]

Haym Salomon, a Jewish banker from Philadelphia, arranged for the Jews of the thirteen colonies to respond with financial aid that turned the tide of the war and enabled General Washington to defeat the British. Salomon believed that until Jerusalem would once again welcome the Children of Israel, America could be the Promised Land for the Jews. It has been estimated that Salomon loaned this country from $600,000 to $800,000. He died bankrupted for the American cause.[127]

Washington was so appreciative of the Jewish contribution to the birth of America that he instructed the engravers of the American one-dollar bill to engrave a tribute to the Jewish people over the head of the bald eagle. It you look carefully, above the eagle's head you'll see the Star of David surrounded by the brilliant light of the Shekinah glory that dwelled above the Mercy Seat in the Holy of Holies in the Jewish Tabernacle.[128]

United States Leaders Supported Israel

The United States was the first country to recognize Israel officially after her creation in 1948. President Harry Truman recognized Israel's right to exist and endorsed the UN's approval for Israel to become a nation. The two countries have a strong bond in values and democracy. The United States pledged to stand firmly behind Israel for many years. Both Democrats and Republicans in Congress have supported Israel in the past. The United State has used her veto power forty-one times to protect Israel.

In 1973, President Richard Nixon saved Israel from defeat during the Yom Kippur War when Israel was attacked by four Arab nations. Nixon airlifted an arsenal of military equipment to Israel overnight. Many military experts say this intervention saved Israel from destruction.

President Ronald Reagan said, "Israel has a right to exist in peace behind secure and defensible borders; and it has a right to demand of its neighbors that they recognize those facts. I have personally followed and supported Israel's heroic struggle for survival, ever since the founding of the State of Israel. In the pre-1967 borders Israel was barely ten miles wide at its narrowest point. The bulk of Israel's population lived within artillery range of hostile Arab armies. I am not about to ask Israel to live that way again."

Israel – A Strategic Ally of the United States

Israel has been a strong and loyal ally of the United States, not just in the Middle East, but in the entire world. They are the only democracy in Middle East. Israel is surrounded by antagonistic Islamic countries, who desire to destroy them. In the war against terrorism and in her stance for freedom from tyranny, America will never have a stronger ally than Israel.

Washington understands that Israel remains its most reliable ally in the Middle East and the eastern Mediterranean. There is no other state in the Middle East where in the near future, an American airplane can count with certainty on being welcomed. Even American allies such as Egypt, Jordan, Saudi Arabia and Turkey may have second thoughts about hosting an American presence, and all of them have a record of denying the U.S. military use of their facilities.[129]

Israel is a roadblock to terrorism. The war we are now facing is not against a sovereign nation; it is against a group of terrorists who are very fluid, moving from one country to another. They are almost invisible. That is whom we are fighting against today. We need every ally we can get. If we do not stop terrorism in the Middle East, it will be on our shores.[130] Israel had coped with terrorists threats for decades. This intensifies our need to cooperate with Israel to defend our homeland from terrorist attacks.

America's Support for Israel

Support for Israel in America significantly increased following the terrorist attacks of 9-11. According to an annual poll conducted by Gallup, 59 percent of Americans support Israel, the highest percent of support since the first Gulf War.[131]

A majority of American oppose the granting of economic aid to the Palestinians. Since Hamas won the elections in the Gaza Strip, expectations for peace in the Middle East have dropped significantly.

Support for Israel among Americans is at its highest point in five years, while the image of Palestinians has grown increasingly negative during the past few months, according to the results of a new survey. Over 60 percent of Americans now believe that the US should support Israel, up from a low point of 23% in 2003. [132]

Evangelical Christian Support for Israel

Christians owe a debt of eternal gratitude to the Jewish people for our Christian heritage. Through them we received the Bible, which has been preserved down through the centuries. Jesus Christ, the Savior of the world, was a Jew. The apostles were Jews. Most of the men who wrote the Old and New Testaments were Jews.

Evangelical Christians are by far the most assertive in their support of Israel because of their strict interpretation of the Bible, both Old and New Testaments. Evangelicals are important to the pro-Israel movement because they number some 50 million in the U.S. alone, compared with five million U.S. Jews, many of whose support for Israel is tentative at best.[133]

The New Testament recognizes that Christians have received spiritual blessings from the Jews. The apostle Paul makes the following statement in Romans 15:27, "If the Gentiles have shared in the Jews' spiritual blessings, they owe it to the Jews to share with them their material blessings." Christians owe a great debt of gratitude to the Jews. After centuries of neglect, many Christians are now motivated to support Jewish ministries.

Evangelistic Christians support Israel because Israel has been willing to compromise to make peace. In July 2000, Israel offered the Palestinians over 90% of the West Bank and all of the Gaza Strip, with a flag flying in East Jerusalem. Yasser Arafat stormed out the meeting, flatly rejected this plan, and made no counterproposal. Soon after that he began his terrorist attacks on Israeli civilians.

After hundreds of years of anti–Semitism, persecution and genocide at the hands of Christians, it's no surprise that many Jews question the motivations of Christians who support Israel today. Most Jews simply cannot understand how the tiger could change his stripes---and many Jews harbor more than a small suspicion that pro-Israel Christians have an unspoken ulterior motive, that their support of Israel primarily serves "selfish" interests.[134]

Error of Replacement Theology

For hundreds of years many mainline Protestant Denominations embrace the idea that God is finished with the Jews. They believe when Israel failed to obey God, she fell under the curse of the law and has remained under God's discipline since then. They teach that when Israel was destroyed in A.D. 70, the everlasting covenant ended and all God's promises to Israel were annulled.

This heresy teaches that the Jews are no longer God's chosen people. They believe that the Jews are no different than any other group of people. They are no different than the Spanish, African or Arab. Many denominations proclaim that God is finished with Israel and the Church has taken her place.

It is thought that at over seventy percent of the established church teach this doctrine. They believe that the New Testament does not even suggest that Christians should support Israel. This doctrine is contrary to biblical teachings.

Such organizations as the Roman Catholic Church and the World Council of Churches have for the last half century, taken positions favoring the Arab and Moslem enemies of Israel. A vital part of this bias is based on the theological convictions that cannot abide the resurrection of Israel from the ashes of the Dispersion. Part of Christianity has expressed delight with the modern Israel, while part has been very negative toward Israel's very existence.[135]

They believe that the Church has replaced Israel and that God has no future plans for the nation of Israel. It is thought that the New Testament does not even suggest and Christians should support Israel. This doctrine is contrary to biblical teachings. Jeremiah claims that the nation of Israel will remain forever.

"Thus says the LORD, Who gives the sun for a light by day, The ordinances of the moon and the stars for a light by night, Who disturbs the sea, And its waves roar (The LORD of hosts *is* His name): If those ordinances depart from before Me, says the LORD, *Then* the seed of Israel shall also cease from being a nation before Me forever. Thus says the LORD: If heaven above can be measured, and the foundations of the earth searched out beneath, I will also cast off all the seed of Israel for all that they have done, says the LORD" (Jeremiah 31:35-37).

The Rise of the Intifada

In the aftermath of the Gulf War, the fanatic Islamic Arabs began and intensified a new tactic against Israel. They had tried to defeat and dislodge the Jewish state unsuccessfully in four wars. Those efforts ended in humiliating failure. At this point they began a new tactic called the Intifada. This was a public relations campaign for world opinion, in which the Arabs who lived in Judea and Samaria (the so-called West Bank) staged riots against Israel, coupled with terrorist attacks against civilians in Israeli cities.[136]

Ever since the Six Day War in 1967, the Israelis had been constructing Jewish settlements in Judea, Samaria and the Golan Heights for security purposes. These settlements were not glorified trailer parks, but beautiful suburban developments with lovely homes, schools and parks. Israelis live in these settlements and commute to work in Jerusalem, Tel Aviv or Tiberias. One of the primary goals of the Intifada was to stop the spread of these Jewish settlements. Gradually, the Intifada gained the sympathy and support of the world press and governments. Israel, the classic underdog of world history, was transformed in the eyes of the world into being the oppressor of the underdog Arabs, who assumed the name "Palestinians."[137]

Unending Arab Aggression against Israel

Israel is a tiny country about one-fourth the size of New York, with a Jewish population of a little over seven million. They are surrounded by 22 Arab counties with a population of over one billion who make up the majority of the population in over 50 nations. Arab countries have land that is 650 times the size of Israel. Their combined land is the size of the United States, all of Central America, and Mexico.

These antagonistic Islamic counties' goal is the final destruction of the Jewish people. Arab propaganda has convinced the world that Israel is the aggressor in the Middle East Conflict, despite the disparity in size and population. It seems ironic that seven million Jews in Israel could cause any mortal danger to the Arab population.

The Arab nations attempted to destroy Israel in 1948, 1967, and 1973. The remarkable victories of Jewish armies against overwhelming odds are clearly miracles of God.

Although many neighboring Arab countries today still wish to destroy Israel, Israel still seeks peace. Israel has forged peace agreements with Egypt (1979) and Jordan (1994), and have lived in peace with these countries ever since. The West Bank (Judea and Samaria) and Gaza were never controlled by any Palestinian government or organization until 1993, when Israel agreed to give the Palestinian Authority certain controls under the Oslo Peace Accord.[138]

At no time do they, or their allies in the Muslim world, acknowledge the sovereignty of Israel over even on square inch of territory in the Middle East. If a Palestinian State is created in the heart of Israel, with sovereign power to deploy troops, import modern weapons–even weapons of mass destruction–and operate with full secrecy and diplomatic immunity, the ability of the State of Israel to defend itself will be fatally compromised.[139]

The war Israel has fought, is fighting, and will fight to the end of this age is the war between the forces of Satan and the forces of God. The God of Abraham, Isaac and Jacob—the God of Israel is His name. The enemy of Israel as well as America, is not Hezbollah, Hamas, the Palestinians, Syria, Iran, Islam or Allah, Rather, the enemy is and always has been the one who desires worship to no one but himself--Satan.[140]

Long after Hamas and Hezbollah have been buried in the bone yard of human history, long after the crises with Iran has been resolves, the Flag of Israel will still be flying over the ancient walls of the sacred city and Jerusalem and Israel will be the praise of all the earth. Make no mistake-the entire world is being convulsed by a religious struggle. The fight is not about money or territory. No-the struggle is whether the Moon God of Mecca, known as Allah, is supreme, or whether the Judeo-Christian Jehovah God of the Bible is Supreme.[141]

If God's chosen people turn over to Allah control of their most sacred sites-if they surrender to Muslim vandals the tombs of Rachel, of Joseph, of the Patriarchs, of the ancient prophets-if they believe their claim to the Holy Land comes only from Lord Balfour of England and the ever fickle United Nations rather than the promises of Almighty God-then in that event, Islam will have won the battle. Throughout the Muslim world the message will go forth-"Allah is greater than Jehovah. The promises of Jehovah to the Jews are meaningless.[142]

Pray for the Peace of Jerusalem

With much of the world turning against Israel, who will stand in the gap to intercede on their behalf? God is looking for intercessors, for watchmen on the wall, who will cry out day and night for Israel, for Jerusalem. "O Jerusalem, I have posted watchmen on your wall; they will pray day and night, continually. Take no rest, all you who pray to the Lord. Give the Lord no until he completes his work, until he makes Jerusalem the pride of the earth." (Isaiah 62:6-7 NLT).

› CHAPTER 12
PROPHETIC SIGNS OF PERILOUS TIMES

"Don't be naive. There are difficult times ahead. As the end approaches, people are going to be self-absorbed, money-hungry, self-promoting, stuck-up, profane, contemptuous of parents, crude, coarse, dog-eat-dog, unbending, slanderers, impulsively wild, savage, cynical, treacherous, ruthless, bloated windbags, addicted to lust, and allergic to God. They'll make a show of religion, but behind the scenes they're animals. Stay clear of these people" (2 Timothy 3:1-5 MSG).

This scripture gives a description of mankind in the last days. The apostle Paul warned of spiritual conditions that characterize people as they cast off moral restrains and society begins to disintegrate. This prophetic list shows symptoms of the disintegrating condition of American society.

Apostasy – Falling Away from the Faith

"The Holy Spirit tells us clearly that in the last times some will turn away from the true faith; they will follow deceptive spirits and teachings that come from demons. These people are hypocrites and liars, and their consciences are dead" (1 Timothy 4:1-2 NLT).

Over the past 40 years or so we have seen the nation's theological views slowly become less aligned with the Bible. Even so-called Christians have increasingly adopted spiritual views that come from other religions. The passing on of a Christian heritage from one generation to the next has rapidly dissipated in America, until America is no longer considered to be a Christian nation. America has abandoned the God of the Bible and are more and more becoming enamored with other gods! Continuing religious research among young people shows that the national trend is away from traditional biblical doctrine in favor of a more popular culture-based theology that is ecumenical at its core. Considering that God says that he is a God that changes not (Malachi 3:6), one must wonder why all the changing.[143]

According to March 13, 2007 Barna Update, one hundred million people in the United States are unchurched. Approximately one-third of the people in our nation never attend church.

Increase in Godlessness

The Apostle Paul said, "People will love only themselves and their money. They will be boastful and proud, scoffing at God, disobedient to their parents, and ungrateful. They will consider nothing sacred. They will be unloving and unforgiving; they will slander others and have no self-control. They will be cruel and hate what is good. They will betray their friends, be reckless, be puffed up with pride, and love pleasure rather than God. They will act religious, but they will reject the power that could make them godly. Stay away from people like that!

Increase in Immorality

The 2000 census reported that eleven million people were living with an unmarried partner. 9.7 million Americans were living with an unmarried different-sex partner and 1.2 million were living with a same-sex partner. Over 40 percent of American women, ages 15-44 have cohabited or (lived with an unmarried different-sex partner) at some time.[144] Many experts think the numbers are much higher because some couples are reluctant to report their living arrangements. The number of unmarried couples living together increased tenfold between 1960 and 2000.

Pornography Sweeping the Churches

Pornography is sweeping through our churches like a tsunami leaving families torn apart in its wake. Many church goers who are struggling to break free from porn use feel isolated and completely helpless. A study in 2009 revealed that 68% of churchgoing man view porn on a regular basis. When you watch porn, powerful neurotransmitters such as dopamine are released, which bond you to the images.[145]

A CNN Report revealed that 50% of Christian males are addicted to pornography. 70% of Christian males visit pornographic websites.

According to neuropsychologist, Dr. Tim Jennings, "Any type of repetitive behavior will create trails in our brain that are going to fire on an automatic sequence." The result is years of bondage. This is how 68% of Christian men can love the Lord, but be in bondage to porn. The repeated viewing of porn literally changes the physical structure of their brain.[146]

Godlessness in the Media and Courts

It seems today that one of the greatest weapons against godliness and morality in America is being waged in the courts. In 1962, the Supreme Court outlawed prayer from public schools. Later they ruled against Bible reading in public schools. Is it any wonder school systems in the United States are failing since the Bible and prayer have been taken out of public schools?

On June 26, 2015 the Supreme Court ruled in favor of Gay Marriage. A recent Gallup poll found that, for the first time, Americans who favor the rights of gay and lesbian couples to marry outnumber those who oppose it. When asked the question if same-sex marriage should be recognized by law, 53 percent of respondents said yes while 45 percent said no.[147]

Increase in Abortion and Child Abuse

Roe vs. Wade changed the face of America. In 1950 abortion was a crime. In recent years, abortion is one of the most common surgical procedures in American, with taxpayers funding most of them. Since 1973 there have been 60 million abortions in the United States, approximately 4,000 each day. Abortion is the leading cause of death and account for more than 37% of in the United States.

In the United States, approximately 6,677 people died per day in 2009 (the most recent data available) of all causes (not including abortion). About 4,000 babies die per day by abortion in the US alone. If we add the victims of abortion to the death rate (making the deaths per day 10,677), they account for more than 37% of deaths in the United States.[148]

Thirty percent of all pregnancies end up in an abortionist's clinic. Worldwide there are 126,000 abortions daily stacking up to nearly 46 million each year. Grant Jeffrey states in his book, *Armageddon: Appointment with Destiny*, that the combined worldwide death toll from abortion since 1945 exceeds the battlefield casualties in all of the wars during these decades.

Planned Parenthood commits nearly 300,000 abortions each year. That's 900 babies murdered everyday – 37 slaughtered every hour. It brags it has "40 percent of the abortion market." Yet it still receives an astonishing $500 million in taxpayer dollars.

Statistics estimate that close to 43% (1 out of 3) women of childbearing age have experienced an abortion. These are your sisters, mothers, wives and friends. These women carry an incredible burden of silence and heartache. Many struggle for years with repressed memories, guilt, shame and depression. Most women feel that they are not allowed to talk about their abortion experience, especially in church.

Increase in Lawlessness

"Men will be lovers of themselves, lovers of money, boasters, proud, blasphemers, disobedient to parents, unthankful, unholy, unloving, unforgiving, slanderers, without self-control, brutal, despisers of good, traitors, headstrong, haughty, lovers of pleasure rather than lovers of God (2 Timothy 3:2-4).

A war is raging for the hearts and souls of your family. Writers and producers of movies, songs, talk shows and other television productions have an agenda that is diametrically opposed to the moral and religious values of the average North Americans. The air waves are flooded with vile, profane, violent and blasphemous programs that enter our homes through our TV sets. The truth is that there's an enemy in the camp.[149]

Human trafficking is a worldwide epidemic, and a national shame. Experts put the number of victims around the globe at 27 million people; their average age is only 12 years old. It is estimated that more people, especially children, are enslaved today than at any other time in history. Modern-day slavery is fueled by a variety of circumstances: poverty, war, natural disasters, abductions, immigrant labor, and false adoptions. Human sex trafficking is big business—global profits are estimated at $32 billion and climbing.[150]

It is unbelievable the lawlessness in our society today. Every day the newspapers across America report of murders. Our prisons are fuller than ever before. Even with falling crime rates in some areas and slower prison population growth, the tremendous number of Americans incarcerated is astounding.

The United States is the world's leader in incarceration with 2.2 million people currently in the nation's prisons or jails—a 500% increase over the past thirty years. These trends have resulted in prison overcrowding and state governments being overwhelmed by the burden of funding a rapidly expanding penal system, despite increasing evidence that large-scale incarceration is not the most effective means of achieve public safety.[151]

Chuck Colson, chairman of Prison Fellowship Ministries in Washington, D.C. said, "The moral collapse in America is so overwhelming that it is causing an institutional crisis. We can't build prisons fast enough. Unless we deal with the moral roots of the problem, it will destroy us." The moral breakdown of our society is overwhelming.

According to figures released by Amnesty International in February, 2002, the prison population in the USA topped two million. This accounts for 25% of the world's prison population yet the USA accounts for only 5% of the world's population. The USA's per capital prison population is 565 prisoners per 100,000 people.[152] The United States has now overtaken Russia with the highest percentage of its citizens behind bars. We have the highest incarceration rate of any country in the world.

This generation is the first generation to see widespread terrorism throughout the world. The US was attacked on American soil on 9-11 when 19 terrorists with box cutters, caused the death of thousands of people. Consider what could have happened if they had real weapons!

Since then, some people wonder if we will ever be safe again. In a recent Newsweek Pool, over 75% say more attacks on a major US city or landmark are likely in the near future.

Increased Persecution of Believers

"These things I have spoken to you that you should not be made to stumble. They will put you out of the synagogues; yes, the time is coming that whoever kills you will think that he offers God service. And these things they will do to you because they have not known the Father or Me. But these things I have told you, that when the time comes, you may remember that I told you of them" (John 16:1-4).

Jesus Christ of Nazareth told us that there would be a tremendous increase in religious persecution before His return. Christ forewarned us that the day would come when people would think they are doing a favor to their God to kill believers. Today is that day!

The World Christian Encyclopedia estimated that there have been 70 million Christian martyrs since the beginning of Christianity, with more than 45 million martyred in the 20th century alone. Where is the outcry for such a tragedy? For the most part, the world has remained silent.

Nine out of the ten countries ranked the most oppressive for Christians to live in were due to Islamic extremism, according to Open Doors annual World Watch List. With the exception of North Korea-ranked No. 1 for the 12th year in a row- every other country on the Top 10 List had as its source of persecution, Islamic extremism. According to the report, the countries with the most extreme persecution beside North Korea are: Somalia, Syria, Iraq, Afghanistan, Saudi Arabia, Maldives, Pakistan, Iran and Yemen.

In June 2010, World Net Daily reported that researcher, Bert Hickman, with the Center for the Study of Global Christianity, confirmed that 105,000 people are killed every year because of their Christian faith. This means that one Christians is killed every five minutes. Furthermore, over the past 10 years, an average 100,000 Christians have been slain for their faith annually. The vast majority is murdered by radical Islamists.

As the battle over the persecution of Christian's worldwide rages – estimates are that 200 million Christians around the globe are subject at any time to punishments up to and including death simply for believing.

Tom Doyle, author of a new book about Christians facing persecution in the Middle East, said that, in spite of the advance of Islamic State, God is changing the hearts of people in the region as Christians continue to boldly share the gospel message in spite of the risks and violence. He also challenges Christians in free nations to live with the same boldness and faith, and reminds us that believers facing persecution are praying for Christians in America.

ISIS Torture of Christians

The terrorists of ISIS--once known as al-Qaeda in Iraq--control territory as large as an entire nation-state, with much of northern Syria and northern Iraq under its control. It is brutal beyond imagination to anyone—Christians, Jews, and even Shiite Muslims—who are not aligned with its jihadist form of Sunni Islam. In Syria, ISIS has slaughtered Shiites and Christians. In Iraq, it has done the same, giving Christians in conquered territories a chilling ultimatum; "Convert, leave your homes or die."[153]

ISIS is stronger than any jihadist group in world history. Americans have long—and rightly—feared al-Qaeda. After all, it carried out the most devastating attack ever on American soil. But if we have feared and fought al-Qaeda, consider the following facts about ISIS.[154]

- ISIS is so brutal that al-Qaeda tried to persuade ISIS to change its tactics.
- ISIS is the world's richest terrorist group.
- ISIS controls more firepower and territory than any jihadist organization in history.

Christians Fleeing the Middle East

Tens of thousands of Christians fled Iraq. Most of them went to Erbil with nothing more than the clothes on their back. Some of the Christians were buried alive, others were beheaded. Christians are not just facing persecution today, they are facing genocide. ISIS forced Christians in Iraq to convert to Islam, pay an enormous fee or die by the sword. Many believers have been beheaded.

Millions of people of various religions have fled, including nearly 4 million Syrian refugees now living in Egypt, Jordan, Lebanon and Turkey. Another 6.5 million Syrians are internally displaced—meaning half of the country's pre-war population of around 20 million has been forced from their homes. A European Parliament resolution in March condemning attacks on Christians and other minorities said more than 700,000 Syrian Christians were among those who have fled the country.[155]

At this moment, for the sake of the Gospel of Jesus Christ, men and women are being bullwhipped into submission, tortured, imprisoned, beaten, battered, and broken. Homes are being burned, families are being executed, and other lives lost through hateful revenge. If you believe that torture and murder because of belief in Jesus Christ is a thing of the past, then you are tragically mistaken. Across our globe, the blood of Christians runs down cobblestone streets, dirt paths, paved alleys, and concrete prison floors.[156] Please pray for these persecuted believers. Donate money to ministries who provide food and clothing to our fellow believers who are being persecuted.

God Promised Revival in the Last Days

"In the last days it shall be, God declares that I will pour out my Spirit on all flesh, and your sons and your daughters shall prophesy, and your young men shall see vision, and your old men shall dream dreams. In those days I will pour out my

Spirit, and they shall prophesy. I will show wonders in the heavens above and signs on the earth below, blood and fire, and vapor of smoke; the sun shall be turned to darkness and the moon into blood, before the Lord comes, the great and magnificent day. It shall come to pass that everyone who calls upon the day of the Lord shall be saved" (Acts 2:17-21 ESB).

All praise to God, the Father of our Lord Jesus Christ. It is by his great mercy that we have been born again, because God raised Jesus Christ from the dead. Now we live with great expectation, and we have a priceless inheritance—an inheritance that is kept in heaven for you, pure and undefiled, beyond the reach of change and decay. Through your faith, God is protecting you by his power until you receive this salvation, which is ready to be revealed on the last day for all to see. So be truly glad. There is wonderful joy ahead, even though you must endure many trials for a little while. These trials will show that your faith is genuine. It is being tested as fire tests and purifies gold—though your faith is far more precious than mere gold. So when your faith remains strong through many trials, it will bring you much praise and glory and honor on the day when Jesus Christ is revealed to the whole world. You love him even though you have never seen him. Though you do not see him now, you trust him; and you rejoice with a glorious, inexpressible joy" (1 Peter 1:3-8 NIV).

❯ CHAPTER 13
PROPHETIC SIGNS IN THE HEAVENS

"God said, 'Let there be lights in the expanse of the heavens to separate the day from the night, and let them be for signs and for seasons and for days and years; and let them be for lights in the expanse of the heavens to give light on the earth and it was so'" (Genesis 1:14–15 NASB).

It was God (not some other deity) who created the light. Israel originality came from Mesopotamia, where the celestial bodies were worshipped, and more recently from Egypt, where the sun was worshipped as a primary deity. God was revealing to then that the very stars, moon and planets which Israel's neighbors had worshipped were the products of His creation.[157]

"God counts the stars and calls them all by name" (Psalm 147:4 TLB). "Seek him who created the Seven Stars and the constellation Orion, who turns darkness into morning and day into night, who call forth the water from the ocean and pours it out as rain upon the land. The Lord, Jehovah, is his name" (Amos 5:8 TLB).

Some people feel that the concept of "signs in the heavens" refers to godless astrology or pagan ritual. The Bible says that God employs celestial signs to warn His people of imminent earthshaking events. A sign in the sky enabled the wise men to locate the newborn babe, born in a manager long ago. If a sign in the sky foretold of the Messiah's first advent, do you think it strange that a sign in the sky will foretell of Christ's Second Coming?

Great Cosmic Signs Important to Christianity, Judaism and Islam

The signs of the end times are an important part of the eschatology of these three religions. They all believe that great cosmic activity will occur, including signs in the sun, moon and stars, along with comets and other heavenly omens as heavenly indicators of the approaching end. Devout Jews recognize total lunar eclipses or "blood moons" as a bad omen for Israel.[158]

Muslims in many countries observe total eclipses when they fall on the Islamic sacred month of Ramadan, the month, when Mohammad allegedly received his revelation recorded in the Koran. According to many Muslims, the anticipated Mahdi will appear on the world scene when there are two eclipses in the month of Ramadan[159]

People are anxious to know when and how he will rise; what they must do to receive this worldwide salvation. According to Shiites, the 12th Imam disappeared as a child in the year 941. When he returns, they believe, he will reign on earth for seven years, before bringing about a final judgment and the end of the world.[160]

Many Iranians Have Accepted Yeshua as Their Messiah

It is thought that as many as seven million Iranians have accepted Yeshua as their Messiah. The Jesus film was showed in one town in Iran. When the people saw the picture of the crucifixion, they explained that this was the man that appeared to them in a vision. The entire city accepted Yeshua as their Messiah.[161]

The Star of Bethlehem

The Star of Bethlehem led the Magi to Bethlehem to find the baby Jesus. "Jesus was born in Bethlehem, in Judea, during the reign of King Herod. Magi from the east came to Jerusalem and asked, 'Where is the one who has been born king of the Jews? We say His star when it rose and have come to worship him'" (Matthew 2:1-2 NIV).

The Star of Bethlehem, also called the Christmas Star, revealed the birth of Jesus to the Biblical Magi, and later led them to Bethlehem. The star appears only in the nativity story of the Gospel of Matthew, where magi "from the east" are inspired by the star to travel to Jerusalem. There they meet King Herod of Judea, and ask where the king of the Jews had been born. Herod, following a verse from the Book of Micah interpreted as a prophecy, directs them to Bethlehem. The star leads them to Jesus' home in the town, where they worship him and give him gifts. The wise men are then given a divine warning not to return to Herod so they return home by a different route.[162]

Super Star Appeared in 2015

On June 30th, 2015 Jupiter and Venus, the two brightest stars in the universe, merged into what is known as a Super Star. When the two stars merged together, they appeared to be a bright double-star in the night sky. This is the first time since 3-2 B.C. that the Super Star has appeared in the night sky.

The planet Jupiter was known as the King Planet. Jesus Christ is King of Kings and Lord Revelation 19:16). Venus was considered the bright morning star in ancient cultures. Jesus was called the bright Morning Star in Revelation 22:16).

The Moon is God's Faithful Witness in the Sky

"If his children forsake my laws and don't obey them, then I will punish them, but I will never completely take away my loving-kindness from them, nor let my promise fail. No, I will not break my covenant; I will not take back one word of what I said. For I have sworn to David (and a holy God can never lie) that his dynasty will go on forever, and his throne will continue to the end of time. It shall be eternal as the moon, my faithful witness in the sky!" (Psalm 89:30-37 TLB).

Jewish Rabbis believe a solar eclipse is a sign of trouble for the world and a lunar eclipse is a sign of trouble for Israel. Since Israel is on a lunar calendar based on the cycles of the moon—any eclipse on the moon is considered a cosmic sign for Israel.

Four Blood Moons

Blood Moons are when the moon appears red due to a lunar eclipse. They occur when the earth is positioned between the sun and the moon. The earth's shadow blocks the sun's light, which would normally reflect off the moon. The delicate layer of dusty air surrounding our planet reddens and redirects the light of the sun, filling the dark behind the Earth with a sunset-red glow.[163] When the earth's shadow completely covers the moon it will turn red during the total portion of an eclipse.

A lunar eclipse occurs when the moon passes behind the earth so that the earth blocks the sun's rays from striking the moon, which can occur only when the sun, earth, and moon are aligned exactly, or very closely so, with the earth in the middle. Hence, a lunar eclipse can only occur the night of a full moon. Unlike with a solar eclipse, no special equipment is required to view a lunar eclipse safely, and it may be viewed with the naked eye.[164]

The Babylonian Talmud, written almost two thousand years ago, records Jewish thinking that whenever the sun is in total eclipse, it is a bad omen for the nations. When the moon is in total eclipse, it is a bad omen for Israel. All through history, civilizations such as the Egyptians and the Mayans have looked to the heavens for patterns and celestial signs, trying to understand if they told of coming events on earth. Eclipses have always had a profound effect on people. I believe God placed the wonder in our DNA so we would understand what He is saying.[165]

Jewish tradition has mixed views on the mystical and eschatological meaning of lunar eclipses. On the one hand, the Talmud (Tractate Sukkah 29a) says that lunar eclipses are a sign of Divine wrath against the Jewish people for moral failings, while solar eclipses are a bad sign for non-Jewish nations; the Jews date their calendar based on the phases of the moon, while the non-Jews base theirs on the solar year. On the other hand, Jewish tradition repeatedly says that astrological and astronomical signs do not affect the Jewish people, and that the Jews' direct relationship with God overcomes any "natural" effects of the movement of heavenly bodies that could affect other nations.[166]

Blood Moon Tetrads in History

- AD 32–33 when Christ was crucified.
- A.D. 70 when the Jewish Temple was destroyed
- 1492 during the Spanish Inquisition
- 1948–1950 – Israel's War of Independence
- 1967- 1968- Israel's 6 Day War

Four Blood Moons of 2014-15 [167]

1. Passover, April 15, 2014
2. Feast of Tabernacles, October 8, 2014
3. Passover, April 4, 2015
4. Feast of Tabernacles, September 28, 2015

There were two blood moons in 2014 and 2015 on Jewish Holy Days. The April 2014 Jewish Passover and 2014 Sukkot Lunar Eclipses took place on the same dates as the A.D. 70 Jewish Passover & Sukkot – Feast of Tabernacles lunar eclipses which occurred when the Roman Army destroyed the 2nd Jewish Temple effectively ending over 1,000 years of Jewish rule in the Nation of Israel ![168] These are the last Blood Moon Tetrads in the next five hundred years. What is God trying to tell us?

The Disciples Ask for a Sign

The disciples were looking for a sign to foretell of Christ's return when they privately asked him; "Tell us," they said, "when will this happen, and what will be the sign of your coming and of the end of the age" (Matthew 24:3 NIV)?

Jesus said that the cosmic signs indicated the Second Coming of Jesus Christ. He told His disciples that there will be signs in the heavens announcing His return and the End of the Age. Jesus Himself said "There will be signs in the sun, in the moon, and in the stars; and on the earth distress of nations, with perplexity, the sea and the waves roaring; men's hearts failing them from fear and the expectation of those things which are coming on the earth, for the powers of heaven will be shaken. Then they will see the Son of Man coming in a cloud with power and great glory (Luke 21:25-27). When these events occur, the world will know that Christ's return is imminent.

On the Day of Pentecost, Peter said, "It shall come to pass in the last days, says God, that I will show wonders in heaven above and signs in the earth beneath: Blood and fire and vapor of smoke. The sun shall be turned into darkness, and the moon into blood, before the coming of the great and awesome day of the Lord. It shall come to pass that whoever calls on the name of the Lord shall be saved" (Acts 2:19-21).

The Apostle John said "The sun will become black and the moon will become like blood. The stars of heaven will fall to the earth and the sky will recede as a scroll with it is rolled up. Every island and mountain will be moved out of their place.... The sky receded as a scroll when it is rolled up, and every mountain and island was moved out of its place. Then every island fled away, and the mountains were not found" (Revelation 6:14; 16:20).

Shortly before the Second Coming signs will appear in the heavens. All natural lights in the heavens will be extinguished. Christ, the true light of the world, will appear in a cloud in the heaven, just as the lightning comes from the east and flashes to the west.

This spectacle in the heavens will be of such magnitude that all will acknowledge its divine origin. Fear will grip men's hearts. The ungodly will seek a place to hide, but none will be available. When these events occur, believers will know that Christ's return is imminent. When these things begin to happen, look up and lift up your heads, because your redemption draws near.

What does the Future Hold?

No one knows for sure. Some have thought it could be the Psalm 83 War. Others think it could refer to the signing of the Seven Year Covenant with the Palestinians. Each time the blood moon tetrads have occurred in history has involved a difficult times for Israel.

❭ CHAPTER 14
COMPARE CHRISTIANITY, JUDAISM AND ISLAM

The Middle East is extremely important to the religions of Judaism, Christianity and Islam. These three religions are followed by three billion people, almost half of the world's population. How tragic that many of the wars have been fought over differences in religion. In order to understand what this generation is facing we need to see how different religions see the end of days.

Three Religions with Similar Eschatology

The three monotheistic religions all trace their roots to Abraham: Judaism, Christianity and Islam. Judaism traces its roots through Abraham's son Isaac, his grandson, Jacob, and the twelve tribes of Israel. Religious Jews look for the arrival of the Messiah to bring peace to the world.

The signs of the end time are varied, but some are the same among the followers of all three religions. All three groups believe that great cosmic activity occur, including signs in the sun, moon and stars, along with comets and other heavenly omens as heavenly indicators of the approaching end. Devout Jews recognize total lunar eclipses or "blood moons" as a bad omen for Israel.

Christianity has its roots in the Torah and the Old Testament prophets, but believe that Jesus Christ provided salvation for all mankind. Christians believe that Jesus Christ is the Messiah, who came to earth as the Lamb of God and gave His life for the sins of the entire world. We believe He will soon return as King of kings and Lord of lords and rule from Jerusalem for a thousand years.

Islam, on the other hand, originated among many of the Arabian tribes and people in Iraq, Syria, Egypt and Lebanon. The early followers were mostly descendants of Ishmael, Abraham's son through Hagar and Esau, Abraham's grandson. Twelve dukes came through the direct bloodline of Esau (Genesis 36), and twelve princes descended from Ishmael (Genesis 25:12-16).

Do Christians and Muslims Worship the Same God?

Many people today believe that the world's three major religions—Judaism, Christianity, and Islam—follow the same god and there is no reason why the three religions cannot exist side by side today in peace. Nothing is further from the truth!

Islam worships Allah, the Moon God, and believes that Allah alone is God and Muhammad is his prophet. Christ said "I am the way, the truth and the life.

No one comes to the Father except through me" (John 14:6). How can they both be correct?

Like the early Christians who believed the Lord was coming soon, Muslims of the seventh century, when Islam was still in its infancy, rode out to conquer the world because they were convinced the end was near. Notice the difference, however, Christians sought to win the world through the gospel of love. Muslims sought to win the world through domination and conquest.[169]

Muslim's View of End Times

Islam follows a theology of triumphalism—"the dominance of one's nations, ideology, or religious creed over another." Islam teaches that Muhammad superseded the patriarchs and Christ. To a Muslim, it is Allah's will for Islam to rule the world. The word Islam does not mean peace—its means submission. Their objective is for everyone to be in submission to them.[170] Islam literally means "submission to the will of Allah." The Qur'an, Islam's holy book, is often spelled Koran. It literally means "that which is to be read."

The Qur'an is the Muslim holy book, but Muslims also reference the Old and New Testaments of the Bible. Their prophet was a seventh-century illiterate man who was supposedly chosen to receive the revelation. He was tasked with converting the pagan people in the Arabian Peninsula, and later worldwide, into Muslims. Islam is the second-largest world religion at 23.2 percent of the population, following Christianity.[171]

The Qur'an sees the world as divided into two, one part, which has come under Islamic rule, and one part, which is supposed to come under Islamic rule in the future. Their division of the world is very clear. Every single person who starts studying Islam knows it. The world is described as Dar al-Islam (the house of Islam), that's the place where Islam rules and the other part which is called Dar al-Harb, the house of war. Not the house of non-Muslim, but the house of war. It is this house of war which has to be, at the end of time, conquered. The world will continue to be in the house of war until it comes under Islam rule.[172]

Islam teaches that the only destiny for the Jews is that of absolute and total slaughter. There is a very persistent hatred for the Jews similar to the ideology expressed through Nazism. This ideology is fully supported and nurtured throughout the Qur'an and Islamic traditions.

For a Muslim, Muhammad is the only absolute truth. It is unthinkable that he was wrong, and because Israel would not adhere to the teaching of Muhammad and convert to Islam, Israel must be defeated. Mohammad is the only one who made war against Israel holy! If Israel survives, then Islam would be wrong, a failure and that is an unthinkable position.[173]

The 12ᵗʰ Imam (Muslim Messiah)

Millions of Muslims around the world are waiting for an Islamic Messiah called the Madhi or the 12ᵗʰ Imam, who will come on the scene at the end of time. He will reign on the earth for seven years, before final judgment and the end of the world. Some Muslims teach that the Madhi will be accompanied with the lesser prophet, Jesus Christ. This Islamic savior will convert the world, including Jews and Christians to Islam. Different branches of Islam have different beliefs about the Madhi. Sunni Muslims believe that their savior will be Muhammad's successor.

People are anxious to know when and how he will rise; what they must do to receive this worldwide salvation. According to Shiites, the 12th Imam disappeared as a child in the year 941. When he returns, they believe, he will reign on earth for seven years, before bringing about a final judgment and the end of the world.[174]

Former Iranian President, Mahmoud Ahmadinejad and others in Iran are deadly serious about the imminent return of the 12th Imam, who will prompt a global battle between good and evil (with striking parallels to biblical accounts of Armageddon.[175] Iranians are preparing for the coming of the Mahdi by turning the country into a mighty and advanced Islamic society. All Iran is buzzing about the Mahdi, the 12th imam, and the role Iran will play in his anticipated return.

Islam's Concept of Eternity

In the end of days, Islam sees a world that is totally Muslim, completely Muslim under the rule of Islam, a complete and final victory. Christians will not exist, because according to many Islamic traditions, the Muslims who are in hell will have to be replaced by somebody and the Christians will replace them. The Jews will no longer exist, because before the coming of the end of days, there is going to be a war against the Jews where all Jews should be killed.[176]

In Islam, hell is a crater of fire beneath a narrow bridge that all souls must cross to go to paradise. Those whom Allah judges unworthy fall in and suffer endless physical torments in one of seven layers of hell. The Qur'an uses Bible-like imagery to describe hell's attributes: It is a "lake of fire", a "burning bed of misery" where the wicked and infidels suffer endlessly, apart from God, with only "boiling, fetid water" to drink.[177]

Palestinian youth believe much more strongly in heaven than they did twenty years ago. They believe that if killed, fighting in the name of Islam, they will go straight to the seventh level of heaven and delight in the company of beautiful virgins. This idea of heaven gives the martyrs comfort and power.[178] The Jewish Old Testament prohibits killing in the Ten Commandments and totally deplores suicide.

Judaism's View of End Times

Judaism is based on a divine revelation from God, experienced by the entire nation, whereas Islam is based on the prophetic claims of a single individual who subsequently convinced others to follow his ways.

Several Old Testament writers believed in the resurrection of the dead. They believed they would be raised to life and see God. They believed in the goodness of God and that the righteous dead will again see God. Job declared, "For I know that my Redeemer lives, and He shall stand at last on the earth; and after my skin is destroyed, this I know, that in my flesh I shall see God" (Job 19:25-26).

Daniel wrote "Many of those who sleep in the dust of the earth will awake, some to everlasting life, some to shame and everlasting contempt" (Daniel 12:2).

Zechariah prophesied that the Messiah will return to the Mount of Olives in Jerusalem with power and great glory (Zechariah 14:4). Some Jews believe so strongly that the Messiah will return that they pay a high price to be buried on the Mount of Olives, close to where the Jewish Messiah is expected to return.

Many Old Testament prophets prophesied that one day the Jewish Messiah would come to Israel, bless the Jewish people and bring peace to the entire world. The hope of Judaism is that the next age will begin with the Jewish Messiah comes to rule the world. There will be peace between nations, not just one nation.

"Now it shall come to pass in the latter days that the mountain of the Lord's house shall be established on the top of the mountains; and shall be exalted above the hills; and all nations shall flow to it. Many people shall come and say, 'Come, and let us go up to the mountain of the Lord, to the house of the God of Jacob. He will teach us His ways and we shall walk in His paths. For out of Zion shall go forth the law and the word of the Lord from Jerusalem. He shall judge between the nations and rebuke many people. They shall beat their swords into plow shares, and their spears into pruning hooks. Nation shall not lift up sword against nation; neither shall they learn war anymore'" (Isaiah. 2:2-4).

The Jews have not forgotten prophecies that the Messiah will return and sit on the throne of David. Many of them wonder why the Messiah hasn't come. They long for His return to redeem the earth from sorrow and suffering.

Seymour Siegel once commented, "The central problem of Christianity is: If the Messiah has come, why is the world so evil? For Judaism, the problem: If the world is so evil, why does the Messiah not come? Israel's only hope has been that someday the Messiah would come and deliver their people".

Songs on the radio in Israel proclaim a longing for the coming of Messiah and the age of redemption. One song that the young people sing says: "O Mashiach, how we want you now. Hurry and open the gates. Please return us to our homeland Yisroel. Ad Mosai, how long must we wait?"[179]

Grant Jeffrey wrote in "Heaven, The Mystery of Angels: "While visiting in Israel I talked to many Israelis who spoke of the need for Messiah to come to solve the terrible problems Israel and the world face. Bumper stickers in Jerusalem stated, in Hebrew, "We want Moshiach Now." Even in New York City these stickers are now appearing: "We want Messiah Now." Every few day a speaker in the Israeli parliament, known as the Knesset, will refer to the coming of the Messiah. The Jerusalem Post and other secular newspapers continually refer to the need for Messiah to come and lead to "the peace of Israel." A growing number of bookstores in Jerusalem contain books that refer to the Talmudic and biblical teachings about the Messiah.[180]

Christian's View of End Times

Christians who know and understand biblical prophecy recall the words of the Luke: "I will cause wonders in the heavens above and signs on the earth below-- blood and fire and clouds of smoke. The sun will become dark, and the moon will turn blood red before that great and glorious day of the Lord arrives. Everyone who calls on the names of the lord will be saved" (Acts 2:19-21 NLT).

The Bible teaches that the final seven years of this age will begin when the Antichrist signs a seven-year covenant with Israel. In the middle of the seven years, he will pollute the rebuilt Jewish Temple and demand worship. In anger, he will vigorously attack the Jews, as well, as all true followers of Christ. This period of time is often referred to as the "Time of Jacob's Troubles" (Jeremiah 30:7) or the "Great Tribulation" (Matthew 24:21).

Christianity sees the next age much like the Jews. We look forward to the return of our blessed Savior, Jesus Christ. When Christ returns, the dead in Christ will arise first and all true believers will meet the Lord in the air. All believers will be evaluated by the Lord at the Judgment Seat of Christ and receive their reward.

Shortly after His return, Christ will lead the great Heavenly Hosts to destroy the Antichrist and his one-world empire in the awesome Battle of Armageddon. Christ will set up an earthly kingdom in Jerusalem and rule and reign as King of kings and Lord of lords for a thousand years. The Jewish people will understand that Yeshua is their Messiah and turn to Him. The world will finally experience peace. Nations will know war no more. The lion will lay down with the lamb.

Jewish and Gentile believers will be a part of the Kingdom of Heaven, "I say to you that many will come from the east and the west and will take their place at the feast with Abraham, Isaac and Jacob in the kingdom of heaven" (Matthew 8:11 NIV). Following the thousand year reign of Christ, believers will live with Christ in His presence forever and ever. What a blessed hope!

> CHAPTER 15
GOD'S PROPHETIC TIME TABLE

"The Lord our God has secrets known to no one. We are not accountable for them, but we and our children are accountable forever for all that he has revealed to us, so that we may obey all the terms of these instructions" (Deuteronomy 29:29 NASB).

The ninth chapter of Daniel is one of the most remarkable chapters in the entire Bible. It has been called the backbone of bible prophecy. It was given to Daniel from the angel Gabriel to reveal a clear understanding of what would transpire in the future. It pinpoints the exact time in history when Yeshua, the Jewish Messiah, presented himself to the Jewish people, over five hundred years before the event took place. This chapter is one of the strongest evidences to prove the divine inspiration of the Bible.

In the seventeenth century a very learned Jew published a book in which he set forth the claims of Jesus Christ to be the Jewish Messiah. He told how he himself had been converted by listening to a debate between a knowledgeable Jew and a Christian convert from Judaism over the meaning of this passage in Daniel nine. The moderator of the debate was a learned rabbi, and as the Christian pressed the claims of this passage home it became so clear that the passage was pointing to Jesus Christ. The rabbi closed the debate with these words: "Let us shut up our books, for if we go on examining the prophecy we shall all become Christians."[181]

Daniel in Babylon

Daniel is the greatest of the ancient prophets of Israel, both in his unblemished character as a man of God and in his unparalleled ability to see through the veil of time to describe the future. It is impossible to exaggerate the importance of the prophet Daniel in terms of his influence on the prophetic views of both Jews and Christians during the last two thousand years[182]. It paints a beautiful picture of a man of God who lived out his commitment in very troubled times.

Daniel was a teenager, when he was taken from Jerusalem to Babylon. When he received this prophecy, he was in his 80s and had lived over fifty years in Babylon. He was studying Jeremiah's prophecy concerning Israel's exile in Babylon and realized that the seventy years captivity would soon come to an end. Even though Daniel was a prophet, he also studied the scriptures.

The Lord God of Hosts says, "Because you have not listened to me, I will gather together all the armies of the north under Nebuchadnezzar, king of Babylon and I will bring them against this land and its people...This entire land shall become a desolate wasteland; the world will be shocked at the disaster that befalls you. Israel and her neighboring lands shall serve the king of Babylon for seventy years" (Jeremiah 25:8, 9, 11 TLB).

Israel's Seventy Years Captivity

Why did the Children of Israel go into captivity in Babylon for seventy years? God promised that if they did not observe the Sabbath and the Sabbatical Year, He would send them into captivity. They failed to keep seventy sabbatical years over a period of 490 years, so God sent them into captivity for seventy years. "The message of the Lord spoken through Jeremiah was fulfilled. The land finally enjoyed its Sabbath rest, lying desolate until the seventy years were fulfilled, just as the prophet had said" (2 Chronicles 36:21 NLT).

Daniel's Prayer for His People

"O Lord, you are a great and awesome God! You always fulfill your covenant and keep your promises of unfailing love to those who love you and obey your commands. But we have sinned and done wrong. We have rebelled against you and scorned your commands and regulations. We have refused to listen to your servants the prophets, who spoke on your authority to our kings and princes and ancestors and to all the people of the land. But the Lord our God is merciful and forgiving, even though we have rebelled against him" (Daniel 9:4-6, 9 NLT).

This prayer is a model prayer for people who are concerned over national decay. If you are concerned about the state of our country today, I suggest that you read Daniel's prayer and see how beautifully and wonderfully he gathers up the whole situation, realistically appraises it, and lays it before God. This is a searching, penetrating prayer of confession, of praise, and of earnest petition to God.[183]

While Daniel was praying and confessing his sins and the sin of Israel, the angel Gabriel appeared to give Daniel to give him understanding regarding the future. Gabriel explained events that would transpire concerning identify of the Messiah, Jerusalem's destruction and the final seven years of this age.

God sent Gabriel to Daniel to outline His time-table for the future spiritual redemption of His Jewish people and all humanity, a redemption that would come through the Jewish Messiah. Then Gabriel went on to relate what will happen to the nation of Israel in the very last days. This entire timetable is laid out in Daniel 9, perhaps the most significant passage of prophecy in the entire Bible.[184]

Daniel's Seventy Weeks Prophecy

Daniel's Seventieth Week will begin after the Church Age when the focus will be on the Jewish people for a period of seven years. This seven years period is sometimes referred to as Jacob's Trouble. It will begin when the Antichrist signs a seven year covenant with Israel.

"He (Antichrist) shall enter into a strong *and* firm covenant with the many (Jews) for one week [seven years]. In the midst of the week he shall cause the sacrifice and offering to cease [for the remaining three and one-half years]; and upon the wing *or* pinnacle of abominations [shall come] one who makes desolate, until the full determined end is poured out on the desolator" (Daniel 9:27 AMP).

"Seventy weeks are determined for your people and for your holy city, To finish the transgression, To make an end of sins, To make reconciliation for iniquity, To bring in everlasting righteousness, To seal up vision and prophecy, and to anoint the Most Holy" (Daniel 9:24).

Gabriel told Daniel that there would be 490 years of Gentile domination concerning Israel and Jerusalem before these six events would be fulfilled. Gabriel also told Daniel that the   Messiah would be cut off after 69th week.

Six Events Determined for Israel

1. To Finish the Transgression – Christ provided salvation for all mankind, but the Jewish leaders did not recognize Him as their Messiah. A future fountain will be opened for the Jews.
2. To make reconciliation for Iniquity – God provided redemption through the death and resurrection of Yeshua, the Messiah.
3. To Make an End To Sin – When Messiah returns, the Israelites will repent and accept Yeshua as their Messiah
4. To Bring in Everlasting Righteousness – Christ will return and set up an eternal kingdom.
5. To Seal up Prophecy – All prophecies and vision will be fulfilled.
6. To Anoint the Most Holy – The Shekinah glory of God will again fill the Jewish Temple and the Messiah will rule over all the earth.

Edict to Rebuild Jerusalem

"Know therefore and understand that from the going forth of the command to restore and build Jerusalem until Messiah the Prince, there shall be seven weeks and sixty-two weeks; The street shall be built again, and the wall even in troublesome times" (Daniel 9:25).

The identity of the starting point of this prophecy is essential to correctly understand it. During the first forty nine years of this prophecy, Jerusalem was to be constructed in troubled times.

The only decree that fits the prophecy was the decree issued by King Artaxerxes. The Bible records the date as "the month Nisan, in the twentieth years of

King Artaxerxes" (Nehemiah 2:1) or, the 20th year of his reign on the first day of the month of Nisan. The Greenwich Observatory confirmed the date as March 5, 444 B.C. Anderson's calculations were among the first to recognize the Hebrew lunar calendar was a 360-day years, 12 months of 30 days each.[185]

King Artaxerxes allowed Nehemiah, his cupbearer, to return to Jerusalem and rebuild the city (Nehemiah 2:1-5). When Nehemiah arrived in Jerusalem, he examined the walls and gates of Jerusalem and encouraged the Israelites to build Jerusalem and restore the city walls. This was the starting point of Daniel's Seventy Weeks Prophecy.

Sir Robert Anderson, Chief Inspector and investigator for Scotland Yard, wrote a book, entitled, *The Coming Prince,* in Great Britain in 1894. His remarkable contribution has been unmatched in current time.

Sir Isaac Newton said that all nations, before the just length of the solar year was known, reckoned months by the course of the moon, and years by the return of winter and summer, spring and autumn; and in making calendars for their festivals, they recorded thirty days to a lunar month and twelve lunar months to a year.[186]

Length of an Old Testament Year

How long was a Biblical Year? In the Old Testament a year was 360 days. Noah's flood started on the 17th day of the second month (Genesis 7:11) and the ark rested on the 17th day of the seventh month (Genesis 8:4). Noah's flood was on the earth for five months or 150 days (Genesis 7:24). Divide 150 divided by 5 = 30 days. When you multiply 30 days x 12 months, it equals 360 days.

The Jews measure time in units of seven. The Hebrew word for seven is *shabua,* a "week" – a period of time. The word "weeks" occurs hundreds of times in the Old Testament and indicates a period of seven. It could be seven days, seven months or seven years depending on the context.

Seventy weeks means seventy sevens or 490 years. A prophetic week corresponds to seven years, with each day in "week" representing a year. The seventy weeks are divided into three periods; 7 weeks + 62 weeks + 1 week = 70 weeks. (1 week = 7 years, 62 weeks = 434 years, 70 weeks = 490 years).

Messiah Crucified

"Then after the sixty-two weeks [of years] the Anointed One will be cut off [and denied His Messianic kingdom] and have nothing [and no one to defend Him], and the people of the [other] prince who is to come will destroy the city and the sanctuary. Its end *will come* with a flood; even to the end there will be war; desolations are determined" (Daniel 9:26 AMP).

The interesting fact about the seventy weeks of Daniel is that sixty-nine seventieths of it have already been fulfilled. We can go back into history and trace the literal, detailed fulfillment of the sixty-nine weeks. This gives us complete confidence to believe that what God has done in the first part of the prophecy He will surely do in the last part.[187]

The Messiah had to be cut off before the 70th week of Daniel could begin. Daniel's prophecy said "The people of the prince who is to come (Antichrist) will destroy the city and the sanctuary" (Daniel 9:26). This happened in A.D. 70 when Titus, a Roman ruler, destroyed Jerusalem and burned the Jewish Temple.

What is the Gap?

Daniel Prophecy of 483 years stopped with the death of Christ and the destruction of Jerusalem.	**THE GAP**	Final 7 Years will begin when Israel confirms a seven year covenant with the Antichrist.

God's prophetic time clock stopped over 1900 year ago with the death and resurrection of Christ and the destruction on the Jewish Temple. No one knows how long this gap will last. God did not disclose the length even to Daniel. We are living in the interval between the 69th and the final 70th week.

How do you explain the gap between the 69th and 70th weeks? If the Jews had accepted Yeshua as their Messiah, perhaps the Millennium would have started. This gap has become known as the "Church Age" or the "Age of Grace".

More than ever before, the church can expect Daniel's "70 week" to begin. World conditions are rapidly building to a crisis. War in the Middle East, ISIS invading Iraq and persecuting Christians, crises in Syria and numerous other disasters around the world make us wonder, "What is going on"? It is time for believers to understand the significance of this prophecy.

Daniel's Seventieth Week

Daniel's Seventieth week is a period of seven years which is sometimes referred to as Jacob's Trouble. It will begin when the Antichrist signs a seven year covenant with Israel.

"He (Antichrist) shall enter into a strong *and* firm covenant with the many (Jews) for one week [seven years]. In the midst of the week he shall cause the sacrifice and offering to cease [for the remaining three and one-half years]; and upon the wing *or* pinnacle of abominations [shall come] one who makes desolate, until the full determined end is poured out on the desolator" (Daniel 9:27 AMP).

Daniel's Seventieth week is a period of seven years which is sometimes referred to as Jacob's Trouble. It will begin when the Antichrist signs a seven year covenant with the Jews.

The Great Tribulation will begin at the mid-point of the final seven years, after the Antichrist pollutes the rebuilt Jewish Temple. Jesus said, "When you see the Abomination of Desolation spoken by Daniel the prophet, standing in the holy place…then there will be Great Tribulation, such as has not been from the beginning until now" (Matthew 24:15, 32 ESV).

The Antichrist will play a prominent role in the 70th week of Daniel's prophecy, which remains to be fulfilled. After the completion of the 70 prophesied weeks the transgression will be truly finished, an end of sins will be indeed be made, reconciliation for iniquity will be initiated, and everlasting righteousness brought in to God's children.

Review of Daniel's Seventy Weeks

Decree to Rebuilt Jerusalem Nehemiah 2:1-5	Jesus entered Jerusalem as the Messiah. John 12:12-15	The Messiah was cut off at the Crucifixion. Luke 23:33	Jerusalem was destroyed by Titus, a Roman ruler, in A.D. 70.	Final 7 Years Israel confirms a covenant with the Antichrist. Daniel 9:26-27

All Israel Will Be Saved

The deliverer will come from Zion; he will turn godlessness away from Jacob. This is my covenant with them when I take away their sins" (Romans 11:27 NIV).

The Messiah will return to earth and reign for 1,000 years. The Jews will accept Yeshua as their Messiah. What a glorious time that will be. This old sin-cursed world will experience universal righteousness and universal peace. We have many reasons to pray "Thy kingdom come."

〉CHAPTER 16
PRE-TRIBULATION RAPTURE: FACT OR FALLACY

About the Time of the End, a body of men will be raised up who will turn their attention to the prophecies, and insist upon their literal interpretation, in the midst of much clamor and opposition. - Sir Isaac Newton

Doctrine of Early Church Fathers

The early Church fathers were not experts on prophecy and the major doctrines of scripture. Most of them did not have access to all the books in the Bible. It took them sometime to get a census on the major doctrines of the Church.

    The Didache, a Church manual written around A.D. 110, clearly taught that the Antichrist would rise to power before the Rapture of the Church. They did not teach the doctrine of imminence, and none taught a clear Pre-Tribulation Rapture doctrine. They admonished Christians to "watch" for the rise of the Antichrist before the return of Jesus Christ.[188]

Quotes from Early Church Leaders

Justin Martyr -A.D. 100-165- argued for the principle of literal interpretation of the Bible and especially in the understanding of prophecy. He believed that the Antichrist would rise to power and persecute Christians before the return of Jesus Christ.[189]

    These early church father understood that the Antichrist would come to power before the Rapture took place. They referred to "false prophets" being multiplied and lawlessness increasing (Matthew 24:15-21). The context shows that the early church fathers who wrote the Didache believed that the Church would go through the Tribulation. Barnabas who traveled with the apostle Paul (Acts 13:1-5) did not believe the Rapture was an imminent event. He believed it would not take place for another 2000 years.[190]

    Perhaps Barnabas considered that there had been about 4,000 years of human history from Adam to the birth of Jesus and there would be about 2,000 more years until the return of Jesus. Christ died around A.D. 33. Two thousand year from A.D. 33 would be 2033, just 17 years from now.

Rise and Spread of Pretribulationism

Pretribulationism arose in the 1830's in Europe when a small group of men concerned about the spiritual condition of the Protestant Church met for pray and fellowship. Other groups in Europe soon sprang up after that.

While speaking in tongues, a young woman named Margaret Macdonald, went into a trance and received a revelation she thought was from God. This vision concerned the Second Advent of Christ. She revealed that Christ's return would be split into two distinct stages. The Rapture would occur before the Tribulation and the Second Coming would occur after the Great Tribulation.

In 1830, a tiny English Protestant sect known as the Irvingites proclaimed this new doctrine. This idea was immediately adopted by John Nelson Darby, a leader of the small British sect known as the Plymouth Brethren. Darby traveled to the United States several times teaching this new concept. Many of the seminaries and other schools used this material to prepare the next generation of ministers.

In the 1880's, this doctrine was spread among Baptist, some Evangelical and Pentecostal churches. Some godly men, who accepted it, later admitted they could not find this doctrine in the Word of God.

The Doctrine of Imminence

This doctrine teaches that nothing has to occur before the Rapture. Christ could return at any moment in a secret, silent rapture, invisible to anyone other than those who are raptured.

The apostle Paul disputed this doctrine in his second letter to the Thessalonians when he revealed that the great apostasy (falling away) and the Antichrist will be revealed before Christ returns. He wrote; "Now, brethren, concerning the coming of our Lord Jesus Christ and our gathering together to Him, we ask you, not to be soon shaken in mind or troubled, as though the day of Christ has come. Let no one deceive you by any means, for that Day will not come unless the falling away comes first and the man of sin is revealed, the son of perdition, who opposes and exalts himself above all that is called God or that is worshipped so that he sits as God in the temple of God, showing himself that he is God" (2 Thessalonians 2:1-4).

Before Christ returns, the falling away will occur and the Antichrist will make his appearance. The Jewish Temple will be rebuilt and the Antichrist will exalt himself and sit in the temple of God, declaring that he is God. This scripture tells us that the Antichrist (the son of perdition) will be revealed before Christ returns.

Will the Holy Spirit be removed at the Rapture?

Some prophecy teachers believe the *one who holds back lawlessness* is the Holy Spirit. They believe that when the church is raptured prior to the Great Tribulation, the Holy Spirit is also removed. Where does the Bible teach that the Holy Spirit will be removed or that Christians will be raptured before the Great Tribulation? We should never build a doctrine on just one or two verses of scripture, especially if that doctrine is disputed.

Who is the Restrainer?

The apostle Paul said, "The mystery of lawlessness is already at work; only he who now restrains will do so until he is taken out of the way. Then that lawless one will be revealed whom the Lord will slay with the breath of His mouth and bring to an end by the appearance of His coming; that is, the one whose coming is in accord with the activity of Satan, with all power and signs and false wonders, and with all the deception of wickedness for those who perish, because they did not receive the love of the truth so as to be saved" (2 Thessalonians 2:7-10 NASB). There is no mention of the Holy Spirit being the restrainer.

Will Believers be kept from the Hour of Trial?

One of the hallmarks of Pre-Trib doctrine is that the Church will be preserved from the hour of trial (tribulation). "Because you have kept My command to persevere, I also will keep you from the hour of trial which shall come upon the whole world, to test those who dwell on the earth" (Revelation 3:10).

This scripture is part of the letter to the Church at Philadelphia. It may or may not apply to Christians in every generation. At first glance, this seems to indicate that the Church will be removed from the Great Tribulation.

Dr. George Eldon Ladd in his book, *The Blessed Hope*, explains this verse. The language of this verse, taken by itself could be interpreted to teach complete escape from the coming hour of tribulation. The language is, "I will keep you out of the hour of trial". This neither asserts nor demands the idea of bodily removal from the midst of the coming trial.

This is proven by the fact that precisely the same words are used by our Lord in His prayer that God would keep his disciples "out of the evil" (John 17:15). In our Lord's Prayer, there is no idea of bodily removal of the disciples from the evil world, but of preservation from the power of evil even when they are in its very presence. A similar thought occurs in Galatians 1:4, where we read that Christ gave Himself for our sins to deliver us from this present evil age. This does not refer to a physical removal from the age but to deliverance from its power and control.[191]

Pre-Tribulation Doctrine

Pretribulationism teaches that the second advent of Christ is divided into two aspects which, it is assumed are separated by the Great Tribulation. These two events are called the Rapture and the Revelation. The Rapture, or catching up of the Church to meet the Lord in the air, is a different event from the Revelation when He will appear in the manifestation of His glory. The Rapture occurs before the Tribulation, while the Revelation occurs when Christ comes to end the Great Tribulation and execute righteous judgment upon the earth.[192]

Since the Rapture precedes the Tribulation, it is assumed that it may occur as any moment; but the Revelation cannot occur until after the appearance of Antichrist and the Great Tribulation. The failure to make this distinction has led to great confusion among commentators on this subject. The coming of Christ for the Rapture of the Church will be a secret coming and will be invisible to anyone except the church; while the Revelation will be a glorious outshining which will be evident to the entire world.[193]

This theory places the Revelation of Christ at the end of the Tribulation when Christ comes in glory to judge the world. They teach that the rapture of the church will have already occurred and the saints have already received their rewards and entered into glorious presence of Christ. If this true, the Rapture is the hope of the church, not the glorious appearance of Christ.

Is this view really taught in the Word of God? If the scriptures do not clearly teach the two aspects in Christ's coming, we shall be forced to conclude that His return will be a single, glorious event.

Jesus Warned His Disciples of Persecution

Jesus warned of a time of persecution such as not occurred since the beginning of the creation which God created until now, and never will. Jesus warns His disciples that they will be hated and ultimately put to death as a result of their identification with Him. Jesus said in Matthew 24:9. "You will be handed over to be persecuted and put to death, and you will be hated by all nations because of me".

"For in those days there will be suffering, such as has not been from the beginning of the creation that God created until now, no, and never will be. If the Lord had not cut short those days, no one would be saved; but for the sake of the elect, whom he chose, he has cut short those days" (Acts 3:19-20 NRSV). If believers are raptured before the Great Tribulation, why will be days be shortened?

Fate of the Disciples[194]

How you ever wondered what happened to the disciples of Jesus? According to tradition…

- Philip was scourged and crucified.
- Matthew was nailed to the ground with spikes and beheaded.
- Jude was beaten to death with sticks and clubs.

- Simon was tortured and crucified.
- John, the Son of Zebedee, was tortured and exiled.
- James, the brother of John, was beheaded.
- James, the brother of Jesus, was pushed from the top of a building and then his broken body was beaten to death.
- Andrew, Peter's brother, hung on a cross for three days before dying.
- Bartholomew was beaten and skinned alive before being beheaded.
- Thomas was speared with a javelin.
- Peter was crucified –upside down.

Persecution of Christians in the Roman Empire

Nero, one of Rome's Emperors, hated the Christians. It was reported that he used the Christians as human torches to light his gardens. Other Christians were merely covered with skins and feed to the lions. Rome had a Coliseum where 50,000 people watched while Christians were thrown to wild beasts.[195]

The Thompson Chain Reference Bible states that Christians sought refuge in the secret underground tunnel in the sand pits, known as Catacombs. They took their shovels, picks and hoes and extended the tunnels to fashioned rooms, chapels and burying places. The Catacombs soon became their only safe retreat. They lived there, worshipped there, and were buried there.

Christian Persecution Today

Two thousand years ago Jesus Christ of Nazareth said there would be tremendous increase in religious persecution in the last days. Christ warned that the day would come when people would think they are doing a favor to their god to kill anyone who does not believe in their religion.

"The hour is coming when those who kill you will think they are doing a holy service to God. This is because they have never known the Father or Me. Yes, I'm telling you these things now, so that when they happen, you will re- member my warning" (John 16:2-4 NLT).

Who would have believed that this generation would see the day when another religion would believe they are favoring their god by killing unbelievers? Today we see the Muslim extremists are killing Jews and Christians for the sake of their god. It is considered a great honor to Allah to kill a non–believer (anyone who is not Muslim).

The year 2015 was the most violent year for Christians in modern history rising to "a level akin to ethnic cleansing," according to a new report by Open Doors USA, a watchdog group that advocates for Christians. The survey found that more than 7,100 Christians were killed in 2015 for "faith-related reasons," up

3,000 from the previous year, according to the group's analysis of media reports and other public information as well as external experts. Open Door's report is independently audited by the International Institute of Religious Freedom. It is an organization that works with Christians worldwide to "equip and encourage" those living under persecution while also helping churches in America advocate for the persecuted around the world.[196]

The group's report defines Christian persecution "as any hostility experienced as a result of one's identification with Christ." Open Doors found this persecution ranged from imprisonment, torture, beheadings and rape to the loss of home and assets, the loss of a job, or even rejection from a community. Much of the persecution faced by Christians occurs in predominantly Muslim nations.[197]

At this moment, for the sake of the Gospel of Jesus Christ, men and women are being bullwhipped into submission, tortured, imprisoned, beaten, battered, and broken. Homes are being burned, families are being executed, and other lives lost through hateful revenge. If you believe that torture and murder because of belief in Jesus Christ is a thing of the past, then you are tragically mistaken. Across our globe, the blood of Christians runs down cobblestone streets, dirt paths, paved alleys, and concrete prison floors.[198]

Bob Unruh reported in World Net Daily: "As the battle over persecution of Christian's worldwide rages – estimates are that 200 million Christians around the globe are subject at any time to punishments up to and including death simply for believing."[199]

The Bible League, a non-profit Christian service organization, has placed 160 million Bibles and New Testament in the hands of people in more than 80 countries around the world. They reported that 400 believers are being martyred daily around the world.

According to Voice of the Martyrs 2002 Special Issue Magazine, more Christians in China are in prison or under detention than in any other country in the world. The confiscation of church property and Bibles continues. The house church movement (illegally unregistered church), which comprises approximately 90 percent of China's Christians, endures unimaginable persecution, yet stands on its commitment to preach the gospel no matter the cost. Despite the Chinese government's persecution of the church, an estimated 1,200 Chinese come to Christ every hour. Bibles are still in great demand as well as other teaching material.

Corrie ten Boom's Comments

Corrie ten Boom said, "I have been in countries where the saints are already suffering terrible persecution. In China the Christians were told, 'Don't worry, before the tribulation comes, you will be translated—(raptured). Then the terrible persecution came. Millions of Christians were tortured to death.[200]

Later she heard a bishop from China say, sadly, "We have failed. We should have made the people strong for persecution rather than telling them Jesus would come first." Turning to me, he said, "You still have time. Tell the people how to be strong in times of persecution, how to stand when the tribulation comes--to stand and not faint." Corrie ten Boom felt that she had a divine mandate to go and tell the people of this world that it was possible to be strong in the Lord Jesus Christ. She said, "We are in training for the tribulation." She went to prison for the sake of Christ and came out victorious.[201]

In Billy Graham warned Christians to get ready to suffer until Armageddon in his book *Til Armageddon*. Armageddon happens at the end of the Great Tribulation.

Ruth Graham's Comments on the Rapture

The news from around the world of Christians suffering unbelievably is bound to make a "Pre-Tribber" do some serious thinking. Of course, I am sure they would say that the tribulation they have undergone is nothing to be compared with the "Great Tribulation" and they are right. However, I would rather prepare myself to go through the tribulation and be happily surprised by an unexpected rapture, than expect to be raptured only to find myself going through the tribulation. Perhaps, not a very scholarly way of approaching the problem, but true none the less.[202]

What we are now witnessing is unprecedented in the history of America and modern culture. In the 1970s Ruth Graham made the statement: "If God doesn't judge America, He'll have to apologize to Sodom and Gomorrah." Those words were spoken at a time when the Ten Commandments were still displayed in public schools and government buildings, when marriage was overwhelmingly upheld, when the idea that God and Jesus could be mocked on national television as the object of comedy, would be unimaginable, when the idea that there would come a time when half or more of American children would be born out of wedlock and the president of the United States would be endorsing homosexuality would be unimaginable. Yet if Ruth Graham would speak of God's judgment on the America of that day, how much more true is it now, and how much farther is this nation down the road to judgment?[203]

Timing of the Rapture of Great Importance

The Timing of the Rapture is not essential to salvation, nor should we argue regarding various theories. If you feel the Great Tribulation will not occur in your lifetime, it may not be of great concern to you. But if we are the generation that will most likely be alive when Christ returns to earth, then the question of whether or not Christians will go though the Tribulation should be vitally important to you.

"When you see all these signs, all taken together, coming to pass, you may know of a surety that He is near, at the very door. Truly I tell you, this generation (the whole multitude of people living at the same time, in a definite, given period) will not pass away till all these things taken together take place" (Matthew 24:33-34 AMP).

Ministers today need to prepare Christians in the Western World regarding the likelihood that we will have to endure at least some of the Tribulation. Believing that some difficult times are ahead is a strong motivation to seek God diligently. We need to search the scriptures and commit portions to memory. It is essential to learn to hear and obey God's voice.

Believers find Relief from Persecution

When do believers will find relief from persecution? The Apostle Paul said that believers will be given rest when Christ returns at the end of this age in glory in flaming fire to reward believers and punish the ungodly.

"It is a righteous thing with God to repay with tribulation those who trouble you, and to *give* you who are troubled rest with us when the Lord Jesus is revealed from heaven with His mighty angels in flaming fire taking vengeance on those who do not know God, and on those who do not obey the gospel of our Lord Jesus Christ. These shall be punished with everlasting destruction from the presence of the Lord and from the glory of His power, when He comes, in that Day, to be glorified in His saints and to be admired among all those who believe" (2 Thessalonians 1:6-10).

When do Saints Receive Their Rewards?

Pretribulationism teaches that believers will be invited to the Marriage Supper of the Lamb and receive their rewards before the Great Tribulation. God's Word tells us that believers receive their rewards when God begins to reign, not before the Great Tribulation.

Believers Receive Their Rewards at the Judgment Seat of Christ.

At the end of Paul's life, he expresses that he has fought a good fight and looks forward to receiving his reward at the Judgment Seat of Christ. He said "There is in store for me the crown of righteousness, which the Lord, the righteous Judge, will award to me on that day—and not only to me, but also to all who have longed for his appearing" (2 Timothy 4:7-8 NIV).

"The kingdoms of this world have become the kingdoms of our Lord and of His Christ, and He shall reign forever and ever!" The twenty-four elders who sat before God on their thrones fell on their faces and worshiped God, saying: 'We give You thanks, O Lord God Almighty, The One who is and who was and who is to come because You have taken Your great power and reigned. The nations were angry, and Your wrath has come, and the time of the dead, that they should be judged, and that You should *reward Your servants the prophets and the saints*, and those who fear Your name, small and great, and should destroy those who destroy the earth'" (Revelation 11:15-18).

"I charge you to keep this command without spot or blame until the appearing of our Lord Jesus Christ, which God will bring about in his own time—God, the blessed and only Ruler, the King of kings and Lord of lords, who alone is immortal and who lives in unapproachable light, whom no one has seen or can see. To him be honor and might forever" (1 Timothy 6:14-16 NIV).

The Second Coming of Christ is our Blessed Hope

The Blessed Hope of the church is the glorious Second Coming of Jesus Christ. "For the grace of God that brings salvation has appeared to all men, teaching us that, denying ungodliness and worldly lusts, we should live soberly, righteously, and godly in the present age, looking for the blessed hope and glorious appearing of our great God and Savior Jesus Christ" (Titus 2:11-13).

"I thank my God always concerning you for the grace of God which was given to you by Christ Jesus, that you were enriched in everything by Him in all utterance and all knowledge, even as the testimony of Christ was confirmed in you, so that you come short in no gift, eagerly waiting for the *revelation of our Lord Jesus Christ,* who will also confirm you to the end, that you may be blameless in the day of our Lord Jesus Christ" (1 Corinthians 1:4-8).

End Time Martyrs in the First Resurrection

"Then I saw thrones, and they sat on them, and judgment was given to them. I saw the souls of those who had been beheaded because of their testimony of Jesus and because of the word of God, and those who had not worshipped the beast or his image, and had not received the mark on their forehead and on the hand, and they came to life and reigned with Christ for a thousand years. The rest of the dead did not come to life until the thousand years were complete. *This is the first resurrection.* Blessed and holy is the one who has a part in the first resurrection; over these the second death has no power, but they will be priests of God and of Christ and will reign with Him for a thousand years" (Revelation 20:4-6 NASB). Believers who will rule with Christ are not restricted to those who come out of the Great Tribulation, but will include all believers who are faithful to Christ.

The End of This Age Occurs After the Resurrection.

God's Holy Word tells us clearly that the resurrection is followed by the end of this age, when Christ sets up His earthly Kingdom. God's Word cannot be any clearer. The Apostle Paul said; "For as in Adam all die, so also in Christ all will be made alive. But each in his own order: Christ the first fruits, after that those who are Christ's at His coming, then comes the end, when He hands over the kingdom to the God and Father, when He has abolished all rule and all authority and power" (1 Corinthians 15:22-24 NASB).

Be Ready for His Return

The fact of His coming is certain. We have this blessed hope that someday we will see our Lord. If you have not accepted Christ as your personal Savior, do so to-day! Someday every knee will bow and every tongue will confess that Jesus Christ is Lord. Won't you bow before him today and make Him your Lord and Savior?

Pray this prayer with me. "Lord Jesus, I bow my knee to you today. Forgive my sins. Cover me with your previous blood. Make me your very own. I acknowledge you today as my personal Lord and Savior. Thank You for coming into my life Make me the person you want me to be."

Living in a state of suspense and expecting the Lord to return shortly produces a purifying affect and promotes godly living. The scriptures are very clear concerning Christ's return. It tells us over and over, Be prepared; Be ready; Be patient; Don't be deceived; He's coming back soon!

❯ CHAPTER 17
THE ANTICHRIST AND FALSE PROPHET

Our world is approaching a crisis today. Both sacred and secular voices alike, agree that we are approaching an unprecedented time of trouble. World famine seems inescapable. Crime and violence is escalating at tremendous proportions. The increase in natural disasters and spread of violence all point to the soon appearance of some remarkable individual who can offer a solution to the world's problems.

Many prophecies are unfolding before our eyes today that in all possibilities, the Antichrist and False Prophet are alive today. They may already be in some position of power and we already know their name. They will soon come to power and their true nature will become evident. Daniel, the Old Testament prophet, said that the Antichrist would achieve power through flattery, intrigue and deceit.

This man will appear as a great leader, speaking great words or wisdom, and will draw all unbelievers to worship him. To them he will be the sum of wisdom, with the answers to all their problems.

He will be a warrior of world-wide renown, a statesman of unrivalled skill, a man of transcendent genius, before whom the exploits of Caesar, Charlemagne and Napoleon will appear trifling. Kings will be his toys and thrones his playthings. Toward the close of his reign he will throw off his mask, no longer assuming to be the real Christ, but standing forth in his own colors he will deny both God the Father and God the Son, will seek to exterminate the Jews and everything else which bears witness to the living God. He will set up his image in the rebuilt Temple at Jerusalem and compel all to worship it.[204]

Compare Christ and Antichrist

CHRIST	ANTICHRIST
Christ is the Son of God.	Antichrist is the Son of Perdition.
Christ is the Seed of the woman.	Antichrist is the Seed of the Serpent.
Christ is the Lamb of God.	Antichrist is the beast.
Christ is the Holy One.	Antichrist is the Wicked One.
Christ is the man of sorrows.	Antichrist is the Man of Sin.
Christ is the Prince of Peace.	Antichrist is the evil prince.
Christ came from heaven.	Antichrist will come from the abyss.
Christ was slain for the people.	Antichrist will slay the people.
Christ received power from God.	Antichrist's power will come from Satan.

Christ humbled Himself.	Antichrist will exalt himself.
Christ cleansed the temple.	Antichrist will defile the temple.
Christ honored the God of His fathers.	Antichrist will not acknowledge God.
Christ was received up into heaven.	Antichrist will go to the Lake of Fire.

The Antichrist Will Confirm a 7-Year Covenant with Israel

"This king will make a seven-year treaty with the people, but after half that time, he will break that pledge and stop the Jews from all their sacrifices and their offerings; then, as a climax to all his terrible deeds, the Enemy shall utterly defile the sanctuary of God. But in God's time and plan, his judgment will be poured out upon this Evil One" (Daniel 9:27 TLB).

A world dictator will arise who is given power by Satan (dragon) and claim to be God. A False Prophet will assist him and perform signs and wonders.

"People worshipped the dragon (Satan) because he had given authority to the beast (Antichrist), and they also worshipped the beast and asked, 'Who is like the beast? Who can wage war against it?' The beast was given a mouth to utter proud words and blasphemies and to exercise its authority for forty-two months. It opened its mouth to blaspheme God, and to slander his name and his dwelling place and those who live in heaven. It was given power to wage war against God's holy people and to conquer them. It was given authority over every tribe, people, language and nation. All inhabitants of the earth will worship the beast—all whose names have not been written in the Lamb's book of life, the Lamb who was slain from the creation of the world" (Revelation 13:4-8 NIV).

For an antichrist figure to come into the modern world there must be a breakdown of the world system as we know it now. There would have to be breakdowns in currency, in law and order, and in the power structures of national states. A financial panic could help pave the way for him. So could a nuclear war. Such disasters could leave people crying out for a man of peace, who will be Satan's counterfeit to Jesus Christ. This man will seem to be like Jesus, until such time as he is ready to show his true self. Then he will be incredibly cruel (Daniel 7:8). e HHe will be the most hideous example of dictatorial power that the world has ever known.[205]

At the beginning of the Antichrist's reign, he will enjoy great popularity. Perhaps his popularity and political power could stem from the fact that he appears to bring peace to a troubled Middle East. The main reason the Bible discusses the Antichrist is not to encourage idle speculation, but to warn believers not to be misled by his deceit.

This time of great distress will be greater when anything that the world has ever seen or will ever see again. Mark 13:20 said; "Unless the Lord had shortened those days, no flesh would have been saved; but for the sake of the elect, whom He chose, He shortened the days". If the saints and elect are in heaven, why will the Great Tribulation have to be shortened?

The Book of Revelation was written when Christians were being persecuted for their faith. Roman Emperors considered themselves to be gods and required worship. The Antichrist will consider himself to be God and demand worship.

The Antichrist is called by several names in the Bible. There are over fifty prophecies about him. It seems obvious that God wants people to recognize him.

Names of the Antichrist

Daniel 8:23	A King of Fierce Countenance
Daniel 9:26	A Prince that shall come
2 Thess. 2:3-4	The Man of Sin
2 Thess. 2:3	The Son of Perdition
1 John 2:18, 22. 1 John 4:3; 2 John 1:7	The Antichrist – Mentioned 4 x by name
Revelation 13:1-4	A Beast out of the Sea

The Antichrist Will Come to Power among Ten Kings

"I saw a beast rising out of the sea, with ten horns and seven heads, with ten diadems on its horns and blasphemous names on its heads. The beast that I saw was like a leopard; its feet were like a bear's, and its mouth was like a lion's mouth. And to it the dragon gave his power and his throne and great authority" (Revelation 13:1-2 ESV).

The Antichrist will come to power among ten nations (ten horns) who will give their power to him. He is called the "the little horn" because in the beginning of his rule, he is small in comparison to the other kings. Soon the ten kings will give their allegiance to him.

The Antichrist is described as a beast over 20 times in the book of Revelation. This reveals his terrible nature and character. This is in great contract to our blessed Lord who is called the "Lamb" many times in that some book. The Lamb describes the gentleness of Christ in contract to the vicious, cruel nature of the Antichrist.

The beast comes up out of the sea, symbolic of the nations. He is described as having seven heads (representing wisdom) and ten horns (representing power). The dragon (Satan) gives him power. The Antichrist will briefly rule over all the nations of the world. This is the last world empire to rule over the world prior to the Second Coming of Jesus Christ, the Messiah.

The Antichrist is the Son of Perdition

"Let no one deceive you by any means; for *that Day will not come* unless the falling away comes first, and the man of sin is revealed, the son of perdition, who opposes and exalts himself above all that is called God or that is worshiped, so that he sits as God in the temple of God, showing himself that he is God: (2 Thessalonians 2:3-4).

This scripture identifies the awful nature of the Antichrist. He is the man of sin, a very wicked and vile person. He is Satan's masterpiece, who will go to any length to carry out Satan's plans. He has all the evil, cunning and power of the Devil incorporated in one man. Perdition means "the loss of the soul", "eternal damnation". He is doomed to spend eternity in hell fire.

The Antichrist Will Display Counterfeit Miracles

The coming of the lawless one is according to the working of Satan, with all power, signs and lying wonders, and with all unrighteous deception among those who perish, because they do not receive the love of the truth, that they might be saved.

Just as God gives gifts of the Spirit to His followers, Satan will empower the Antichrist with deceptive signs and wonders. The counterfeit miracles seem miraculous to the world. People who are not grounded in God's Word will be deceived by the Antichrist's lying wonders.

The main reason the Bible discusses the Antichrist is to warn people not to be misled by his deceit. When the Antichrist appears it will be very difficult for the faithful. He will wage war against anything that is holy causing much wickedness and suffering, but his doom is sure.

The Antichrist is an Intellectual Genius.

"Then I (Daniel) desired to know the truth concerning the fourth beast, which was different from all the rest, exceedingly terrifying, with its teeth of iron and claws of bronze, and which devoured and broke in pieces, and stamped what was left with its feet; and concerning the ten horns that were on its head, and concerning the other horn, which came up and to make room for which three of them fell out—the horn that had eyes and a mouth that spoke arrogantly, and that seemed greater than the others. As I looked, this horn made war with the holy ones and was prevailing over them" (Daniel 7:19-21 NRSV).

The Antichrist will have a superior intelligence. He was described as "A horn that has eyes." The horn represents strength while the eyes speak of intelligence. He will have a brilliant mind and worldly wisdom that will baffle even the educated.

In Daniel 7:20 we are told that he has "a mouth that spoke very great things". He will have a perfect command and flow of language. His oratory will not only gain attention, but command respect. Revelation 13:2 declares that his mouth is "as the mouth of a lion" which is a symbolic expression telling of the majesty and awe producing effects of his voice. The voice of the lion excels that of any other beast. So the Antichrist will out rival orators ancient and modern.[206]

The Antichrist's number is 666.

"He (Antichrist) required everyone—small and great, rich and poor, free and slave to be given a mark on the right hand or on the forehead. And no one could buy or sell anything without that mark, which was either the name of the beast or the number representing his name. Wisdom is needed here. Let the one with understanding solve the meaning of the number of the beast, for it is the number of a man. His number is 666" (Revelation 13:16-18 NLT).

Six in biblical numerology is the number of man—just short of perfection, whereas seven is the number of perfection. Revelation tells us that the number 666, or the mark of the Antichrist, is going to be stamped upon the hand and forehead of every person in the world during the reign of the Antichrist.[207] If anyone takes the Mark of the Beast, he will share the fate of the Antichrist and be tormented with fire and brimstone forever and ever (Revelation 14:11).

In the Hebrew language, superlatives are expressed by repeating the word or phrase, the ultimate being its repetition three times. Thus, when Isaiah saw the Lord lifted up and exalted in the Temple, he heard Seraphim singing, "Holy, holy, holy is the Lord of hosts" (Isaiah 6:1-3). The number 666 therefore represents the number of Man carried to its zenith.[208]

The number 666 is used because of its symbolism in Jewish thinking. The Bible tells us that in the year in which King Solomon received 666 talents of gold, he turned his back on God and became obsessed with women, horses, and money (1 Kings 10:14 and 2 Chronicles 9:13). Thus, in Jewish history, the number 666 came to stand for apostasy.[209]

This number is related to the fact that in both Hebrew and Greek, the letters of the alphabet also stand for numbers. This makes it possible to add up a numerical value for every name. The Antichrist's name will add up to 666 in either Greek or Hebrew (or perhaps both) and will thus be an expression of the ultimate apostasy — presenting one's self as a substitute for the real Messiah.[210]

Through the years, Bible scholars have tried to numerically identify the antichrist, checking the names of contemporary world figures to see if any of their names contain a numeric value of 666. (Using this kind of formula, one group has proven that the words "purple dinosaur" contain a numeric value of 666, thus concluding that the antichrist is none other than Barney!) Others have tried to discern the identity of this man by evaluating the characteristics of infamous individuals who seem to possess traits similar to those of the antichrist.[211] Perhaps we shouldn't waste time trying to identify him before his appearance.

Fate of those Who Take the Mark of the Beast

Locusts with faces and hair like people will torment people who have the mark of the beast. These hideous creatures are demonic in nature. They come from the abyss or the bottomless pit to torment all who have the mark of the beast. Foul and loathsome sores will come upon those who worship the beast and receive his mark. An even worse fate awaits those who accept the mark of the beast. They will spend eternity in the lake of fire (Revelation 16:1-4).

Miniature Computer Chips Available

Recently scientists have developed a miniature computer chip so powerful that it will hold up to five gigabytes of information in a chip the size of a dime. This tiny chip will hold as much information as contained in thirty complete sets of the Encyclopedia Britannica. This chip could also be configured in a shape the size of two grains of rice that could be injected beneath the skin. How could the apostle John have known that the future would hold such incredible technology unless God inspired him to write the words recorded in Revelation?

This generation is the first generation with the technology available to fulfill the prophecy of a "cashless" society. Technology for a computer chip to be placed under the skin is now available and patented at the U.S. Patent Office.

The Antichrist Blasphemies God and Demands Worship

"He was given a mouth speaking great things and blasphemies. He was given authority to continue for forty-two months. He opened his mouth in blasphemy against God, to blaspheme His name, His tabernacle, and those who dwell in heaven" (Revelation 13:5-6).

The Antichrist will show contempt, and blaspheme the name of God. He hates everything God stands for. He will pollute the Jewish Temple and demand worship. "Let no one deceive you by any means; for that Day will not come unless the falling away comes first, and the man of sin is revealed, the son of perdition, who opposes and exalts himself above all that is called God or that is worshiped, so that he sits as God in the temple of God, showing himself that he is God" (2 Thessalonians 2:3-4).

The Antichrist will claim to be God, set up his own image in the Jewish temple and demand worship. When the Jews refuse to worship him, the Antichrist will turn against the Jewish people in vengeance.

The Antichrist Will Persecute the Saints

"Then he (Antichrist) opened his mouth in blasphemy against God, to blaspheme His name, His tabernacle, and those who dwell in heaven. It was granted to him to make war with the saints and to over them. And authority was given him over every tribe, tongue and nation. All who dwell on the earth will worship him, whose names have not been written in the Book of Life of the Lamb slain from the foundation of the world" (Revelation 13:6-8).

The Antichrist will be a vile, evil person who sets himself up against Christ and God's people (the saints) during the last days just before the Second Coming of Christ.

The Antichrist attacks the Jewish people, but when God provides a place of sanctuary for them in the wilderness, he makes war against the remnant of her seed, which keep the commandments of God, and have the testimony of Jesus Christ. The Antichrist offers temporal salvation to those who receive the mark of the beast. Christ offers eternal salvation to those who do not accept the mark of the beast.

Thank God that the reign of the Antichrist is a short one. He will be allowed to persecute the godly for a "time" (one year) and "times" (two years) and "half a time" (six months) equaling (3 ½ years). He will speak great words against the most High and viscously attack the saints of God.

Unholy Trinity

There will be two major players in the tribulation aiding Satan (dragon). They are the Antichrist and the False Prophet. These three, Satan, the Antichrist and the False Prophet form an unholy trinity.

The False Prophet

The False Prophet has two horns like a lamb, posing like a true prophet. His main goal is to cause people to worship the Antichrist and receive his mark. The Devil, the Antichrist, and the false prophet form an unholy Trinity, counterfeiting Father, Son, and Holy Spirit. He will be able to perform great miracles, even causing fire to come down from heaven (Revelation 13:13). God called down fire upon Sodom and Gomorrah. Elijah called down fire on Mount Carmel. This mighty display of power, is Satanic in origin, and will deceive many.

The False Prophet will set up an image of the first beast (Antichrist) in the holy place in the rebuilt Jewish temple and demand that the world worship him.

The image will have power to kill those who refuse to worship him. This image is mentioned seven times in Revelation. Many scholars believe that the setting up of this abomination or image in the Jewish temple will signal the beginning of the Great Tribulation.

The 13ᵗʰ Chapter of Revelation Tells How the False Prophet Will Aid the Antichrist.

- He poses as a true prophet (v 11).
- He causes all to worship the Antichrist (v 12).
- He performs miracles & calls fire down from heaven (v 13).
- He deceives people into following the Antichrist (v 14).
- He makes an image of the Antichrist for people to worship (v 14).
- He puts to death those who do not worship the Antichrist (v 15).
- He causes people to take the Mark of the Beast (v 16).

The scriptures repeatedly warn against Israel accepting the false messiah who presents himself to the Jews as the legitimate messiah in the last days. It is illogical and virtually impossible that any gentile could possible present himself to the Jewish people of Israel as a credible candidate.[212]

Jesus declared that He, as the Jewish Messiah and Son of David, presented Himself to Israel, but was rejected. Yet in the last days "another" of the same background would be accepted as the promised Messiah. Another reason the Antichrist may be Jewish related to the very name that the scriptures assign to him. The name "Antichrist" indicates that this individual will be opposed to Jesus Christ, but will impersonate Jesus Christ by posing as a messianic figure.[213]

Nationality of the Antichrist

What is the nationality of the Antichrist? Some scholars have thought the Antichrist will be a Gentile since the beast comes out of the sea. The sea is thought to refer to the Gentile nations. The Hebrew people distrusted a large body of water. The sea was a perilous and forbidding place to them. The sea became a symbol of the nations of the world and the troubled lives of the unrighteous.

Daniel 9:26 tells us that the Antichrist will come from the people that destroyed Jerusalem and the Jewish Temple. The Romans were responsible for destroying Jerusalem and the Temple in A.D. 70. In the Holy Roman Empire, the spiritual leader was always the Pope. The Antichrist could come out of the Roman Empire with a prior Jewish heritage. No one knows for sure.

The Roman Empire as a whole spanned hundreds of years, and territorial boundaries shifted during that time. Not all countries that are listed were held by

Rome during the entirety of the empire, but all were occupied for at least some amount of time. Over time Rome occupied nearly all of Europe, the Middle East and the northern coast of Africa.[214]

Because of this, many people believe that the Antichrist will come from a revitalized Roman Empire and restore it to world power. Today the Roman Empire lives on in the nations of Europe. Like Humpty-Dumpty, it feel apart, but never died. It is slowly coming on the world scene as a powerful collision.

This sinister demon-inspired leader will dominate the world in the end time. He will persecute the saints, seek to destroy the Jews and banish all that is holy. He intends to wreck God's plan for the restoration of Israel and the Messianic Kingdom of peace on earth.

Safe Countries from the Antichrist

"He shall enter also into the glorious land, and many countries shall be overthrown: but these shall escape out of his hand, even Edom, and Moab, and the chief of the children of Ammon" (Daniel 11:41).

During the last part of the Great Tribulation, many Jews will find refuge in desolate mountains and wilderness places. Some of them could seek refuge in Jordan, the former lands of the Amorites, Edomites and Moabites. Perhaps God-fearing Gentiles will help the persecuted Jews find safety as Corrie ten Boom did during the Holocaust.

Final Outcome of the Antichrist and False Prophet

"The devil who deceived them was thrown into the lake of fire and brimstone, where the beast and the false prophet are also; and they will be tormented day and night forever and ever" (Revelation 20:10 NASB).

God is still in control! This awesome truth is revealed in every chapter John writes. If it penetrates every area of your life, it can make a difference in your life. You can trust your future to God and trust Him, because He loves you. He is ultimately in control of the universe.

› CHAPTER 18
FOUR HORSEMEN OF THE APOCALYPSE

The four horsemen is a prophetic description of what will occur in the Last Days prior to the return of Jesus Christ. Horses are often associated with biblical prophecy. The four horsemen represent the first four seals in the sixth chapter of Revelation. The first is white, the second is red, the third is black and the fourth is pale. They tell the story of God's intervention in human affairs.

Billy Graham in his book, *Approaching Hoofbeats: The Four Horsemen of the Apocalypse* interpret the first horse to be false religion or false christs. Revelation tells us that the second horse is war. The third is famine and the fourth is death. Christ described these same conditions in the same order in Matthew 24.

Jesus answered and said to them: "Take heed that no one deceives you. For many will come in My name, saying, 'I am the Christ, (*white horse)* and will deceive many. You will hear of wars and rumors of wars (*red horse*). See that you are not troubled; for all these things must come to pass, but the end is not yet. For nation will rise against nation, and kingdom against kingdom. And there will be famines, (*black horse*) pestilences, (*pale horse*) and earthquakes in various places. All these are the beginning of sorrows" (Matthew 24:4-8). *Emphasis added.*

Each horseman brings judgment on the earth with increased severity as the Second Coming of Christ approaches. The Four Horsemen ride not only to warn us, but also to awaken us. They come to show us the proper path. They tell us about events that will transpire in the last days. They let us know that God is in control.

In the book of Revelation, we see not the will of God to judge humanity, but the will of God to deal consummately and conclusively with the affairs of this planet, to bring things to a head and a finish. They cannot be brought to a head and a finish without the visitation of appropriate judgment upon those who resist and have no responsiveness or will to hear the heart of the Creator or feel His desire to reach to them in love, inviting them into a relationship with Him, which will bring redemption.[215]

White Horse – Antichrist

"Then I saw the Lamb open one of the seven seals, and I heard one of the four living creatures call out, as with a voice of thunder, 'Come!' I looked, and there was a white horse! Its rider had a bow; a crown was given to him, and he came out conquering and to conquer'" (Revelation 6:1-2 RSV).

The Antichrist enters the world astride a white stallion. He does not appear as a villain. He chooses a white horse, symbolic of a conqueror, but does not reveal his identify. He brings temporary, counterfeit peace, but goes out to conquer. He carries a bow without arrows. A crown is given to him. He goes out to conquer. The Antichrist will appear to solve the world's problems and be received as the Great Liberator.

The platform of the Antichrist is world unity and peace. Many Jews will accept him as their Messiah. He comes to power with a promise of peace, but in reality his promises are lies. The world will believe they are entering a time of peace but actually; they are entering the Great Tribulation.

The rider on the white horse is the counterfeit Christ, or the Antichrist, who will gain control of ten kingdoms. He will conquer without war. Revelation 13:4 says, "Who is like the beast? Who can make war against him"? No one will be able to fight him.

Jesus Christ Rides on a White Horse

"Now I saw heaven opened, and behold, a white horse. He who sat on him was called Faithful and True, and in righteousness He judges and makes war. His eyes were like a flame of fire, and on His head were many crowns. He had a name written that no one knew except Himself. He was clothed with a robe dipped in blood, and His name is called The Word of God. He has on His robe and on His thigh a name written; King of kings and Lord of lords" (Revelation 19:11-16).

The apostle John told of a second rider on a white horse. This rider comes to judge and make war. His eyes are a flame of fire and on His head are many crowns. His robe is dipped in blood and His name is The Word of God. This rider is Christ, the King of kings and Lord of lords.

The crown that the Antichrist wears in Revelation 6:2 is *stephanos*, which means "the victor's crown". The crown that Jesus Christ wears is *diadema*, the "kingly crown" (Revelation 19:12). The Antichrist will never wear the *diadema*, because it belongs only to the Son of God.[216]

Red Horse –War

"When he opened the second seal, I heard the second living creature say, 'Come!' And out came another horse, bright red; its rider was permitted to take peace from the earth, so that men should slay one another; and he was given a great sword" (Revelation 6:3-4 RSV).

The second rider comes on a fiery red horse. Red depicts the color of fire and blood. This rider takes peace from the world. There will be assassinations, rebellions, revolts and massacres. Many people will be killed. Wars spring up all over the world.

Some underdeveloped countries spend as much on armament as they do to feed their people. The rider of the red horse, who brings war, paves the way for the rider on the black horse who brings famine, disease and starvation.

Black Horse - Famine

"When He opened the third seal, I heard the third living creature say, 'Come and see.' So I looked, and behold, a black horse, and he who sat on it had a pair of scales in his hand. And I heard a voice in the midst of the four living creatures saying, A quart of wheat for a denarius, and three quarts of barley for a denarius; and do not harm the oil and the wine" (Revelation 6:5-6).

A voice calls out to the third horseman, who rides the black horse and carries the scale of judgment. This seems to indicate that food will be difficult to obtain and very costly. In times of scarcity, every kernel of grain counts. This means the weight of food is critically important.

The silver denarius was the basic unit of Roman money, equivalent to a day's wages. The third horseman said a day's wages for a loaf of bread. How will the worker's family be fed?

This scripture also said; "Do not touch the oil and the wine." Oil and wine have been associated with wealth. This shows a picture of famine coexisting with luxury. While some of the world suffers in hungry, others will be living in luxury as presented by the oil and wine

There have been famines since the beginning of time, but today the population of the earth is growing at astronomical rate. The problem of hungry has greatly increased. Only a few countries, the United States, Canada and Australia produce more food than they consume.

In 2009, the sky rocking cost of food was a wake-up call for the planet. Between 2005 and the summer of 2008, the price of wheat and corn tripled and the price of rice climbed five-fold, spurring food riots in nearly two dozen countries and pushing 75 million more people into poverty.[217]

For most of the past decade, the world has been consuming more food that it has been producing. With our surging population, food prices may escalate many times their normal level. Many of the poor are spending over fifty percent of their income on food.

David Wilkerson sent an urgent message to everyone on his mailing list in 2009. He instructed believer to get a thirty-day supply of non-perishable food, toiletries and other essentials. In major cities, grocery stores are emptied in an hour at the sign of an impending disaster. Others are calling for several months supply of food and water to prepare for an emergency.

Grocery stores are often emptied at the sign of an impending disaster. The stores in Houston, Texas were emptied when the streets were flooded in 2015.

Green Horse – Death

"When the Lamb broke the fourth seal, I heard the fourth living being say, 'Come!' I looked up and saw a horse whose color was *pale green* like a corpse. Death was the name of its rider, who was followed around by the grave. They were given authority over one-fourth of the earth, to kill with the sword and famine and disease and wild animals" (Revelation 6: 7-8 NLT).

The rider on the fourth horse was named death. He kills with the sword, famine, pestilence and wild beasts. Pestilence means any fatal infectious disease such as the aids virus. Permission is given to kill one fourth of the population of the earth with the sword, hunger, and wild beasts.

Violent Deaths in the 20th Century

The 20th Century was the bloodiest century in the history of mankind. Before the 20th Century, a war had never claimed 1 million lives. Then came World War I with its 8 million deaths. Twenty short years later, World War II resulted in 52 million fatalities. These two wars along qualify the 20th Century to be labeled the "century of death".[218]

The Economist magazine, September 11, 1999, reported that the governments of the Soviet Union, China, Germany and Japan combined have killed, during this century, 170 million in political purges. When we add to that the 8 million killed in World War I and the 52 million in World War II, the level of inflicted deaths becomes absolutely staggering![219]

The total population of the earth at the beginning the 20th century was only 1.6 billion people. During the last quarter century, approximately 1.14 one billion babies were killed by abortion. Add to that the 8 million killed in World War I and 50 million killed in World War II, plus 170 million died by political purges; it is absolutely staggering the large number of deaths by violence. There were 1,144,000,000 needless fatalities in the 20th century.

Violent Death in the 20th Century

- World Population in 1900 – 1.6 billion
- Causalities in WWI – 8 billion
- Causalities in WWII – 52 billion
- Political Purges – 170 billion people
- Deaths by Abortion – 1.14 million babies

Are we living in the era of the green horse? Is the era of the green horse over? You can answer these questions for yourself. Many times we are unaware of prophecies being fulfilled before our eyes. Pray for spiritual discernment to discern the signs of the time.

Vision of the Four Chariots

Zechariah, the Old Testament prophet, had a vision of the Four Chariots with the same four horses. These chariots are described as four spirits that go out before the Lord of all the earth.

"I looked up again, and there before me were four chariots coming out from between two mountains—mountains of bronze. The first chariot had red horses, the second black, the third white, and the fourth dappled—all of them powerful. I asked the angel who was speaking to me, "What are these, my lord?" The angel answered me, "These are the four spirits of heaven, going out from standing in the presence of the Lord of the whole world. The one with the black horses is going toward the north country, the one with the white horses toward the west, and the one with the dappled horses toward the south." When the powerful horses went out, they were straining to go throughout the earth. And he said, "Go throughout the earth!" So they went throughout the earth. Then he called to me, "Look, those going toward the north country have given my Spirit rest in the land of the north" (Zechariah 6:1-8 NIV).

Is the Green Horse Islam?

The Greek word for green is choros, where we get the English word chlorophyll. The pale green horse appears to be the color of a human corpse.

The color green has a special place in Islam. Flags in Islamic countries are predominantly green. Muslim stores have green trim. Green is often used to decorate mosques. The binding of the Quran is green. Many of the flags of Islamic countries are predominantly green. The Temple Mount is trimmed with green. The fear of green, Islam's color, has replaced the fear of red, communism's color.

This horseman was given permission to kill one fourth of the population of the earth with the sword, hunger, and wild beasts. The rider on the fourth horse was named death and Hell follows. He kills with the sword, famine, pestilence and wild beasts. Pestilence means any fatal infectious disease such as the Ebola virus or the Aids virus.

This rider is given power to kill one-fourth of the population of the earth with the sword, famine, pestilence and wild animals of the earth. In December, 2015, the population of the world was 7.4 billion people. This horse will kill 1.8 billion people. That is more people than live in North America, Central American and South American combined.

Conquering tyrants who bring the world war, famine and pestilence are certainly nothing new. Suffering people from the days of the Roman Empire to the most recent war can easily recognize anticipations of these four dreaded horsemen. The book of Revelation has been a source of encouragement to suffering believers throughout history. As they see the Lamb opening the seals, they realize that God is in control and that His purposes will be accomplished. [220]

Islam's Modern Day Terrorism

The Apostle John said believers in Jesus would suffer much persecution in the last day, even by being beheaded. Christians are not just facing persecution today, they are facing genocide. ISIS forced Christians in Iraq to convert to Islam, pay an enormous fee or die by the sword.

ISIS has emerged as not just the most ruthless of the Sunni jihadist organization in Iraq and Syria; it is also the most successful. ISIS is so extreme that other well-known, radical Islamist and jihadist groups have not only distanced themselves from ISIS, they have also publicly condemned ISIS's actions and even fought ISIS fighters directly.[221]

ISIS is brutal beyond imagination to anyone—Christians, Jews, and even Shiite Muslims—who are not aligned with its jihadist form of Sunni Islam. In Syria, ISIS has slaughtered Shiites and Christians. In Iraq, it has done the same, giving Christians in conquered territories a chilling ultimatum; "Convert, leave your homes or die."[222] Hundreds of thousands of believers have fled the Middle East recently.

Islam fulfills the prophecy of the pale green horse that will dominate the world in the last days. Are we living in the era of the pale green Horse? Is the era of the pale green horse over? You can answer these questions for yourself. Many times we are unaware of prophecies being fulfilled before our eyes. Pray for spiritual discernment to discern the signs of the time.

ISIS Claims Victory after Terrorist Attacks

ISIS celebrated killing 224 civilians in a Russian Plane Crash on October 30, 2015. On November 15, 2015, ISIS terrorist attacks left 129 people dead and more than 350 injured in Paris. ISIS promised additional attacks against Paris.

On November 16, 2015 ISIS suffered a major defeat, just hours after the terrorist attack in Paris, with reports that coalition forces destroyed the militant group's headquarters in Iraq in an attack that left 250 militants dead.[223]

Martyrs Beheaded in the Last Days

"I saw thrones on which were seated those who had been given authority to judge. I saw the souls of those who had been beheaded because of their testimony for Jesus and because of the word of God. They had not worshiped the beast or his image and had not received his mark on their foreheads or their hands. They came to life and reigned with Christ a thousand years" (Revelation 20:4).

This scripture described the end-time martyrs who will be beheaded for their witness for Jesus Christ in the Last Days.

The Cry of the Martyrs

The martyrs cried out, "O Sovereign Lord, holy and true, how long before you judge the people who belong to this world and avenge our blood for what they have done to us?" Then a white robe was given to each of them. They were told to rest a little longer until the full number of their brothers and sisters—their fellow servants of Jesus who were to be martyred—had joined them." (Revelation 6:10-11 NLT).

The Greek word *martus*, which gives us our English word *martyr,* simply means witness. The souls of the martyrs "under the altar" indicate that their lives were given sacrificially to the glory of God. These saints were slain by the enemy because of their witness to the truth of God and the message of Jesus.[224]

The 2001 World Christian Encyclopedia edition estimates that since the beginning of time, there have been 70 million Christian martyrs, but over 45.5 million were martyred in the 20th century. Can you imagine what it would be like to be put in jail or beaten for reading your Bible or attending a worship service? Remember these persecuted believers in your prayers and support groups, like Voice of the Martyrs who help persecuted believers.

Victory for Martyrs

Martyred believers will give glory to God when they sing the last song recorded in God's Word. "Great and marvelous *are* your works, O Lord God, the Almighty. Just and true *are* your ways, O King of the nations. Who will not fear you, Lord, and glorify thy name? For you alone *are* holy. All nations will come and worship before you; for your righteous deeds have been revealed" (Revelation 15:3-4 NLT).

The kingdom of this world will become the Kingdom of our God and His Messiah! He will rule forever and ever! Even so, come Lord Jesus!

› CHAPTER 19
FINAL SEVEN YEARS UNTIL ARMAGEDDON

The final seven year of this age will begin when the Jewish people sign a seven year covenant of peace with the Antichrist. In the middle of the seven years, the Antichrist violates the covenant, pollutes the rebuilt Jewish Temple and stops the daily sacrifices.

Abomination of Desolation

"He (Antichrist) shall enter into a strong *and* firm covenant with the many for one week [seven years]. And in the midst of the week he shall cause the sacrifice and offering to cease [for the remaining three and one-half years]; and upon the wing *or* pinnacle of abominations [shall come] one who makes desolate, until the full determined end is poured out on the desolator" (Daniel 9:27 AMP).

The Great Tribulation

The Great Tribulation will begin when the Antichrist stops the daily sacrifices and pollutes the Jewish Temple. "When you see the abomination of desolation spoken of by the prophet Daniel, standing in the holy place...Then there will be great tribulation, such as has not been from the beginning of the world until now, no, and never will be. If those days had not been cut short, no human being would be saved. But for the sake of the elect those days will be cut short" Matthew 24:15, 21-22 ESV).

The Great Tribulation is an intense period of suffering and distress in the last days. The Bible teaches that it will be a future, worldwide time of persecution like none other. It will be a time of disasters occurring throughout the world. Jeremiah called it "Jacob's Troubles" while Daniel called it a "Time of Trouble". The Great Tribulation is the wrath of the Antichrist. The wrath of God will not be poured out until the Messiah return to execute judgment on the ungodly.

Length of the Great Tribulation

Daniel said "He (Antichrist) shall speak pompous words against the Most High, shall persecute the saints of the Most High, and intend to change times and law. Then the saints shall be given into his hands for a time and times and half a time" (Daniel 7:25). Time is one, times are two and half a time is one-half. The Antichrist will rule for three and one-half years.

The Revelation of John gives us additional information regarding the length of the Great Tribulation. The Holy City will be trampled down by Gentiles for

42 months– 3 ½ years (Rev. 11:2). The Antichrist (beast) will exercise authority for 42 months - 3 ½ years (Rev. 13:4-5). The two witnesses will prophecy for 1,260 days - 3 ½ years (Rev. 11:3). The woman (Israel) fled into the wilderness for 1,260 days - 3 ½ years (Rev. 12:6).

The Antichrist

A great world leader will appear in the last days. He will be empowered by the dragon (Satan). He will appear on the world scene in a very inconspicuous way. Flattery and intrigue are his tactics to achieve power. God will allow the Antichrist to operate for forty-two months, which is three and one-half years.

"The beast (Antichrist) was given a mouth to utter proud words and blasphemies and to exercise its authority for forty-two months. It opened its mouth to blaspheme God, and to slander his name and his dwelling place and those who live in heaven. It was given power to wage war against God's holy people and to conquer them. And it was given authority over every tribe, people, language and nation. All inhabitants of the earth will worship the beast—all whose names have not been written in the Lamb's book of life, the Lamb who was slain from the creation of the world" (Revelation 13:5-8 NIV).

He will be very charismatic, messianic-type man who will dazzle the world with his miracles. He believes he is God incarnate and demands that the world worship him. He briefly rules over all the nations of the world and attempts to destroy the Jews and all true believers. The Bible warns believers not to be misled by the Antichrist's tactics.

Contrast Christ and Antichrist

Jesus Christ	Antichrist
Came from Heaven (Mark 1:11)	Came from the Bottomless Pit (Rev. 11:7)
Son of God (Mark 1:1)	Son of Perdition (2 Thess. 2-3)
Seed of the Woman (Genesis 3:15)	Seed of Satan (Genesis 3:15)
Glorified God (John 17:4)	Blasphemes God (Rev. 13:6)
Came to do His Father's will (John 5:30)	Came to do his own will (Daniel 11:36
Cleanses the Jewish Temple (John 2:15)	Desecrates the Temple (Daniel 11:31).
Called the Lamb (Isaiah 53:7)	Called the Beast (Rev. 13:1)
Called the "Holy One (Mark 1:24)	Called the Lawless One (2 Thess. 2:8)
Prince of Peace (Isaiah 9:6)	Wicked Prince of Israel (Ezek. 21:25)
Good Shepherd (John 10:11)	Idol Shepherd (Zech. 11:17)
Humbles Himself (Phil. 2:8)	Exalts himself (2 Thess. 2:3-4)
Worked Miracles (Acts 2:22)	Works Miracles (2 Thess. 2:9
Rides on a white horse (Rev. 19:11)	Rides on a white horse Rev. 6:2)

The False Prophet

The Antichrist will be assisted by a False Prophet who will do miraculous signs in the name of the Antichrist. The False Prophet will be able to perform great miracles, even causing fire to come down from heaven (Revelation 13:13). This mighty display of power is satanic in origin, and will deceive many.

The False Prophet will imitate Christ. He will come in with two horns like a lamb, but will speak like a dragon. His primary objective will be to cause people to worship the Antichrist.

The Mark of the Beast

"He causes all, both small and great, rich and poor, free and slave, to receive a mark on their right hand or their foreheads, and that no one may buy or sell except one who has the mark or the name of the beast, or the number of his name. Here is wisdom. Let him who has under-standing calculate the number of the beast, for it is the number of a man. His number is 666" (Revelation 13:16-18).

God's Word tells us that the Antichrist will cause all people, small and great, rich or poor, free or bond, to receive a mark in their foreheads or their right hand. No one will be able to buy or sell without the mark of the beast. The Antichrist offers temporal salvation to those who receive the mark of the beast. Christ offers eternal salvation to those who do not accept the mark of the beast.

"If anyone worships the beast and its image and receives its mark on their forehead or on their hand, they, too, will drink the wine of God's fury, which has been poured full strength into the cup of the wrath. They will be tormented with burning sulfur in the presence of the holy angels and of the Lamb" (Revelation 14:10 NIV).

Fate of Those Who Take the Mark of the Beast

Locusts with faces and hair like people will torment people who have the mark of the beast. These hideous creatures are demonic in nature. They come from the abyss or the bottomless pit to torment all who have the mark of the beast. Foul and loathsome sores will come upon those who worship the beast and receive his mark. An even worse fate awaits those who accept the mark of the beast. They will spend eternity in the lake of fire.

The Two Witnesses

"I will give power to my two witnesses, and they will be clothed in burlap and will prophesy during those 1,260 days. These two prophets are the two olive trees and the two lamp stands that stand before the Lord of all the earth. If anyone tries to harm them, fire flashes from their mouths, and consumes their enemies. This is how anyone who tries to harm them must die" (Revelation 11:3-5 NLT).

Two great witnesses will make their appearance during the Great Tribulation. The witnesses are clothed in sackcloth like John the Baptist. They call fire down from heaven like Elijah. They perform miracles and show wonders similar to those done in Egypt by Moses. They turn the rivers and oceans into blood and send plagues on the Antichrist Kingdom. They are able to withhold rain from the earth. If anyone tries to harm them, they call down fire from heaven and consume them. They are given great power to witness for 1,260 days.

They perform miracles and show wonders similar to those done in Egypt by Moses. They turn the rivers and oceans into blood and send plagues on the Antichrist Kingdom. They are able to withhold rain from the earth. If anyone tries to harm them, they call down fire from heaven and consume them.

Two Witnesses will be Killed

"When they finish their testimony, the beast that comes up out of the bottomless pit will declare war against them, and he will conquer them and kill them. Their bodies will lie in the main street of Jerusalem, the city where the Lord was crucified. For three and a half day, all peoples, tribes, languages, and nations will stare at their bodies. No one will be allowed to bury them. All the people who belong to this world will gloat over them and give presents to each other to celebrate the death of the two prophets who had tormented them" (Revelation 11:7-10 NLT).

Their bodies are left to decay in the street of Jerusalem for three-and one half days. People all over the world can view their dead bodies, (possibly through television). During this time the ungodly rejoice by giving presents to each other to celebrate the death of the two prophets.

Two Witnesses Will be Resurrected

"After the three and a half days, the breath of life from God came into them, and they stood on their feet; and great fear fell upon those who were watching them. [12] And they heard a loud voice from heaven saying to them, "Come up here." Then they went up into heaven in the cloud, and their enemies watched them" (Revelation 11:11-13 NASB).

144,000 Sealed by God

"I saw another angel coming up from the east, having the seal of the living God. He called out in a loud voice to the four angels who had been given power to harm the land and the sea. Do not harm the land or the sea or the trees until we put a seal on the foreheads of the servants of our God. Then I heard the number of those who were sealed: 144,000 from all the tribes of Israel" (Revelation 7:2-4 NIV).

144,000 were sealed by God in order to be protected during the Great Tribulation. It seems obvious that they are Jewish believers in Christ. The name of Christ and the name of the Father are written on their foreheads. They are composed of 12,000 men from each of the twelve tribes of Israel. During the Great Tribulation these Jews will preach the Gospel to the nations.

Mountain of Megiddo

Armageddon is the Hebrew word meaning "the Mountain of Megiddo." Megiddo is a city in Israel that overlooked the Valley of Jezreel. It lies east of Mount Carmel in the northern part of Israel on the main road that linked Egypt and Syria. From this vantage point you can see a great extended plain stretching from the Mediterranean Sea eastward across the northern part of Israel. It is approximately seven miles wide, fifteen miles long and fifty miles north of Jerusalem. Today it is known as the bread basket of Israel.

During Old Testament times, major traffic traveled past Megiddo, making it a strategic military stronghold. History tells us this region in Israel was the setting for many ancient battles. Napoleon looked at Armageddon and described it as the most natural battlefield on the face of the earth. Hugh Armies were able to maneuver easily over the empty plains.

A few years ago, I stood on Megiddo, the small mountain beside Armageddon, It was a beautiful setting. I looked at the fertile land, the fruit trees and farms. I thought that in the near future this scene will be drastically changed. Someday soon a 200 million man army of the Antichrist, along with all the nations of the world, will come against Israel at the Battle of Armageddon.

The Bible teaches that the world is not headed for peace and unity, but toward a final cataclysmic war known as the Battle of Armageddon. The ungodly will continue to fall deeper and deeper into sin and wickedness, until this climactic holocaust.

Satan will make a desperate, but futile attempt, in a final showdown. He sends out "spirits of demons, performing signs and wonders to gather the kings of the earth together in a final attempt to defeat the armies of the living God. This battle is a symbol of the conflict between God and the forces of evil. On the plains of Israel the Antichrist will join with his armies to fight against Israel. Nations of the world will fight with the Antichrist against Israel (probably over the status of Jerusalem). This confrontation will be so large that soldiers will look like locusts on the plains of Megiddo.

Battle of Armageddon

"These miracle-working demons conferred with all the rulers of the world to gather them for battle against the Lord on that great coming Judgment Day of God Almighty…They gathered all the armies of the world near a place called, in Hebrew, Armageddon, and the Mountain of Megiddo. Then the seventh angel poured out his flask into the air; and a mighty shout came from the throne of the temple in heaven, saying, 'It is finished!' Then the thunder crashed and rolled, and lightning flashed; and there was a great earthquake of a magnitude unprecedented in human history…Islands vanished, and mountains flattened out, and there was an incredible hailstorm from heaven; hailstones weighing a hundred pounds fell from the sky onto the people below, and they cursed God because of the terrible hail" (Revelation 16:14, 16-17, 20-21 TLB).

How the 200 Million Army is Destroyed

1. Fire and sword– Isaiah 66:15-16
2. Mammoth Hailstones – Revelation 6:21
3. Darkness on the earth – Zechariah 14:6
4. Flesh will dissolve – Zechariah 14:12
5. Great panic and people will attach each other – Zechariah 14:12

Zechariah gave an excellent description of what will occur at Armageddon. "God will march out against the godless nations and fight—a great war! That's the Day he'll take his stand on the Mount of Olives, facing Jerusalem from the east. The Mount of Olives will be split right down the middle, from east to west, leaving a wide valley. Half the mountain will shift north, the other half south. Then you will run for your lives down the valley, your escape route that will take you all the way to Azal. You'll run for your lives, just as you ran on the day of the great earthquake in the days of Uzziah, king of Judah. Then my God will arrive and all the holy angels with him. What a Day that will be! No more cold nights—in fact, no more nights! The Day is coming—the timing is God's—when it will be one continuous day. Every evening will be a fresh morning. God will be king over all the earth, one God and only one. What a Day that will be!" (Zechariah 14:3–9 MSG).

Why Armageddon?

Why does God allow the Great Tribulation and the worst battle of the ages? God allows time for kings, nations and people to accept Him. He allows Satan to make a one last-ditch effort to set up his kingdom. It seems that Satan is winning, but

God is in total control.

- God wants to prove the falseness of Satan's claim (Isaiah 14:12–15).
- God will punish the ungodly (Revelation 19:15).
- God wants to prepare the earth for the Millennial Reign (Revelation 16:20).
- God will prepare a great-martyred multitude for heaven (Revelation 7:9, 14).
- God desires to purge Israel (Zechariah 13:8–9).
- God wants the entire world to know that He is God.
- God will establish the Millennial Reign and bring peace to the earth (Daniel 9:24).

The Antichrist and His forces show great strength but their defeat will come quickly. The battle belongs to the Lord. "He who keeps Israel shall neither slumbers nor sleeps" (Psalms 121:4). When it looks like Israel is being totally defeated, their Messiah will descent from heaven with His army of angels and totally crush the Antichrist's army. The Lord intervenes supernaturally to destroy the armies of Satan and pours out His wrath and the forces of evil will be completely destroyed (Revelation 16:19).

The Messiah Will Destroy the Antichrist.

"Then the Lord will go forth and fight against those nations, as He fights in the day of battle. In that day His feet will stand on the Mount of Olives, which faces Jerusalem on the east. The Mount of Olives shall be split in two, from east to west, making a very large valley…Thus the Lord my God will come, and all the saints" (Zechariah 14:3–5).

Christ will lead the great Heavenly Hosts to destroy the Antichrist and his one-world army in the awesome Battle of Armageddon. This great slaughter will occur in Megiddo in northern Israel. This will be the worst battle ever to occur in the world. God will destroy this great host in one day.

"Now I saw heaven opened, and behold, a white horse. He who sat on him *was* called Faithful and True, and in righteousness He judges and makes war. His eyes *were* like a flame of fire, and on His head *were* many crowns. He had a name written that no one knew except Himself. He *was* clothed with a robe dipped in blood, and His name is called The Word of God. The armies in heaven, clothed in fine linen, white and clean, followed Him on white horses. Now out of His mouth goes a sharp sword, that with it He should strike the nations. He Himself will rule them with a rod of iron. He Himself treads the winepress of the fierceness and wrath of Almighty God. He has on *His* robe and on His thigh a name written King of kings and Lord of lords" (Revelation 19:11–16).

> CHAPTER 20
IMPORTANCE OF THE RESURRECTION

"Blessed be the God and Father of Our Lord Jesus Christ, who according to His great mercy has caused us to be born again to a living hope through the resurrection of Jesus Christ from the dead, to obtain an inheritance which is imperishable and undefiled and will not pass away, reserved in heaven for you" (1 Peter 1:3-4 NASB).

Down through the generation mankind has believed in the hope of a general resurrection. Greek philosophers, such as Plato, believed that an immortal soul inhabited a body. At death the soul left its bodily prison and soared upward to God.

The Bible tells us that someday following death our bodies will be resurrected. Have you ever noticed that there are some similarities between sleep and death? A sleeping body and a dead body look very similar. People sometimes say at a funeral that the deceased looks like he is asleep. When a believer dies, he is really just asleep awaiting the resurrection. Sleep is temporary, and so is death for the believer in Jesus Christ.

Old Testament Concept

The Jewish people believed in the goodness of God and that the righteous dead would again see God. Several Old Testament writers believed they would be raised to life and see God.

Isaiah wrote: "Those who belong to God will live; their bodies will rise again! Those who sleep in the earth will rise up and sing for joy! For God's light of life will fall like dew on his people in the place of the dead" (Isaiah 26:19 NLT).

The Psalmist also said, "As for me, I will see your face in righteousness; I shall be satisfied when I awake in your likeness" (Psalm 17:15).

Daniel wrote "Many of those who sleep in the dust of the earth will awake, some to everlasting life, some to shame and everlasting disgrace" (Daniel 12:2 NLT).

New Testament Concept

In the New Testament there was a controversy regarding the resurrection. The Pharisees believed in the resurrection but the Sadducees didn't. The Sadducees said here is no resurrection--and no angel or spirit; but the Pharisees confess both.

The Apostle said: "I admit to you, that according to the Way which they call a sect I do serve the God of our fathers, believing everything that is in accordance with the Law and that is written in the Prophets; having a hope in God, which these men cherish themselves, that there shall certainly be a resurrection of both the righteous and the wicked" (Acts 24:14-15 NASB).

Jesus said there would be a resurrection of the just and the unjust. "Don't be so surprised! Indeed the time is coming when all the dead in their graves shall hear the voice of God's Son, and shall rise again—those who have done good, to eternal life; and those who have continued in evil, to judgment" (John 5:28-29 TLB).

Christ Foretold of His Resurrection

Jesus said, "I am the resurrection and the life. Whoever believes in me will live, even though he die, yet shall he live" (John 11:25 ESV).

On several occasions Christ predicted His death and resurrection. "Listen," He said, we're going up to Jerusalem, where the Son of Man will be betrayed to the leading priests and the teachers of religious law. They will sentence him to die. Then they will hand him over to the Romans to be mocked, flogged with a whip, and crucified. But on the third day he will be raised from the dead" (Matthew 20:18-19 NLT).

Christ also explained that His authority extended over all, both living and dead. Christ is able also to resurrect all from the dead. "Christ both died and rose again for this very purpose – to be Lord both of the living and the dead" (Romans 14:9 NLT).

The Bible gives a deal of evidence that Christ arose from the dead. Christ appears to a large number of people following the resurrection. He appeared to Peter, the twelve disciples and later to a group of 500 people.

"I delivered to you as of first importance what I received; that Christ died for our sins in accordance with the scriptures, that he was buried, that he was raised on the third day in accordance with the scriptures, and that he appeared to Cephas, then to the twelve. Then he appeared to more than five hundred brothers at one time, most of whom are still alive, though some have fallen asleep. Then he appeared to James, then to all the apostles" (1 Corinthians 15:3-7 ESV).

Importance of the Resurrection

"If Christ has not been raised, our preaching is useless and so is your faith. More than that, we are then found to be false witnesses about God, for we have testified about God that he raised Christ from the dead. But he did not raise him if in fact the dead are not raised. For if the dead are not raised, then Christ has not been raised either. If Christ has not been raised, your faith is futile; you are still in your sins. Then those also who have fallen asleep in Christ are lost" (1 Corinthians 15:14-18 (NIV).

The resurrection of Jesus is the most important event in human history. If Christ did not arise from the dead then our hope in Christ is futile. The great hope of the Christian faith is the resurrection. Even the death of Christ is mean-ingless without the resurrection. Paul, the apostle, explains the importance of the resurrection by saying that if our hope is in this life only, we are of all men most pitiable. If Christ is not raised from the dead, there is no hope for a future life and those who have already died have perished.

A Christian should never view life as ending in death. This life is not all there is. We can look beyond the sunset to the sunrise believing we will spend eternity with Christ. We should remember that we will again see our loved one.

"I do not want you to be ignorant, brethren, concerning those who have fallen asleep, lest you sorrow as others who have no hope. For if we believe that Jesus died and rose again, even so God will bring with Him those who sleep in Jesus" (1 Thessalonians 4:13-14).

Christ died for our sins. He was buried and rose again the third day accord-ing to the scriptures. The entire New Testament rests upon this historical fact.

Timing of the Resurrection

When will the resurrection occur? Three times in the sixth chapter of John, we are told that the resurrection will occur on the last day.

"This is the will of Him who sent Me, that of all that He has given Me I lose nothing, but raise it up on the last day. For this is the will of My Father, that everyone who beholds the Son and believes in Him will have eternal life, and I Myself will raise him up on the last day…No one can come to Me unless the Father who sent Me draws him; and I will raise him at on the last day…He who eats my flesh and drinks My blood has eternal life, and I will raise him up on the last day" (John 6:39, 40, 44, 43 NASB).

It seems significant that the same thing is repeated four times in one chapter. The same exact statement is made in the 11th chapter of John. Jesus said to Martha, "Your brother will rise again." Martha said to Him, "I know that he will rise again in the resurrection on the last day" (John 11:23-24 NASB). Jesus did not correct her.

Believer's Resurrection

"The Lord Himself will descend from heaven with a shout, with the voice of an archangel, and with the trumpet of God. And the dead in Christ will rise first. Then we who are alive and remain shall be caught up together with them in the clouds to meet the Lord in the air. And thus we shall always be with the Lord" (1 Thessalonians 4:16-17).

The resurrection and the rapture occur on the same day according the Apostle Paul. If the resurrection occurs on the last day, how are believers raptured before the Great Tribulation?

"I saw the souls of those beheaded because of their witness to Jesus and the Word of God, who refused to worship either the Beast or his image, refused to take his mark on forehead or hand—they lived and reigned with Christ for a thousand years! The rest of the dead did not live until the thousand years were up. This is the first resurrection—and those involved are most blessed, most holy. No second death for them! They're priests of God and Christ; they'll reign with him a thousand years" (Revelation 20:4-6 MSG).

When Christ returns, the dead in Christ will be resurrected and meet the Lord in the air along with believers who are still alive. Those who are martyred and those who did not receive the Mark of the Beast during the tribulation are included in the first resurrection. The first resurrection for the righteous occurs when Christ returns. The second resurrection is for the ungodly, which does not occur until after the Millennial Reign of Christ.

If the resurrection occurs on the last day and those who were martyred during the tribulation are in the first resurrection, how can the rapture and resurrection occur before the Great Tribulation?

What our resurrected body will become is not clear. Some believe it will not be subject to time or space, like Jesus when he went through closed doors. Whatever the situation, we can be sure that our immortal bodies will be suited for eternity to live forever.

Believers will live forever

Believers will become immortal and live forever. The word mortal means "subject to death". Immortal means the opposite—imperishable. The term "immortal soul" is not used once in the entire Bible! The Word of God doesn't teach such a concept. The King James Version uses the expressions "soul" and "spirit" but never once attaches the term "immortal" to either word. Only God is immortal. "The King of kings and Lord of lords…only has immortality (I Timothy 6:15-16)." Believer's moral body will become immortal like Christ's at the resurrection. Our Savior, Jesus Christ, abolished death and brought life and immortality to light through the Gospel.

Two Resurrections

Jesus said there would be a resurrection of the just and the unjust. "Truly, truly, I say to you, an hour is coming and now is, when the dead will hear the voice of the Son of God, and those who hear will live. For just as the Father has life in Himself, even so He gave to the Son also to have life in Himself; and He gave Him authority to execute judgment, because He is *the* Son of Man. Do not marvel at this; for an hour is coming, in which all who are in the tombs will hear His voice, and will come forth; those who did the good *deeds* to a resurrection of life, those who committed the evil *deeds* to a resurrection of judgment" (John 5:25-29 NASB).

The resurrection of the ungodly does not occur until after the Thousand Year Reign of Christ at the Great White Throne Judgment (Revelation 20:11-15). There is a vast difference in the death of the righteous and the death of the wicked. The righteous are freed from all future suffering and sorrow while the wicked have only sorrow ahead.

Characteristics of the Resurrected Body

The Bible gives us some glimpses of what our new spiritual body will be like. Our resurrected bodies will be like Christ. During the 40-day period after Christ's resurrection He looked similar to an ordinary man. He had nail prints in his hands and He ate food.

Christ's resurrected body was different from His physical body. He was recognizable but yet he moved on a much higher level of life. According to Gospel accounts, he was no longer limited to natural laws. Jesus could come or go at will even through closed doors.

The resurrection of saints at the return of Christ is a bodily resurrection. Our bodies will be transformed to a new level of life. At His coming, Christ will transform our bodies to be conformed to the body of his glory. "Our citizenship is in heaven, from which we also eagerly wait for the Savior, the Lord Jesus Christ, who will transform our lowly body that it may be conformed to His glorious body, according to the working by which He is able even to subdue all things to Himself" (Philippians 3:20-21).

The Rapture, the catching up to meet the Lord in the air, is the sign that the living, as well as the dead, has put on the glorious resurrection body. They are no longer earthbound, mortal creatures, but have entered into the fullness of life, which means a new level of existence whose character we can now only faintly discern.[225]"Let me reveal to you a wonderful secret. We will not all die, but we will all be transformed! It will happen in a moment, in the blink of an eye, when the last trumpet is blown. For when the trumpet sounds, those who have died will be raised to live forever. We who are living will also be transformed. For our dying bodies must be transformed into bodies that will never die; our mortal bodies must be transformed into immortal bodies. Then, when our dying bodies have been transformed into bodies that will never die, this scripture will be fulfilled: "Death is swallowed up in victory" (1 Corinthians 15:51-54 NLT).

Our spiritual bodies will be full of the power of the Holy Spirit, perfectly designed for the enjoyment of eternal life. They will be redeemed from weakness, pain and decay, no longer subject to death.

This earthly body that is corruptible, mortal and subject to death will be forever changed to an incorruptible, immortal, imperishable body not subject to sin. What our resurrected body will become is not clear. Some believe it will not be subject to time or space, like Jesus when he went through closed doors. Whatever the situation, we can be sure that our immortal bodies will be suited for eternity.

We know that when this tent we live in now is taken down--when we die and leave these bodies--we will have wonderful new bodies in heaven, homes that will be ours forevermore, made for us by God himself, and not by human hands. How weary we grow of our present bodies. That is why we look forward eagerly to the day when we shall have heavenly bodies which we shall put on like new clothes. We shall not be merely spirits without bodies. Our earthly bodies make us groan and sigh, but we wouldn't like to think of dying and having no bodies at all. We want to slip into our new bodies so that these dying bodies will, as it were, be swallowed up by everlasting life. This is what God has prepared for us. Now we look forward with confidence to our heavenly bodies, realizing that every moment we spend in these earthly bodies is time spent away from our eternal home in heaven with Jesus. We know these things are true by believing, not by seeing. And we are not afraid but are quite content to die, for then we will be at home with the Lord. So our aim is to please him always in everything we do, whether we are here in this body or away from this body and with him in heaven. For we must all stand before Christ to be judged. Each of us will receive whatever he deserves for the good or bad things he has done in his earthly body.[226]

Where are the Dead?

The Apostle Paul said, "We are always confident and know that as long as we are at home in the body we are away from the Lord. For we live by faith, not by sight. We are confident, I say, and would prefer to be away from the body and at home with the Lord" (2 Corinthians 5:6-8 NIV).

This implies that as long as the spirit of the believers remains in the body, it cannot be present with the Lord. However, when the spirit is released from the body, it has direct access to the presence of the Lord.

Redemption of the Universe

The Christian's hope is not only that God will resurrect our physical body, but that He will redeem the physical universe. God's redemption is both the resurrection of the physical body and the renewal of this universe, including Planet Earth. The grand and glorious truth that we will once again walk this physical planet is made abundantly clear in scripture. John's expression "a new heaven and a new earth" is not meant to communicate a place that is totally other than this present earth, but rather this universe renewed.[227]"All creation is waiting patiently and hopefully for that future day when God will resurrect his children. For on that day thorns and thistles, sin, death and decay—the things that overcame the world against its will at God's command—will all disappear, the world around us will share in the glorious freedom from sin which God's children enjoy. For we know that even the things of nature, like animals and plants, suffer in sickness and death as they await this great event. And even we Christians, although we have the Holy Spirit within us as a foretaste of future glory, also groan to be released from pain and suffering. We, too, wait anxiously for that day when God will give us our full rights as his children, including the new bodies he has promised us— bodies that will never be sick again and will never die" (Romans 8:19-23 TLB).

He was supreme in the beginning and—leading the resurrection parade— he is supreme in the end. From beginning to end he's there, towering far above everything, everyone. So spacious is he, so roomy, that everything of God finds its proper place in him without crowding. Not only that, but all the broken and dislocated pieces of the universe—people and things, animals and atoms—gets properly fixed and fit together in vibrant harmonies, all because of his death, his blood that poured down from the cross" (Colossians 1:18-20 MSG).

› CHAPTER 21
GLORIOUS RETURN OF THE MESSIAH

About the Time of the End, a body of men will be raised up who will turn their attention to the prophecies, and insist upon their literal interpretation, in the midst of much clamor and opposition. - Sir Isaac Newton

One of the greatest themes in scripture is the Second Coming. While there are approximately 300 prophetic passages in the Old Testament that foretold the first coming of Christ, there are more than eight times as many verses that describe the Second Coming and His triumphant rule. More than 2,400 verses through the Old and New Testaments reveal God's promises about the return of Christ. The remarkable number of prophetic passages about the Second Advent emphasizes the vital importance of this event in God's plan of redemption for humanity. In light of the recent evidence of the fulfillment of these key prophetic signs, we need to live in daily expectation of Christ's return.[228]

Of the 216 chapters in the New Testament, there are 318 references to the Second Coming, or one out of every thirty verses. Twenty-three of the twenty-seven New Testament books refer to this great event. The four books that do not refer to it are single-chapter letters written to individual persons on a particular subject. The fourth book Galatians, which does not specifically mention the coming of Christ, but certainly implies it. For every biblical prophecy on the first coming of Christ, there are eight concerning His Second Coming.[229]

Christ gave His followers very specific information regarding His Second Coming. If Christ felt it was important for people to know what was going to transpire in the last days, it must be important. Christ's return is vitally important to believers. Consider seriously what the Bible has to say about this event. Christ tells us that the generation who sees the signs will be the generation that sees the return of Christ.

"When you see all these signs, all taken together, coming to pass, you may know of a surety that He is near, at the very door. Truly I tell you, this generation (the whole multitude of people living at the same time, in a definite, given period) will not pass away till all these things taken together take place" (Matthew 24:33-34 AMP).

The saddest thing of all in connection with our subject is that Christian theologians have divided into opposite camps. And yet it need not surprise us that the Second Coming of Christ is a controversial doctrine—what doctrine of scripture is not.[230]

Over a long period the Catholic, Orthodox and the mainline Protestant denominations have gradually de-emphasized their teaching and belief in the literal return of Christ. In contract, the Evangelical, Pentecostal, and Charismatic churches created during the last two centuries have strongly affirmed the biblical truth of the return of Christ and the Millennium. This fundamental core belief in Christ's triumphant return motivated hundreds of millions of believers in these churches to walk in personal holiness as well as the greatest wave of evangelism and missions, the world has ever known.[231]

Old Testament Concept

The scriptures speak of believers (dead and living) being caught up together into heaven at Christ's return. Even Old Testament Saints believed they would be able to see God in the hereafter. God told Daniel: "As for you, go your way until the end. You will rest and then at the end of the days, you will rise again to receive the inheritance set aside for you" (Daniel 12:13 NLT).

One of the most dramatic pictures of the Second Coming is found in the Old Testament Book of Daniel. "I was watching in the night visions, and behold One like the Son of Man, coming with the clouds of heaven! He came to the Ancient of Days, and they brought Him near before Him. Then to Him was given dominion and glory and a kingdom that all peoples, nations, and languages should serve Him. His dominion is an everlasting dominion, which shall not pass away, and His kingdom which shall not be destroyed" (Daniel 7:13-14).

The earliest prophecy concerning the Second Coming of Jesus is recorded in the book of Jude, one of the final books of the New Testament. Jude, the brother of Jesus, made reference to the righteous patriarch Enoch, who was raptured to heaven before the Great Flood. Jude revealed that Enoch prophesied about the Second Coming. "Enoch, the seventh from Adam, prophesied about these men also, saying, "Behold, the Lord comes with ten thousands of His saints, to execute judgment on all" Jude 14-15).

Christ Taught in Parables about His Return

Jesus made it perfectly clear that He would come again, before His death and after his resurrection. He spoke more than twenty times of events concerning His return. Some of the parables concerned His departure, His absence and His return. If Christ does not return, some parables are absolutely pointless.

The parable of the Three Servants (Matthew 25:14-30) indicates there will be a long interval of time before our Lord's return. This parable illustrates that the Kingdom of Heaven is like a man going on a long journey, who gives money to three servants to invest while he is gone. After a long time, the master of the house returns and rewards his servants according to how they invested the money.

In the Parable of the Ten Servants (Luke 19:11-27), a nobleman was called away to a distant land and gave ten pounds of silver to his servants to invest while he was gone. When he returned, he rewarded those who have invested wisely and condemned those who invested poorly.

Believers Kept from the Hour of Trial

"Because you have kept My command to persevere, I also will keep you from the *Hour of Trial* which shall come upon the whole world, to test those who dwell on the earth" (Revelation 3:10). Jesus told believers, "Watch and pray that you may be counted worthy to escape all these things that will come to pass and to stand before the son of Man" (Luke 21:26).

This period is referred to as Daniel's 70th week in Daniel 9:24-27 and the Time of Jacob's Trouble in Jeremiah 30:7. This period is known as the Great Tribulation when Israel will experience a period of difficulty just before Yeshua's return.

Mighty Angels Return with Christ

"Immediately after the tribulation of those days the sun will be darkened, and the moon will not give its light. The stars will fall from the sky and the power of the heavens will be shaken. Then the sign of the Son of Man will appear in the sky, and then all the tribes of the earth will mourn, and they will see the Son of Man Son of Man coming of the clouds of the sky with power and great glory. He will send forth His angels with a great trumpet and they will gather together His elect from the four winds, from one end of the sky to the other" (Matthew 24:29-31 NASB).

The world will soon see the Son of Man coming on the clouds of heaven with power and great glory. When Christ returns, He will bring His angels with Him. This fact is repeated over and over in the scriptures. Gabriel appeared to Mary announcing the birth of our blessed Messiah. Possibly he will be the angel that announces the Second Coming of Christ, our blessed Savior.

John, the Beloved, describes the Second Coming of Christ to earth in power and great glory. "I saw heaven opened, and behold, a white horse, and He who sat on it *is* called Faithful and True, and in righteousness He judges and wages war. His eyes *are* a flame of fire, and on His head *are* many diadems; and He has a name written *on Him* which no one knows except Himself. *He is* clothed with a robe dipped in blood, and His name is called The Word of God" (Revelation 19:11-13 NASB).

The Dead in Christ will Rise First

"If we believe that Jesus died and rose again, even so God will bring with Him those who sleep in Jesus. For this we say to you by the word of the Lord, that we who are alive and remain until the coming of the Lord will by no means precede those who are asleep. For the Lord Himself will descend from heaven with a shout, with the voice of an archangel, and with the trumpet of God. And the dead in Christ will rise first. Then we who are alive and remain shall be caught up together with them in the clouds to meet the Lord in the air. And thus we shall always be with the Lord" (1 Thessalonians 4:14-17).

We can tell you with complete confidence—we have the Master's word on it—that when the Master comes again to get us, those of us who are still alive will not get a jump on the dead and leave them behind. In actual fact, they'll be ahead of us. The Master himself will give the command. Archangel thunder! God's trumpet blast! He'll come down from heaven and the dead in Christ will rise—they'll go first. Then the rest of us who are still alive at the time will be caught up with them into the clouds to meet the Master. Oh, we'll be walking on air! And then there will be one huge family reunion with the Master. So reassure one another with these words (2 Thessalonians 14:15--18 MSG).

The scriptures indicate that when Christ returns He will bring with Him those who sleep in Jesus was well as all His angels. The angels gather up the followers of Christ that are still alive (saints or elect) from the four corners of the earth. Christ returns with his angels and are joined together with the saints of all ages, both Old Testament and New Testament Believers.

Christ Returns to the Mount of Olives

In that day His feet will stand on the Mount of Olives, which is in front of Jerusalem on the east; and the Mount of Olives will be split in its middle from east to west by a very large valley, so that half of the mountain will move toward the north and the other half toward the south (Zechariah 14:4 NASB).

An earthquake will split the Mount of Olives in two, separating the northern part (Mount Scopus) from the southern part (the Mount of Olives proper). The whole of Jerusalem will be lifted up and leveled off, becoming the dominating mountain height in this area. This agrees with the prophecy given both in Isaiah and Micah.[232] "Now it shall come to pass in the last days the mountain of the Lord will be established as the chief of the mountains, and will be raised above the hills; and all nations will stream to it" (Isaiah 2:2 NASB).

Through all the centuries of its history, Jerusalem has never had an adequate water supply of its own. But as a result of these geological upheavals, Jerusalem will become for the first time a source of water. Artesian fountains will be opened there and will flow forth in rivers to the east and to the west. To the east a river will flow through the valley formed by the earthquake in the Mount of Olives, descending through the Judean wilderness to the Dead Sea. This river will bring life and fruitfulness wherever it flows. It is described in detail in Ezekiel 47:1-12).[232]

Glorious Appearance of Jesus Christ

The Divine Creator will soon divinely invade human history. The King of kings will rule over all the earth. God will forever emancipate His saints from warfare. Satan, the archenemy, will be bound for 1,000 years and can no longer tempt the inhabitants of God's Kingdom.

The first time Messiah came He was a baby in a manger, surrounded by donkeys and goats. The next time He comes He will be mounted on a milk-white stallion thundering through the clouds of heaven with the armies of God following Him. On His head will be many crowns, for He will come back to earth as King of kings and Lord of lords.[233]

The first time Jesus came He was brought before Pilate; He was dragged before Herod. He was mocked, spit upon, and forced to wear a scarlet robe of mockery. The next time He comes, Pilate shall be brought before Him. Herod will be dragged before Him. Hitler will be hauled before Him, and that infamous hater of the Jewish people will bow before the King of the Jews and confess that He is Lord to the glory of God, the Father.[234]

The first time the Lamb of God came He was nailed to a bitter rugged cross where He suffered and bled and died alone. The next time He comes He will put His foot on the Mount of Olives and it shall split in half. He will walk across the Kidron Valley and through the Eastern Gate and set His throne up on the Temple Mount. From there He shall reign for one thousand years in the Millennium. Following that will be the Great White Throne Judgment, after which human time shall cease and eternity will begin.[235]

The apostle John recorded the last prophecy in the book of Revelation where Jesus said, Look. "I am coming soon! My reward is with me, and I will give to each person according to what they have done. Yes, I am coming soon! Amen! Come, Lord Jesus" (Revelation 22: 12, 20 NIV).

Why has Christ's return been delayed? One of the reasons is that God wants to give as many people as possible a change to accept him, repent and accept Him as their personal Savior. "The Lord isn't slow about his promise, as some think. No, he is being patient for your sake. He does not want anyone to be destroyed, but wants everyone to repent" (2 Peter 3:9 NLT). Accept Christ today as your personal Savior. Don't delay. Put your faith and trust in him and accept Him as your Lord and Master.

"The dawn of day is breaking, Behold! It streaks the sky, and hearts for Him are waking, who soon shall fill each eye; Soon! Soon! in brightness beaming, "The day-star" shall appear, with glory round Him streaming, Our eyes are looking onward, To see the One we love; Our feet are pressing forward, To tread those courts above; Our hearts do leap with pleasure, as nearer comes the day When love, beyond all measure, shall beckon us away. There "face to face," beholding the One who came to die, His glory all unfolding before each raptured eye, With nothing there to hinder, but all to call forth wonder, and ceaseless bursts of joy. There on His bosom resting, Oh! deep and full repose, No more a time of testing— No more to meet our foes; But there, in brightest glory, to gaze upon His face, and ever tell that story— "The glory of His grace."[236]

❯ CHAPTER 22
THOUSAND YEARS OF PEACE

"Behold, the tabernacle of God is with men and He will dwell with them and they shall be His people and God Himself shall be with them, and be their God. The kingdoms of this world are become the kingdom of our Lord, and of His Christ; and He shall reign forever and ever" (Revelation 21:3; 11:15).

This thousand year period when Christ rules as King over the world is known as the Millennium. It comes from a Latin word meaning 1,000 years. "Millo" means 1,000 and "annum" means years. Together they refer to a period of 1,000 years.

At Christ's first advent, He stood before human courts and was found guilty. When He returns, His Divine glory will be fully manifested. He will come as the Lion of the Tribe of Judah, instead of the gentle Lamb. Instead of humiliation and shame, He will be clothed in honor and royal majesty. Our Lord will be King of kings and Lord of lords and reign in power and majesty over all the earth. What a day that will be!

Three Views Concerning the Millennium

One of the saddest things of all in connection with this subject is that theologians are divided into opposite camps. It is not surprising that the Millennium is a controversial subject—what doctrine of scripture is not? Church history has seen the rise of three competing views concerning the Millennium.

A-Millennialism

A-Millennialism teaches that there is no literal 1,000–year reign of Christ. Instead, the church inherits the millennial blessings promised to Israel, and Christ reigns through the church, right now, in an allegorized millennium. This view was developed and promoted by Augustine in the fourth century.[237] This theory teaches that Satan was bound at the cross and has been bound throughout the history of the church. If that is true, he must be bound with an extremely long chain.

Post Millennialism

Post Millennialism believes that Christ will not return till after the Millennium. They believe in a Millennium brought about by missionary activities, by the preaching of the Gospel, by the prayers of the saints, by the efforts of the churches. They think that ultimately the Church will convert the world. This theory is expressed in different ways and with various modifications and amplifications, but the postmillennialists are agreed that the Kingdom is to be brought in by a united effort of the church. They are also unanimous in interpreting the Messianic prophecies in a non-literal sense. The Kingdom they look for is to be a spiritual one, not literal. Christ's rule is to be internal not external. The King is to govern from heaven and not to reign on earth.[238]

They believe that as more and more people across the globe are converted, the world will gradually be conquered for Christ and Jesus will at last return to earth to take up the throne won for Him by His church. This view flourished until World War I, when it became abundantly clear the world was not getting better.[239]

Pre Millennialism

Pre-millennialism is the oldest view of the three and holds that Christ will physically return to earth to put down His enemies and reign over the earth for a literal 1,000-years period. This view is found in the writings of the earliest church fathers and remains the most common view among evangelicals.[240]

The Messiah in the Millennium

"Many people will say, 'Come, let us go up to the mountain of the Lord, to the temple of the God of Jacob. He (Messiah) will teach us his ways, so that we may walk in his paths. The law will go out from Zion, the word of the Lord from Jerusalem'" (Isaiah 2:3 NIV).

When the Messiah returns He will mount His Throne on Mount Zion and rule gloriously in Jerusalem, in the sight of all His people. The prophecies will be fulfilled concerning the redemption of Israel and the Promised Land. There will be such glory that the brightness of the sun and moon will seem to fade away. The glorious Messianic Kingdom will soon be established. The whole world will be filled with His glory.

Satan in the Millennium

There can never be a thousand years of peace and righteousness on earth, if Satan, the enemy of God's people, remains on this earth. Satan was given the dominion of this world and became the "god of this age" after Adam and Eve sinned. Christ stripped Satan of his authority in the lives of believers at His resurrection.

When Satan gathers the kings of the earth to battle against Israel at Armageddon, God will laugh at his folly and madness. It is foolish to attempt to overcome the plans of God. It would be easier to roll back the ocean than to stop the plans of the Most High.

There is a God in heaven that can rid the world of our ruthless adversary. Revelation 20:1-3 describes the removal of this Arch-Foe from the earth. An angel comes down from heaven, having the key to the bottomless pit and a great chain in his hand. He lays hold of Satan and binds him for a thousand years so he cannot deceive the nations any more till the thousand years are finished.

Satan can no longer harass, hinder or tempt the saints of God. This earth will be rid of the devil for a thousand years. For a thousand years the earth will live in peace. This will end the struggle that man has waged with Satan for the past six thousand years.

Believers in the Millennium

"God raised us up with Christ and seated us with him in the heavenly realms in Christ Jesus in order that in the coming ages he might show the incomparable riches of his grace, expressed in his kindness to us in Christ Jesus" (Ephesians 2:6-7 NIV).

The church occupies a very special place in the Millennium. We will enter the Millennium in our resurrected bodies that will never decay. Our weak, mortal bodies will be changed into glorious bodies like Christ.

Victorious believers, who obey Christ to the very end, will be given authority over the nations (Revelation 2:26). In that day, saints will judge the world and rule and reign with Christ. Those who are martyred during the Great Tribulation will be resurrected and reign with Christ. Blessed and holy are those who share in the first resurrection. The second death does not have any power over them, for they will be priests of God and of Christ and will reign with him for a thousand years.

"The sovereignty, the dominion and greatness of all the kingdoms under the whole heaven will be given to the people of the saints of the Highest One; His kingdom will be an everlasting kingdom, and all the dominions will serve and obey Him" (Daniel 7:27 NASB).

Jesus said to the disciples, "Assuredly I say to you, that in the regeneration (coming age), when the Son of Man sits on the throne of His glory, you who have followed Me will also sit on twelve thrones, judging the twelve tribes of Israel" (Matthew 19:28).

All true believers will sing a new song to the Lord saying: "You are worthy to take the scroll and to open its seals, because you were slain, and with your blood you purchased for God persons from every tribe and language and people and nation. You have made them to be a kingdom and priests to serve our God, and they will reign on the earth" (Revelation 5:9-10 NIV).

Nations in the Millennium

"Many nations will come, saying, 'Come, let us go up to the Lord's mountain of the Lord, to the temple of the God of Jacob. He will teach us his ways, so that we may walk in his paths.' The law will go out from Zion, and the word of the Lord from Jerusalem. He will judge between many peoples and will settle disputes for strong nations far and wide. They will beat their swords into plowshares and their spears into pruning hooks. Nation will not take up sword against nations, nor will they train for war anymore'" (Micah 4:2-3 NIV).

God's plan instituted thousands of years ago will surely come to pass. Nothing can stop it. "This is the plan determined for the whole world; this is the hand stretched out over all nations. For the Lord Almighty has purposed, and who can thwart him? His hand is stretched out, and who can turn it back" (Isaiah 14:26-27).

When Jesus returns to earth, kings will bow down before Him and all nations will serve Him. "Many nations will join themselves to the Lord on that day, and they, too, will by my people. I will live among you, and you will know that the Lord of Heaven's Armies sent me to you" (Zechariah 2:11 NLT).

During this thousand year reign, righteousness will reign in all the earth. Sin and evil will exist, but the evil will be immediately brought to justice. The world will be completely free from the horrors of war.

People from all over the world will go to Jerusalem to worship the Lord. They won't say, "Let's go up to New York or Dallas or Rome." No! They will say, "Come, and let us go up to the mountain of the LORD, To the house of the God of Jacob; He will teach us His ways, and we shall walk in His paths. Out of Zion shall go forth the law and the word of the LORD from Jerusalem" (Isaiah 2:3).

Israel in the Millennium

"For Zion's sake I will not hold My peace, and for Jerusalem's sake I will not rest, until her righteousness goes forth as brightness, and her salvation as a lamp that burns. The Gentiles shall see your righteousness, and all kings your glory. You shall be called by a new name, which the mouth of the LORD will name. You shall also be a crown of glory in the hand of the LORD, and a royal diadem in the hand of your God" (Isaiah 62:1-3).

Israel can't have peace today because her Messiah is not there, but someday soon He will return to Mount Zion. Jerusalem will be called the Faithful City, the Holy Mountain of the Lord. The Lord will be a shelter for his people and strengthen the Children of Israel. Israel will not only enjoy the blessing of their Messiah, but they will be a blessing to all the families of the earth.

It is clear in God's Word that the nation of Israel has been preserved for a purpose. A marvelous future awaits the descendants of Abraham. Jerusalem will no longer be trampled by Gentiles, for the Tabernacle of David will be restored. Israel will no longer be the sport of the nations. She will become the head instead of the tail.

"This is what the Lord Almighty says: "In those day ten men from all languages and nations will take firm hold of one Jews by the hem of his robe and say. 'Let us go with you, because we have heard that God is with you'" (Zechariah 8:23 NIV).

"In that day the Lord will defend the inhabitants of Jerusalem, and the one who is feeble among them in that day will be like David, and the house of David *will be* like God, like the angel of the Lord before them. And in that day I will set about to destroy all the nations that come against Jerusalem. I will pour out on the house of David and on the inhabitants of Jerusalem, the Spirit of grace and of supplication, so that they will look on Me whom they have pierced; and they will mourn for Him, as one mourns for an only son, and they will weep bitterly over Him like the bitter weeping over a firstborn" (Zechariah 12:8-10 NASB).

Once again, old men and women will walk Jerusalem's streets and sit together in the city square. The streets will be filled with boys and girls at play (Zechariah 8:3-5).

Together with martyred believers, they will be a part of leadership in the New Kingdom. "Many will come from the east and west, and shall sit down with Abraham, and Isaac, and Jacob, in the kingdom of heaven" (Matthew 8:11).

"In Jerusalem, the Lord of Heaven's Armies will spread a wonderful feast for everyone around the world. It will be a delicious banquet of clear, well-aged wine and choice meat. There he will remove the cloud of gloom, the shadow of death that hangs over the earth. He will swallow up death forever! The Sovereign Lord will wipe away all tears. He will remove forever all insults and mockery against his land and people. The Lord has spoken!" (Isaiah 25:6-8 NLT).

God's Divine presence will again dwell in Jerusalem. Israel will bless all the nations of the world. The Messiah will soon return and fulfill all the great prophecies concerning the redemption of Israel and the Promised Land. What a glorious day that will be!

Creation in the Millennium

"The wolf also shall dwell with the lamb, the leopard shall lie down with the young goat, the calf and the young lion and the fatling together; and a little child shall lead them. The cow and the bear shall graze; their young ones shall lie down together. The lion shall eat straw like the ox. The nursing child shall play by the cobra's hole, and the weaned child shall put his hand in the viper's den. They shall not hurt nor destroy in My holy mountain" (Isaiah 11:6-9).

"For all creation is waiting patiently and hopefully for that future day when God will resurrect his children. For on that day, thorns and thistles, sin, death and decay—the things that overcame the world against its will at God's command--will all disappear, and the world around us will share in the glorious freedom from sin, which God's children enjoy" (Romans 8:19-21 TLB).

What a wonderful time the Millennium will be for this sin-cursed world! Satan removed, the Antichrist destroyed, Israel penitent and restored, the heathen nations completely evangelized, and creation itself delivered from its bondage of corruption. Christ Himself on the throne, the Holy Spirit poured out upon all flesh, and God's Kingdom spread throughout the world. Yes, indeed, shall it be said, "Lord, it is good to be here".[241] What a wonderful time the Millennium will be for this sin-cursed world! Believers have many reasons to pray "Thy kingdom come,"

❯ CHAPTER 23
NEW JERUSALEM (CITY OF GOD)

When a mortal man speaks anything of that eternal blessedness of the saints in glory, he is like a blind man discoursing about the light which he has never seen, and so cannot distinctly speak anything concerning it. In a way it is akin to a man writing a travel guide for a land he has never visited or seen. It is to attempt to describe the indescribable with words which cannot come close to expressing the glory of heaven (Charles Spurgeon).

The paradise that God has prepared for us, the marvelous Heavenly City, is clearly and explicitly described in His Holy Book, the Bible, in the last two chapters of Revelation, the prophecies of Saint John. It is so amazing, so breathtakingly beautiful, that it is almost beyond description! It is the largest City ever built, built by God Himself! It glows with golden light from its crystal golden beauty and is full of golden mansions for you and me!

Eternity is ushered in following the Thousand Year Reign of the Messiah. It tells of a new era, a new heaven, a new earth, and a New Jerusalem. Christ has prepared a special place for His bride. John saw the New Jerusalem, like a huge, majestic mountain descending out of heaven.

"I saw a new heaven and a new earth, for the first heaven and the first earth had passed away. There was no more sea. John saw the holy city, New Jerusalem, coming down out of heaven from God, prepared as a bride adorned for her husband. I heard a loud voice from heaven saying, "Behold, the tabernacle of God is with men, and He will dwell with them, and they shall be His people. God Himself will be with them and be their God. And God will wipe away every tear from their eyes; there shall be no more death, nor sorry, nor crying. There shall be no more pain, for the former things have passed away" (Revelation 21:1-3).

The Lord Jesus said: "I go to prepare a place for you and if I go and prepare a place for you, I will come again, and receive you unto myself; that where I am there you may be also (John 14:2-3 ESV). This heavenly paradise, this marvelous heavenly city already exists. The departed saints already live there.

The only inhabitants in the New Jerusalem will be God, Jesus Christ and His bride. This includes all who have their name in the Lamb's Book of Life. Some scholars believe this includes all redeemed believers from the beginning of time. Jesus said, "I tell you this, that many Gentiles will come from all over the world—from east and west—and sit down with Abraham, Isaac, and Jacob at the feast in the Kingdom of Heaven" (Matthew 8:11 NLT).

In the ancient world, rulers kept a register of those who were citizens of their kingdom. Only when a man died or lost his right as a citizen, was his name removed. The Book of Life is the register of those who are citizens of the heavenly kingdom. This paradise, this marvelous Heavenly City, has been prepared for believers. It is so breathtakingly beautiful, it is indescribable.

Human history begins in a garden and ends in a city that is like a garden paradise. What began in Genesis is brought to completion in Revelation as the following summary shows:[242]

Genesis	Revelation
Heaven and earth created, 1:1	New heavens and earth, 21:1
Sun created, 1:16	No need of the sun, 21:23
The night established, 1:5	No night there, 22:5
The sea created, 1:10	No more seas, 21:1
The curse announced, 3:14-17	No more curse, 23:3
Death enters history, 3:19	No more death, 21:4
Man driven from the tree, 3:24	Man restored to paradise, 22:14
Sorrow and pain begin, 3:17	No more tears or pain, 21:4

Heaven is a city, without sickness, sorrow, pain or death. It is a city where you never grow old. It is a city without grieves or graves, without sin or sorrow, without births or burials. It is a city where Jesus is King and all the citizens are saints (Author unknown).

Size and Shape of the City

The angel who spoke with me had a gold measuring rod to measure the city, and its gates and its wall. The city is laid out as a square, and its length is as great as the width; and he measured the city with the rod, fifteen hundred miles; its length and width and height are equal (Revelation 21:15-16 NASB).

The New Jerusalem could stretch from the Gulf of Mexico to Canada and from Colorado to the Atlantic Ocean. It also reaches upward the same distance. The shape of the city is a perfect cube. Some translations call it "foursquare", which means equal on all sides.

Dr. J. Vernon McGee asked a mathematician and an engineer involved in the space program to determine what the circumference of the sphere would be. They both came up with the same answer. "To enclose a cube measuring 1,500 miles on each side, the circumference of the sphere would be about 8,164 miles. The diameter of the moon is about 2,150 mile and that of the New Jerusalem sphere is about 2,600 miles. The New Jerusalem will be somewhat larger than the moon and it will be a sphere like the other heavenly bodies."[243]

This heavenly city is twenty times as large as New Zealand, ten times as big as Germany, ten times as big as France, forty times larger than England. It is much larger than India. It is an enormous continent all by its self (David Jeremiah).

Walls and Gates of the Heavenly City

He (the angel) carried me away in the Spirit to a great and high mountain, and showed me the holy city, Jerusalem, coming down out of heaven from God, having the glory of God. Her brilliance was like a very costly stone, as a stone of crystal-clear jasper. It had a great and high wall, with twelve gates, and at the gates twelve angels; and names were written on them, which are the names of the twelve tribes of the sons of Israel. There were three gates on the east and three gates on the north and three gates on the south and three gates on the west. The wall of the city had twelve foundation stones, and on them were the twelve names of the twelve apostles of the Lamb. The one who spoke with me had a gold measuring rod to measure the city, and its gates and its wall. The city is laid out as a square, and its length is as great as the width; and he measured the city with the rod, fifteen hundred miles; its length and width and height are equal (Revelation 21:10-17 NASB).

The walls of the New Jerusalem are designed for beauty rather than protection. They are built of Jasper, a very hard substance. The twelve gates are named for the twelve tribes of Israel. There are three gates on each side of the city of God. The gates of the city are made up of a pearl, but the gates will never be closed (Revelation 21:25) because only the redeemed will live there.

The names of the twelve apostles are on each foundation. The foundation stones are made of precious stones. The twelve apostles helped to lay the foundation for the church of Jesus Christ. Christ was the foundation stone, but the apostles help build on it. They are now being honored in the foundation in the New Jerusalem.

Precious Stones in the City

The construction of its wall was of jasper; and the city was pure gold, like clear glass. The foundations of the wall of the city were adorned with all kinds of precious stones: the first foundation was jasper, the second sapphire, the third chalcedony, the fourth emerald, the fifth sardonyx, the sixth sardius, the seventh chrysolite, the eighth beryl, the ninth topaz, the tenth chrysoprase, the eleventh jacinth, and the twelfth amethyst. The twelve gates were twelve pearls: each individual gate was of one pearl. And the street of the city was pure gold, like transparent glass (Revelation 21:18-21).

The New Jerusalem itself is pure gold that seems like transparent glass. The precious stones in the twelve foundations of the Holy City are copied in the Zodiac.[244] The Zodiac signs are in precisely the reverse order than they are mentioned in the foundation of the New Jerusalem.[245]

The twelve foundations of the city not only have the names of the twelve apostles, but they are twelve different precious stones. The most beautiful and costly articles known to man are precious stones. These stones express in human terms the magnificence of the city. The foundations of the New Jerusalem are constructed of the flashing brilliance of rich and costly gems.[246]

On the inside is Jesus, who when He was here, was the light of the World. There He will be the light of the Universe. Astronauts tell us that in space the colors are entirely gray and black--but wait until you see the New Jerusalem. It is going to light up God's new heavens and new earth as they have never been lighted before.[247] The light of God's glory will shine throughout the entire city.

The city is described as a jasper stone as clear as crystal. The light shinning from within through the jasper stone, acting as a prism would give every color and shade of color in the rainbow--colors that you I have not even thought of yet. The presence of the primary colors suggests that every shade and tint is reflected from this city. A rainbow that appears after a summer shower gives only a faint impression of the beauty in the coloring of the city of light. Oh, what a glorious place this is![248]

Glory of God Illuminates the City

Then he (the angel) showed me a river of the water of life, clear as crystal, coming from the throne of God and of the Lamb, in the middle of its street. On either side of the river was the tree of life, bearing twelve *kinds of* fruit, yielding its fruit every month; and the leaves of the tree were for the healing of the nations. There will no longer be any curse; and the throne of God and of the Lamb will be in it, and His bond-servants will serve Him; they will see His face, and His name *will be* on their foreheads. There will no longer be *any* night; and they will not have need of the light of a lamp nor the light of the sun, because the Lord God will illumine them; and they will reign forever and ever (Revelation 22:1-5 NASB).

In this scripture, there is a river flowing from the throne of God and a garden similar to the Garden of Eden. Man was prevented from eating the Tree of Life in the Garden of Eden. In eternity, man is now allowed to eat from the Tree of Life, which symbolizes abundant life.

"He who overcomes, I will make him a pillar in the temple of My God, and he shall go out no more. And I will write on him the name of My God and the name of the city of My God, the New Jerusalem, which comes down out of heaven from My God. I will write on him My new name" (Revelation 3:12).

We long for a return to Paradise—a perfect world, without the corruption of sin, where God walks with us and talks with us in the cool of the day. Because we are human beings, we desire something tangible and physical, something that will not fade away. And that is exactly what God promises us—a home that will not be destroyed, a kingdom that will not fade, a city with unshakeable foundations, an incorruptible inheritance.[249]

❯ CHAPTER 24
FINAL JUDGMENT

East is east and west is west, and never the twain shall meet, 'Till earth and sky stand presently at God's great judgment seat.
Rudyard Kipling, the English poet

By nature God is holy, just and loving. He is longsuffering and desires to show mercy. Because of God's nature, many people believe that God will never judge mankind. Jesus Christ took upon Himself the sin of all mankind at his death on the cross. Believers who trust in Christ, repent of their sins will not be condemned, but will receive eternal life.

As human being, we have a terminal disease called *mortality*. The current death rate is 100 percent. Unless Christ returns soon, we're all going to die. We don't like to think about death; yet, worldwide, three people die every second, 180 every minute, and nearly 11,000 every hour. If the Bible is right about what happens to us after death, it means that more than 250,000 people every day go to either to heaven or hell.[250]

Jesus said in Matthew 7:13-14: "Enter by the narrow gate; for wide *is* the gate and broad *is* the way that leads to destruction, and there are many who go in by it. Because narrow *is* the gate and difficult *is* the way which leads to life, and there are few who find it".

Many people today have been deceived into believing that if their good works outweigh their evil works they will escape judgment. God's judgment may not be speedily carried out, but you can be sure that Judgment Day is coming and the ungodly will not escape.

God Destroyed the Ancient World by a Flood

"Most importantly, I want to remind you that in the last days scoffers will come, mocking the truth and following their own desires. They will say, 'What happened to the promise that Jesus is coming again? From before the times of our ancestors, everything has remained the same since the world was first created.' They deliberately forget that God made the heavens by the word of his command, and he brought the earth out from the water and surrounded it with water. Then he used the water to destroy the ancient world with a mighty flood. By the same word, the present heavens and earth have been stored up for fire. They are being kept for the day of judgment, when ungodly people will be destroyed'" (2 Peter 3:3-7 NLT).

We need to remember that God destroyed the wicked leaving only Noah and his family on this earth. This earth is being preserved until God pours out His judgment and destroys the heavens and earth with fire along with all the ungodly.

There will be a final judgment, with the reward of eternal life promised to the redeemed and eternal loss in hell to the unregenerate.

"If God did not spare angels when they sinned, but cast them into hell and committed them to pits of darkness, reserved for judgment; and did not spare the ancient world, but preserved Noah, a preacher of righteousness, with seven others, when He brought a flood upon the world of the ungodly; and if He condemned the cities of Sodom and Gomorrah to destruction by reducing them to ashes, having made them an example to those who would live ungodly lives thereafter; and if He rescued righteous Lot, oppressed by the sensual conduct of unprincipled men for by what he saw and heard that righteous man, while living among them, felt his righteous soul tormented day after day by their lawless deeds), then the Lord knows how to rescue the godly from temptation, and to keep the unrighteous under punishment for the Day of Judgment " (2 Peter 2:4-9 NASB).

God is so wonderfully kind, patient and tolerant with people. The awesome magnitude of His love was manifested on the cross, when God's only Son experienced the wrath for our sins. But don't forget that His kindness is intended to turn our hearts to repentance. If you fail to repent; you are storing up terrible punishment for yourself.

Christ, who was without sin, died on the cross for the sins on the world. Believers can rely upon the righteousness of God because our sins were atoned for at Calvary. God doesn't want anyone to perish, but He desire everyone to turn to Him in repentance. When you repent and receive Christ, as your personal Savior, you are justified by His blood and God's wrath will not fall on you. If you fail to put your trust in Christ for forgiveness, your sins will be judged. Do not think that you will escape, if you neglect this great salvation!

"He (God) will give eternal life to those who keep on doing good, seeking after the glory and honor and immortality that God offers. But he will pour out his anger and wrath on those who live for themselves, who refuse to obey the truth and instead live lives of wickedness. There will be trouble and calamity for everyone who keeps on doing what is evil—for the Jew first and also for the Gentile. There will be glory and honor and peace from God for all who do good, for the Jew first and also for the Gentile" (Romans 2:6-10 NLT).

God's Wrath on Unrighteousness

"The wrath of God is revealed from heaven against all ungodliness and unrighteousness of men, who by their unrighteousness suppress the truth. For what can be known about God is plain to them, because God has shown it to them. For his invisible attributes, namely, his eternal power and divine nature have been clearly perceived, ever since the creation of the world, in the things that have been made.

So they are without excuse. Although they knew God, they did not honor him as God or give thanks to him, but they became futile in their thinking, and their foolish hearts were darkened" (Romans 1:18-21 ESV).

Judgments in God's Word

Type of Judgment	Scriptures
Judgment of the Cross	Romans 8:34
Judgment of Angels	1 Corinthians 6:3; 2 Peter 2:4
Judgment of the Church	1 Corinthians 5:13
Judgment Seat of Christ	Romans 14:10; 2 Cor. 5:10
Sheep and Goat Judgment	Matthew 25:32-46
Great White Throne Judgment	Revelation 20:11-15

The Judgment Seat of Christ

"Therefore, God elevated him (Jesus Christ) to the place of highest honor and gave him the name above all other names, that at the name of Jesus every knee should bow, in heaven and on earth and under the earth, and every tongue declare that Jesus Christ is Lord, to the glory of God the Father" (Philippians 2:9-11 NLT).

"Most assuredly, I say to you, he who hears My word and believes in Him who sent Me has everlasting life, and shall not come into judgment, but has passed from death into life" (John 5:24).

The Judgment Seat of Christ does not determine salvation. Believers will be rewarded according to how faithfully they have walked with the Lord, and obeyed his commands.

- How is your prayer life (Matthew 6:6)?
- Have you shared the gospel with non-believers (Matthew 28:18-20)?
- Have you showed concern for the needy (Matthew 25:34-40)?
- How well have you controlled your tongue (James 3:1-9)?
- Have you lived victoriously over sin (Romans 6:1-4)?

Judgment of the righteous dead is called the Judgment Seat of Christ or the Bema Judgment. It is not a judgment for sin. Judgment for sin occurred on earth when the believer became aware of sin in his life and proclaimed Christ as Lord.

The believer is judged in the person and cross of Christ (2 Corinthians. 5:21).[251]

While the resurrected righteous are being rewarded, the unrighteous dead are still in Sheol-Hades. They will not be resurrected until it is time for the Great White Throne Judgment following the Millennium (Revelation 20:11-15). Even though both the righteous and unrighteous dead are resurrected, the events are more than a thousand years apart.[252]

The judgment of the unrighteous dead comes at the end of time as man counts time. According to the Bible, at the end of the millennium, Satan will be released from bondage "for a season." He will entice the nations of the earth to gather together in a great war against Christ and His celestial host. Satan's efforts will fail and lead to final judgment for him and those who have followed him. Resurrection of the unrighteous dead of all ages will occur at this time (Revelation 20:5). They will stand before God in judgment—the small and great, famous and infamous, important and insignificant, citizen and king (Revelation 20:12). No one escapes the searching eye of the eternal judge.[253]

The Ungodly will face Christ as Judge

God's role as judge is reflected in the leadership functions of political officials, who uphold order in society and execute judgment on evildoers. The rulers of Israel bore special responsibility in this respect as do the leaders of the church today. Believers also have a responsibility to judge matters of wrongdoing among themselves, but this should always be done fairly and with compassion. Believers are never to take over the task of judgment that belongs to God alone.[254]

Great White Throne Judgment

"Then I (John) saw a great white throne and Him who sat on it, from whose face the earth and the heaven fled away. And there was found no place for them. And I saw the dead, small and great, standing before God, and books were opened. And another book was opened, which is the Book of Life. And the dead were judged according to their works, by the things which were written in the books. The sea gave up the dead who were in it, and Death and Hades delivered up the dead who were in them. And they were judged, each one according to his works. Then Death and Hades were cast into the lake of fire. This is the second death…Anyone not found written in the Book of Life was cast into the lake of fire" (Revelation 20:11-15)

The Great White Throne Judgment is the final judgment, the ultimate separation of good and evil at the end of history. It is the most dreadful and hopeless of all. This judgment occurs after the Great Tribulation, the resurrection of the dead and the Second Coming of Jesus Christ at the end of time.[255]

Law courts have witnessed some tense and terrible scenes, but the most famous and fearful of these pale into insignificance alongside the staggering scene of the final judgment we are now to consider. This judgment, which occurs after the Millennium and the final disposition of Satan and the present heavens and earth, will be the most solemn and awful ever witnessed. At last the eternal judge is to settle all accounts. Having dealt with Satan, the god of the world, Christ now prepares to deal with the sinners of the world. At last the end of the world is reached, for creation flees from the face of the One sitting upon the throne. Some refer to this as a general judgment, but Revelation knows no general judgment. Any judgment in this book is particular. All people from all ages of earth's history, whether good or bad, are not to gather at this great scene. It is only the wicked dead, just as the judgment of Christ is only for believers.[256]

What kind of throne is this one, set up not on earth or in the heavens? It is not the throne of a sovereign about to reign and rule, but that of a judge about to pronounce doom upon the guilty. Set up for a specific purpose, it is not a permanent throne, for it ceases to be as soon as its judgments have been meted out to the condemned. At this throne the position in Pilate's day will be reversed; then the Creator was judged by the creature, but now the creature appears before the Creator for sentencing. In Pilate's hall Jesus stood speechless before man, but here man is speechless before God. He who stood condemned before the earthly tribunal will now decide the destinies of the human race and will reveal the principles of divine government.[257]

The White Throne Judgment will be nothing like our modern court cases. At the White Throne, there will be a judge, but no jury, a prosecution but no defense, a sentence but no appeal. No one will be able to defend himself or accuse God of unrighteousness. What an awesome scene it will be![258]

Having rejected the great salvation offered by Christ, sinners are now made to stand before God's Great White Throne. It will be great for several reasons; because of the dignity of the Judge Himself: because of the greatness and unparalleled solemnity of the occasion; because of the vastness of the scene; here is the dawn of eternity; because of the eternal consequences involved; and because of the great destinies it will decide.[259]

The throne corresponds to the character of its Occupant, "The Lord reigns forever; he has established his throne for judgment. He will judge the world in righteousness" (Psalm 9:7–8). The Infinite One, before whom the finite must stand, is holy and righteous in the day of God's wrath, when his righteous judgment will be revealed" (Romans 2:5). There will be no unfair, unjust treatment, such as He Himself received at Pilate's hands. Being white, the throne symbolized the purity and righteousness of the judgment of the Judge. It is white because of its immaculate purity. Here we have the undimmed blaze of divine holiness, purity, and justice. How terrible it will be for sinners to face to unapproachable light of the Lord's presence![260]

Hell is the final judgment of God upon the wicked. A classic example of eternal punishment is the destruction of Sodom and Gomorrah. In the New Testament, Jude compared the wicked men of Sodom and Gomorrah, with those who will suffer the vengeance of eternal fire.

Everlasting Punishment

"Then the King will turn to those on the left and say, 'Away with you, you curse ones, into the eternal fire prepared for the devil and his demons'" (Matthew 25:41 NLT).

Hell fire was prepared for the devil and his angels. God never wanted anyone to go to hell. Hell is described as a lake of eternal fire that shall never be quenched, where there will be wailing and gnashing of teeth. Full consciousness will make the anguish worse. There will be probation, no purgatory and no escape.

God is a just God, yet the scriptures teach that God will punish ungodly men with eternal punishment. Today people believe that God is a loving and merciful and they find it hard to believe that God will punish the lost. Men ask the question, "Why does God who is so good, punish men in eternity without a moment's rest?"

Hell is described as the second death. The second death is final, where the spirit is eternally separated from God. Anyone whose name is not written in the Lamb's Book of Life will be cast into the lake of fire" (Revelation 20:15). They will be joined with the Antichrist, the False Prophet and the Devil and be tormented day and night forever and ever.

The greatest sin is rejecting God's Plan of Salvation through Jesus Christ. Let's share the joys of knowing God with others, so they will accept Christ and receive eternal life.

Conclusion

The final Day of Judgment will not result in annihilation of the present order but rather a complete renewal of that order. What will be annihilated is sin; thus the new creation will be the dwelling place of righteousness, a truly blissful home for the children of God. The promise gives the Christian hope and encouragement to remain steadfast in righteousness until the day of the Lord.[261]

❯CHAPTER 25
HORRORS OF ETERNAL HELL

Every day people Google the question, "Is Hell Real?" According to the Bible, hell is very real and the road to destruction is wide. Jesus said, "You can enter God's Kingdom only through the narrow gate. The highway to hell is broad, and its gate is wide for the many that choose that way. But the gateway to life is very narrow and the road is difficult, and only a few ever find it" (Matthew 7:13-14 NLT).

God's Word says that there are two eternal destinations, not one, and we must choose the right road. Jesus said, "No one comes to the Father except through me" (John 14:6). All other roads lead to hell. The Bible teaches that hell will be the destiny of all who reject God's plan of salvation provided through the shed blood of Jesus Christ.

Because God is the source of all good, and hell is the absence of God, Hell must also be the absence of all good. Likewise, community, fellowship, and friendship are good, rooted in the triune God himself. But in the absence of God, hell will have no community, no camaraderie, and no friendship. I don't believe hell is a place where demons take delight in punishing people and where people commiserate over their fate. More likely, each person is in solitary confinement, just as the rich man is portrayed along in hell.[262]

Different Concepts about Hell

The hottest contemporary debates among evangelicals center on question that Christians have struggled with for centuries. Are the "fires" of hell to be understood literally or as a metaphor for something else? Do the torments of damnation last forever, or are the wicked finally destroyed? Are all the people who never had a change even to hear the gospel eternally damned, or do they get a chance to be saved after death?[263]

Judaism's Concept of Hell

In Judaism, the idea of a literal hell has been widely rejected since the 18th century, when Moses Mendelssohn, an influential German philosopher, reasoned that eternal punishment is inconsistent with God's mercy. With the exception of the Orthodox, belief in an afterlife in heaven or hell has all but disappeared from modern Judaism.[264]

Islam's Concept of Hell

In Islam, hell is a crater of fire beneath a narrow bridge that all souls must cross to go to paradise. Those whom Allah judges unworthy fall in and suffer endless physical torments in one of seven layers of hell. The Koran uses Bible-like imagery to describe hell's attributes. It is a "lake of fire," a "burning bed of misery" where the wicked and infidels suffer endlessly, apart from God, with only "boiling, fetid water" to drink.[265]

Pope John Paul II's Concept of Hell

Pope John Paul II said, "Hell is not a place, but a state, a person's state of being, in which a person suffers from the deprivation of God. Rather than a place, hell indicates the state of those who freely and definitely separate themselves from God."

America's Concept of Hell

A U.S. News poll shows that more Americans believe in hell today than did in the 1960s or even 10 years ago. But like the pope, most now think of hell as "an anguished state of existence" rather than as a real place.[266]

Several years ago, Time magazine devoted its cover story to the question of eternity or the afterlife. The results of a Time/CNN poll found that 81% of Americans believe in the existence of heaven. Sixty-three percent of Americans believe that hell exists, although only one percent believes they'll go there. Belief in life after death is still a large part of the American culture.

Sheol, Abode of the Dead

Sheol is an Old Testament word that is thought to be a gloomy, underground region. It is Hebrew word for the place of departed spirits. It is mentioned over 65 times in the New American Standard Bible but is not mentioned in many of the newer translations. It is often translated as hell, grave or pit.

Sheol is generally thought to be "the unseen world" or the abode of the dead. It is the place where the righteous and unrighteous go at death. The Old Testament refers to the body going to the grave, but the soul or spirit of man goes to Sheol.

Sheol is used to refer to both the righteous (Psalm 16:10) and unrighteous (Numbers 16:33). When Lucifer desired to be like God, he was sent down to Sheol, which was described as the lowest depths of the Pit (Isaiah 14:12-15).

The body is never said to be in Sheol or Hades and the spirit is never said to be in the grave. So Sheol and Hades are used consistently in the two testaments to refer to the abode of dead spirits. The grave is just the depository where the body deteriorates and returns to the original dust.[267]

Hades

Hades is the New Testament equivalent to Sheol. It was the place when the spirit of the dead went at death, awaiting the resurrection. Hades consisted of two compartments—Paradise and Torment. There was a fixed gulf that no one could cross over. At death, the righteous went to Paradise while the ungodly went to Torment.

Abraham's Bosom, a compartment in Hades, was a holding place for the righteous, until the death of Jesus. After the resurrection, Jesus emptied Abraham's Bosom, from the heart of the earth, and set the captives free. When believers die now, their spirits go directly to heaven.

Jesus said to the repentant thief on the cross, "Truly I say to you, today you shall me with me in Paradise" (Luke 23:43).

Hell was originally prepared for Satan and His Angels

"The the King will turn to those on the left and say, 'Away with you, you cursed ones, into the eternal fire prepared for the devil and his demons" (Matthew 25:41 NLT).

Some people have the concept that Satan created hell and will be wearing a red suit and carrying a pitch fork. Actually, hell was originally created by God for the devil and his angels to put an end to sin and rebellion. It will be the final abode of the wicked and those who reject God's gracious plan of salvation.

Hell, A Place of Outer Darkness

Our Lord refers to hell as a place of "outer darkness" three times in Matthew's Gospel (Matthew 8:12; 22:13; 25:30). Could this be a spiritual realm into which the light of God never shines? It speaks of physical darkness, in which lost souls grope in terror.

Hell is a place of unrelieved torment and horrible misery. It is a place of impenetrable darkness without light. Have you ever been in the darkness of night and longed for daylight, or been in a dark room and wanted light? Darkness will encompass those who will be in hell for eternity; there will be no hope of ever seeing light.[268]

When our family visited Carlsbad's Caverns in New Mexico, we took a tour of the caves and followed the guide down through rooms of beautiful crystal white stalactites and stalagmites. At one point in the tour, the guide had all the people sit down. When he turned all the lights off, we couldn't see anything, not even our hand in front of our face. I can't imagine the horrors of spending eternity without any light.

Parable Concerning Eternity

"The Kingdom of Heaven can be illustrated by a fisherman—he casts a net into the water and gathers in fish of every kind, valuable and worthless. When the net is full, he drags it up onto the beach and sits down and sorts out the edible ones into crates and throws the others away. That is the way it will be at the end of the world—the angels will come and separate the wicked people from the godly, casting the wicked into the fire; there shall be weeping and gnashing of teeth. Do you understand" (Matthew 13:47-51 TLB)?

Our Lord told this parable that describes the time between his resurrection and return. He allows the wicked and righteous to grow together. He tolerates the evil in the world for this period of time. But someday there will come a time of judgment. At the end of time, God will judge the wicked and condemn them to eternal damnation.

Hell will exist for All Eternity

"These will go away into everlasting punishment, but the righteous into eternal life" (Matthew 25:46 NASB).

The wicked...shall be tormented with fire and brimstone in the presence of the holy angels, and in the presence of the Lamb. The smoke of their torment ascends up forever and ever. They will have no rest day or night, those who worship the beast and his image, and whoever receives the mark of his name" (Revelation 14:10-11 NASB).

The Lord speaks of hell as "everlasting punishment". It is a permanent fate confirmed by the book of Revelation, which described damnation this way: "They will be tormented day and night forever and ever" (Revelation 20:10).

We cannot, perhaps, know what that entire passage means, but it certainly speaks of an unending state of destruction and unceasing death. Hell grants no furloughs and no time off for good behavior. No bribes are accepted. The prayers of the living cannot shorten hell by one split second or alleviate its horror by a degree.[269]

Jesus said that the unrighteous will go away to eternal, everlasting punishment. The essential meaning of the phrase everlasting punishment involves banishment from the presence of God and Christ forever-- a fate worse than death.

Another word that expresses eternity is endlessness. Endlessness is the aspect of hell that reveals that it has no end. After the wicked have suffering millions of years, it will never end. It may be difficult to comprehend that the wicked deserve eternal hell for rejecting the salvation God so graciously provided, but God's Word is true.

Hell is a place of suffering, separation, remorse and divine wrath. There will be no break from the torment, no rest day or night. There will no comfort, no love, no light, and no escape. The misery of hell has absolutely no end. There will be hope of ever escaping.

The wicked will beg for annihilation, but will find none. The Bible teaches eternal punishment just the same as it teaches eternal life. The wicked will earnestly wish to die, so they can escape the wrath of God.

There are two emotional prospects that help keep you stable on earth. They are rest and hope. In hell there is neither rest nor hope. There will be no break from the torment. There will be no break from the flame. There will be no break from the fire. There will be no rest. I pray no one goes to this awful place.[270]

Bottomless Pit or Abyss

"Their king is the angel from the bottomless pit; his name in Hebrew is Abaddon, and in Greek, Apollyon—the Destroyer" (Revelation 9:11 NLT).

Hell is described as the Abyss or the bottomless pit. If you go to that horrible place you'll never touch anything solid. You will be suspended in outer darkness for all eternity. It is the place of disobedient spirits, the world of the dead.

At the present time, Satan and a large number of demons roam in the world, but some fallen angels have been locked in the Abyss, or Bottomless Pit, a deep chasm. They will be judged and consigned to Gehenna, the lake of fire. When Jesus cast the demons out of the man from the Gadarenes, the demons begged not to be sent to the Abyss.

The apostle Peter described this dungeon for the damned angels. "God did not spare even the angels who sinned. He threw them into hell, in gloomy pits of darkness, where they are being held until the Day of Judgment" (2 Peters 2:4 NLT).

During the Millennial Reign of Christ, Satan will be bound for 1,000 year in the Abyss. "I saw an Angel descending out of Heaven. He carried the key to the Abyss and a chain—a huge chain. He grabbed the Dragon, that old Snake— the very Devil, Satan himself!—chained him up for a thousand years, dumped him into the Abyss, slammed it shut and sealed it tight. No more trouble out of him, deceiving the nations—until the thousand years are up. After that he has to be let loose briefly" (Revelation 20:1-3 MSG).

The Lake of Fire

Jesus called the final hell, Gehenna. Gehenna is a Greek term (borrowed from a literal burning dump near Jerusalem) that always refers to hell, a place of torment. It refers to the Valley of Hinnom, a place where dead bodies were burned during the time of King Josiah (2 Kings 23:10). It denotes the eternal state of the lost after the resurrection.

The Lake of Fire is the future home of all who rebel against God. The wicked will be judged at the Great White Throne Judgment and consigned to Gehenna, the Lake of Fire, along with Satan, and the fallen angels. They will forever suffer the torments of eternal Hell.

Who Goes to Hell?

"The cowardly and unbelieving and abominable and murderers and immoral persons and sorcerers and idolaters, and all liars will be in the lake which burns with fire and brimstone" (Revelation 21:8 NASB).

The Bible gives us a great deal of information regarding who will go to hell. Only the people who repent of their sins and accept Christ can be sure they will avoid hell. "The wicked shall be turned into hell, and all the nations that forget God" (Psalm 9:17).

People need to realize that eternal joy in heaven awaits all who turn to Christ in repentance and accept Christ's payment for sin. Eternal torment in hell awaits those who reject Christ.

If statistics are correct, over 6,000 people in the United States will die today and go into eternity. Jesus said, "Heaven can be entered only through the narrow gate! The highway to hell is broad and its gate is wide enough for all the multitudes that chose its easy way. The Gateway to Life is small, and the road is narrow, and only a few ever find it" (Matthew 7:13–14 TLB).

Pray the following prayer: "Lord Jesus, I need you. I repent of my sins. I accept you as my Lord and Savior. Make me the person you want me to be. God is faithful to forgive all your sins and cleanse you from your unrighteousness.

❯ CHAPTER 26
WONDERS OF HEAVEN

"We are citizens of heaven, where the Lord Jesus Christ lives and we are eagerly waiting for him to return as our Savior. He will take our weak mortal bodies and change them into glorious bodies like his own, using the same power with which he will bring everything under his control" (Philippians 3:20-21 NLT).

God loves us enough to tell us the truth—there are two eternal destinations, not one, and we must choose the right path if we are to go to Heaven. Only one does: Jesus Christ said, "No one comes to the Father except through me" (John 14:6). All other roads lead to hell. The high stakes involved in the choice between Heaven and Hell will cause us to appreciate Heaven in deeper ways, never taking it for granted, and always praising God for his grace that delivers us from what we deserve and grants us forever what we don't.[271]

Jesus made it extremely clear that most people are not going to heaven. He said, "Enter through the narrow gate. For wide is the gate and broad is the road that leads to destruction, and many enter through it. But small is the gate and narrow the wary that leads to life, and only a few find it" (Matthew 7:13-14 NIV).

Since there is only one way to Heaven, make sure you have a reservation. You must have your name written down in the Lamb's Book of Life. No one else will be admitted.

The Hope of Eternal Life

"All praise to God, the Father of our Lord Jesus Christ. It is by his great mercy that we have been born again, because God raised Jesus Christ from the dead. Now we live with great expectation, and we have a priceless inheritance—an inheritance that is kept in heaven for you, pure and undefiled, beyond the reach of change and decay. And through your faith, God is protecting you by his power until you receive this salvation, which is ready to be revealed on the last day for all to see" (1 Peter 1:3-5 NLT).

The doctrine of heaven was enormously important to the church until recent years. The Bible was considered the undisputed Word of God with certainly of judgment, the longing for a heavenly home and the dread of hell. This is no longer the case for many people today. People are attempting to chart their path in this world without a fixed point of reference.

There is a farm in the center of the United States. On that farm is a monument marking the exact point of the geographical center of our nation. It is a fixed reference point from which all other geographical points in the nation can be measured. Each of us has his reference point and for me as a Christian, the reference point by which I measure my life is through the Bible, the Holy Scriptures of the Old and New Testament.[272]

Heavenly Minded

"You have been raised with Christ, set your hearts on things above, where Christ is seated at the right hand of God. Set your minds on things above, not on earthly things, for you died, and your life is now hidden with Christ in God. When Christ, who is your life appears, you also will appear with him in glory" (Colossians 3:1-2 NIV).

Many people today spend their time collecting material possessions, seeking worldly pleasures, and trying to keep up with the Jones. They live as they expect to live here forever and make little preparation for eternity. Little is thought of gathering eternal possessions. Only eternity will demonstrate eternal possessions that are stored up.

The Psalmist wrote; "Lord, remind me how brief my time on earth will be. Remind me that my days are numbered--how fleeting my life it. You have made my life no longer than the width of my hand. My entire lifetime is just a moment to you" (Psalm 39:4-5 NLT).

Heavenly Bodies

"We are children of God now, and what we will be has not yet appeared; but we know that when He appears, we shall be like Him, for we shall see Him as He is" (1 John 3:2 ESV).

At death, our mortal bodies die, but our soul continues to live. At the resurrection we will receive our heavenly bodies which are spiritual, imperishable bodies suited to live eternally. Our glorified body will be similar to our present physical body, but much more glorious and suited for eternity. We will be able to eat and drink, just as Christ did after the resurrection. We will never experience suffering, pain, sickness or death. Imagine never being tired or weary!

Heaven's Joy

We are promised that Christ will be able to keep us from stumbling and present us faultless before His presence with great joy. When His glory is revealed, we will have exceedingly great joy. We need to remember that the sufferings of this present age are as nothing compared to the glory that will be revealed to us.

The greatest joy in heaven will be seeing God. I can't imagine what it would be like to see our Lord face to face and continually experience His presence and glory. No words can express what great joy this will be! Heaven will be a place of unspeakable joy.

Heaven is a city without pain, a city without sorrow, without sickness, without death. There is no darkness there. The Lamb is the light thereof. It needs no sun, it needs no moon. The paradise of Eden was as nothing compared with this one. The tempter came into Eden and triumphed, but in that city nothing that defiles shall ever enter. There will be no temper there. Think of a place where temptation cannot come.[273]

Think of a place where we will be free from sin; where pollution cannot enter, and where the righteous shall reign forever. Think of a city that is not built with hands, where the buildings do not grow old with time; a city whose inhabitants no census has numbered except the Book of Life, which is a heavenly directory. Think of a city through whose streets runs no tide of business, where no nodding hearses creep slowly with their burdens to the tomb; a city without griefs or graves, without sins or sorrows, without marriage or mourning, without births or burials; a city which glories in having Jesus for its king, angels for its guards, and whose citizens are saints![274]

Henry Lockyer said, "If you have a dear one in Heaven your heart yearns to see, do not despair, for you will meet again. The voice you loved to hear, you will hear again. The identity of the one you were near to on Earth remains the same and instant recognition will be yours as you meet, never to part again. Your beloved one is only lost awhile".

Heavenly Rewards

"Now if anyone builds on this foundation with gold, silver, precious stones, wood, hay, straw, each one's work will become clear; for the Day will declare it, because it will be revealed by fire; and the fire will test each one's work, of what sort it is. Is anyone's work which he has built on it endues, he will receive a reward. If anyone's work is burned, he will suffer lost; but he himself will be saved, yet so as through fire" (1 Corinthians 3:12-15).

Gold, silver and precious stones indicate heavenly works, good works that God honors – Dedicated spiritual service to the Lord. Wood, hay and stubble indicate inferior works, because these are inferior materials – Shallow activities with no real value.

Crowns that Believers can Win

1. The Incorruptible or Victor's Crown (1 Corinthians 9:14, 25, 27)
2. The Crown of Life (Revelation 2:10) Called the Martyr's Crown
3. The Crown of Righteousness (2 Timothy 4:8)
4. The Crown of Glory (1 Peter 5:2-4).
5. The Crown of Rejoicing or Soul Winner's Crown (1 Thessalonians 2:19-20)

Heavenly Activities

What will we be doing in heaven? Paul tells us that we were created for good works. We will have all eternity to serve the Lord. Since we are the bride of Christ, we will be given great authority in the kingdom, reigning with Christ.

I believe that our talents will be magnified. Whatever your talent, you will be able to use it to the glory of God, whether it be singing, painting, organizing, writing or teaching. Possibly we will be able to explore the universe. It will be greater than Star Wars!

Have you ever wondered how God could keep a record of everything regarding each person here on earth? The massive storage space of modern computers gives us a better concept of this ability. Could God have kept videos of major events in history, like the crossing of the Red Sea, the Great Flood, and the Jewish Temple? We may be able to check these out in God's library.

In heaven there is continual worship of God before His throne in heaven. There are twenty-four elders sitting around the throne of God. They are clothed in white robes with crowns of gold on their heads, each having a harp to worship God. They worship Him who lives forever and ever.

"The twenty-four elders fall down before Him who sits on the throne and worship Him who lives forever and ever, and cast their crowns before the throne, saying: 'You are worthy, O Lord, to receive glory and honor and power; For You created all things, and by Your will they exist and were created" (Revelation 4:10-11).

In heaven there will be choirs of angels. Perhaps there will be fabulous choirs and symphony orchestras worshipping before the Throne of God. Billions of angels and the redeemed will praise God together. If you like feasts and music, you can look forward to great adventure in heaven.

Will I have Family in Heaven?

All Christians are part of God's family, but there is no reason to feel there could not be families in heaven. There will no longer be human procreation in heaven thus requiring the necessity of mating and child bearing. We will probably not be separate family units like husbands, wife and children, although all your family who are believers will be in heaven with you. We as one gigantic family are heirs of God and joint heirs with Jesus Christ. God's Word makes it clear that we will know each other in heaven.

Our entire family, who are believers, will be there. All our relatives, children, parents, ancestors and Christian friends will share Heaven's glory. We will have all eternity to spend together with Christ and other believers. Heaven will be the greatest family reunion we've ever known. We will be able to meet our ancestors whom we have never met. In heaven there will be no good-bys.

We will be able to make new friends and meet those we have read about in the scriptures. What an adventure to speak with Biblical characters, disciples and those who lived long ago! Imagine meeting Christ and having Him say to you; "Well done, thy good and faithful servant".

Heavenly Knowledge

"Now we see things imperfectly, like puzzling reflections in a mirror, but then we will see everything with perfect clarity. All that I know now is partial and incomplete, but then I will know everything completely, just as God now knows me completely" (1 Corinthians 13:12 NLT).

In heaven our knowledge will be greatly increased. We will have much greater insight and fuller knowledge of spiritual things. All our questions will be answered. We will have no greater reward or relationship than being with our wonderful God and seeing him face to face. There will be no good-byes in heaven.

The only inhabitants in the New Jerusalem will be God, Jesus Christ and His bride. This includes all who have their name is in the Lamb's Book of Life. This book contained the names of all redeemed believers from the beginning of time. This paradise, this marvelous Heavenly City that has been prepared for believers, is described in the last two chapters of Revelation. It is so breathtakingly beautiful that it is indescribable.

Everything that is evil will disappear and everything that is good and true will prevail. "Nothing impure will ever enter it, nor will anyone who does what is shameful or deceitful, but only those whose names are written in the Lamb's Book of Life" (Revelation 21:27 NIV).

Some glorious day our heavenly Father will say, "Come you who are blessed by our Heavenly Father, inherit the Kingdom prepared for you from the foundation of the world".

Conclusion

If you're a Christian suffering with great pain and loss, be of good cheer. The new house is nearly ready for you. Moving day is coming. The dark winter is about to be magically transformed into spring. One day soon you will be home—for the first time. Until then, I encourage you to meditate on the Bible's truths about Heaven. Let your imagination soar and your heart rejoice.[275]

Victory for Martyrs

Martyred believers will give glory to God when they sing the last song recorded in God's Word. "Great and marvelous *are* your works, O Lord God, the Almighty. Just and true *are* your ways, O King of the nations. Who will not fear you, Lord, and glorify thy name? For you alone *are* holy. All nations will come and worship before you; for your righteous deeds have been revealed" (Revelation 15:3–4 NLT). The kingdom of this world will become the Kingdom of our God and His Messiah! He will rule forever and ever! Even so, come Lord Jesus!

End Notes

› Chapter 1 Endnotes- Prophecies in Genesis

1   Dr. James Kennedy, *The Real Meaning of the Zodiac*, TCRM
    Publishing, Ft. Lauderdale: 1993), 9.
2   Ibid. 9.
3   Women's Study Bible, Thomas Nelson Publishers, 1979, p. 17.
4   http:///www.bible-truth.org/GEN12HTM
5   J. Vernon McGee, Thru the Bible with J. Vernon McGee, Vol. 5, p. 884
6   http://gracethrufaith.com/selah/as-it-was-in-the-days-of-noah
7   Ibid.

› Chapter 2 Endnotes- Living in the Day of Noah

8   Genesis 6:11-13 ESV.
9   John Funk, *The Days of Noah*, http://www.raptureready.com/featured/funk/noah.html
10   J. L. Robb, http://www.omegaletter.com/articles/articles.asp?ArticleID=7571
11   Merrill F. Unger, *Unger's Bible Dictionary*, (Chicago: Moody Press, 1977, 392.
12   Ibid. 757.
13   www.matthewmcgee.org
14   John Funk, Ibid.

› Chapter 3 Endnotes - God's Covenant with Abram

15   John F. Walvoord, Every Prophecy of the Bible, David C. Cook, 1999, 25.
16   J. Vernon McGee, *Thru the Bible with J. Vernon McGee*, Thru the Bible Radio, Vol. 1, 58.
17   http://www.bible-truth.org/GEN12.HTM
18   Henry H. Halley, *Halley's Bible Handbook* (Grand Rapids: Zondervan Pub), 95.
19   *The Patriarchs and the Origins of Judaism*; http://www.jewfaq.org/index.htm.
20   Ibid.
21   http://blog.beliefnet.com/kingdomofpriests/2009/04/canaanites-for-same-sex-marriage.html#ixz-z10uTL8dFF
22   J. Vernon McKee, Thru the Bible with J. Vernon McKee, Vol. 1 (Pasadena, CA: 1981) 57.
23   Lance Lambert, Israel, *The Unique Land: The Unique People* (Wheaton: Living Books, Tyndall Publishers, 1981, 173.
24   Ibid. 174.

› Chapter 4 Endnotes - Deliverance from Egyptian Bondage

25   H. H. Halley, Halley's Bible Handbook, (Grand Rapids, Zondervan Publishing, 122.
26   Ibid. 121.
27   Clem Clack, *The Bible in Focus*, (Blackburn: Donors, Inc. 1981), 42.
28   John Hagee, His Glory Revealed, (Nashville: Thomas Nelson Pub., 1999), 7.

› Chapter 5 Endnotes – Battle for Jerusalem and Temple Mount

29   Mike Evans, *Jerusalem Betrayed*, (Dallas: Word Publishing, 1997), 114.
30   Jim Gerrish, *The Uniqueness of Israel*, http://biministry.org/article.php?nbr=001
31   John Hagee, *Jerusalem Countdown* (Lake Mary: FRONT LINE, A Strang Communication, 2006), 32.
32   Evans, 129.
33   Ibid. 128.

34   John McTernan, *Israel, God's Anvil*, http://www.focusonjerusalem.com/IsraelGodsAnvil.html
35   Ibid.
36   Dennis Lindsey, *Israel: the Nation of Destiny*, (Maoz Israel Report, August 2007).
37   Ibid.

› Chapter 6 Endnotes – Jewish Temple

38   Paul L. Maier, Josephus, The Essential Writings, Kregel Publications, Grand Rapids, 1988, 247.
39   Mike Evans, *Jerusalem Betrayed* (Dallas: Word Publishing, Dallas). 105-106
40   Unger, Merrill F. *Unger's Bible Dictionary. Chicago, Illinois. Moody Press. pp. 1089-1081.*
41   Unger, 1080.
42   Unger, 1080-1081.
43   http://judaism.about.com/od/holidays/a/tishabav.htm
44   http://www.wujs.org.il/activist/learning/months/av.shtml
45   http://judaism.about.com/od/holidays/a/tishabav.htm
46   Lance Lambert, *Israel, The Unique Land- The Unique People,* (Wheaton: Tyndale Pub., 1981), 161-162.
47   Clarence Wagner, http://focusonjerusalem.com/significantfacts.htm
48   *http://www.sixdaywar.co.uk/hidden_miracles.htm*
49   Gershon Gorenberg, *The End of Days: Fundamentalism and the Struggle for the Temple* Mount (New York: Free Press, 2000, updated 2002)
50   Irvin Baxter – *Prophetic Fulfillments Indicate Nearness of Second Coming*, End Time Magazine, Sept./Oct., 2015, p.4.
51   Irvin Baxter, *Red Heifer and Third Temple*, End Time Magazine, Sept. Oct. 2015, p. 13.
52   Ibid.
53   Ibid.
54   http://www.templeinstitute.org/vessels_gallery_16.htm
55   Irvin Baxter, *Prophetic Fulfillments Indicate Nearness of Second Coming.* End Time Magazine, Sept. Oct. Sept. Oct. 2015, p. 4
56   Women's Study Bible, Thomas Nelson Publishers, 1995, p. 1428.

› Chapter 7 Endnotes – Miracles in the Holy Land

57   J.R. Church, *Hidden Prophecies in the Psalms*, (Oklahoma City, Prophecy Publications, 1986), 72-73.
58   Ibid.
59   Ibid. 74.
60   Sitiveni Rabuka, *Divine Intervention*; http://www.fijitimes.com/story.aspx?id=104343
61   Ibid.
62   Lindsey, Hal, *Planet Earth, the Final Chapter* (Beverly Hills: Western Front, 1998), 20-21.
63   http://www.watchmanbiblestudy.com/Documents/IsraeliMiraclesGod.htm
64   Ibid.
65   A.N. Dugger, *Six Day War,* http://www.watchmanbiblestudy.com/Documents/IsraeliMiraclesGod.htm
66   Sitiveni Rabuka, http://tandi-1964.blogspot.com/2009/11/divine-intervention.html
67   Ibid.
68   Jerry Klinger, http://www.jewishmag.com/167mag/kissinger-nixon-war-watergate/kissinger- nix-on-war-watergate.htm.
69   Alan Greenspan, Against All Odds TV Program
70   http://www.jewishmag.com/167mag/kissinger-nixon-war-watergate/kissinger-nixon-war-watergate.htm
71   Greenspan, Ibid.
72   Ibid.
73   Jerry Klinger, Ibid.
74   http://www.scribd.com/doc/58026067/Miracles-in-Israel-during-the-Gulf-War-of-1991#scribd
75   www.benmelech.org
76   Ibid.
77   Ibid.
78   Ibid.

79   Ibid.
80   www. chabad.org
81   Dr. Renald E. Showers, *The Coming Apocalypse*, Bellmawr, NJ, 2009, 60.

› Chapter 8 Endnotes – Glory of the Lord

82   Alfred Endershim, D.D. PhD, *The Temple, Its Ministry and Services*, Grand Rapids: Wm. Eerdman Publishing Company, 1992, 61.
83   Alexander Jones, Ed., *The Jerusalem Bible*, Garden City, NY, Doubleday and Co. Inc. 1966, p. 695.

› Chapter 9 Endnotes – Battle of Gog and Magog Endnotes

84   Hal Lindsey, Apocalypse Code, (Palos Verges: Western Front Ltd, 1997), 80.
85   Paul Boyer (1992). *When Time Shall Be No More*. Belknap Press of Harvard University, 162.
86   J. Vernon McGee, *Thru the Bible with J. Vernon McGee*, Vol. 3 (Nashville: Thomas Nelson Publishers, 1982), 514-515.
87   Dr. Renald E. Showers, *The Coming Apocalypse*, Friends of Israel Gospel Ministry, Bellmawr, 2009, 102.
88   Ron Rhodes, Northern Storm Rising, (Eugene: Harvest House Publishers, 2008), 102.
89   Jimmy DeYoung, John Ankerberg TV Show, Day Star, 9-13-2011.
90   Showers, Ibid.
91   Mike Evans, *Jerusalem Betrayed*, (Dallas: Word Publishing, 1997), 275
92   Salah Uddin Shoaib Choudhury - http:www.asiantribune.com/index.php?q=node/211
93   *Israel Strikes Oil Deposit*, Israel NationalNews.com, May 6, 2004.
94   Joel Rosenberg, *Epicenter* (Carol Stream: IL: Tyndale, 2006), 63
95   Arnold Fruchtenbaum, *Footsteps of the Messiah* (San Antonio: Ariel, 2006), 111-112.
96   Ron Rhodes, 103.

› Chapter 10 Endnotes - Blessings or Curses

97   http://hallindsey.org/index.php?option=com_content&task=view&id=237&Itemid=56
98   John Phillips, *Exploring the World of the Jews* (Chicago: Moody Press, 1988), 128l.
99   http://www.shema.com/CombatingReplacementTheology/crt-000.php
100 http://www.bdsmovement.net/make-an-impact
101 William Koenig, *Eye to Eye – Facing the Consequences of Dividing Israel* (Alexandria: 2004), 301.
102 Thomas S. McCall, Th.D – Israel: The Center of Divine History,
        http://www.levitt.com/essays/dh.html.
103 Nicole Winfield – The Associated Press- *Pope calls Palestinian leader 'angel of peace'*
        http://news.yahoo.com/pope-calls-palestinian-leader-angel-peace-during-visit.
104 Palestinian Incitement to Terror, Flame http://factsandlogic.org/ad_154/
105 Ibid.
106 John Hagee, *In Defense of Israel* (Lake Mary: FrontLine, a Strang Company, 2007).
107 John P. McTernan, As America Has Done To Israel, (Whitaker House, 2008) 95.
108 http://hallindsey.org/index.php?option=com_content&task=view&id=237&Itemid=56
109 Ibid.
110 Michael D. Evans, *The American Prophecies* (New York: Time Warner Books, 2004), p. 14.
111 Ibid.
112 Salad Uddin Shoaib Choudbury - http://www.asiantribune.com/index.php?q=node/211
113 Spanish Writer Sebastian Vilar Rodrigez, All European Life Died in Auschwitz- 1-15-2008.
114 Hal Lindsey, I Will Bless Them That Bless Thee.

› Chapter 11 Endnotes - Ten Reasons to Support Israel

115 George W. Bush comments at the American Jewish Committee's Centennial Dinner, on May 4, 2006.
116 Lance Lambert, *Israel, The Unique Land- The Unique People*, (Wheaton, Tyndale Publishers, 1981), 73.
117 Dore Gold and Jeff Helmreich, An Answer to the New Anti-Zionists: *The Rights of the Jewish People to a*

Sovereign State in their Historic Homeland (Jerusalem Viewpoints- No. 507, 21 Heshvan 5764- Nov. 16, 2003.

118 U.S. Senator James M. Inhofe from Oklahoma, *Peace in the Middle East*, Senate Floor Statement, March 4, 2002.

119 Jennifer Rosenberg, What Does Holocaust Mean? http://history1900s.about.com/od/holocaust/a/holocaustfacts.htm

120 John Phillip, *Exploring the World of the Jews* (Chicago: Moody Press, 1988), 128.

121 U.S. Senator James M. Inhofe, Ibid.

122 *Gerardo Joffe, Some of Israel's Accomplishments,* Facts and Logic about the Middle East, Joint Action Taskforce, July 8, 2004.

123 Ibid.

124 Farid Ghadry, *Why I Admire Israel*, Facts and Logic about the Middle East, 8-7-2007.

125 http://judaism about.com/ad/americanjewry/a/accomplishments.htm

126 David Allen Lewis, Israel and the USA: *Restoring the Lost Pages of American History: The Story of Haym Solomon, Forgotten Patriot* (Springfield, MO: Menorah Press, 93), 3-10.

127 Ibid.

128 Vendyl Jones, *Will the Real Jesus Please Stand?* (Tyler, TX: Priority Publishing, Institute of Judaic-Christian Research, 1983), 220-28

129 Efraim Inbar, *Israel Remains America's Irreplaceable Ally*, Jerusalem Post, Israel, Oct. 6, 2006.

130 U.S. Senator James M. Inhofe, Ibid.

131 Yitzhak Benhorin – *Most Americans support Israel* , Israel News Poll, February 14-2006, http://www.ynetnews.com/articles/0,7340,L-3215863,00.html

132 Kade Hawkins, Prophecy News Watch Headlines, January 9, 2009, http://us.f818.mail.yahoo.com/ym/showletter. .

133 *Why do Christians Support Israel?* FLAME, April 28, 2007.

134 Ibid.

135 Thomas S. McCall, Th.D – *Israel: The Center of Divine History,* p.16.

136 Ibid.

137 Ibid.

138 Farid Ghadry, Flame, Ibid.

139 Pat Robertson, *Why Evangelical Christians Support Israel*, The Herzliya Conference, Lauder School of Government, Diplomacy, and Strategy, December 17, 2003

140 Dennis Lindsey, *Israel: The Nation of Destiny*, (Maoz Israel Report, Aug. 2007), p. 1.

141 John Hagee's Speech at the American Israel Public Affairs Conference.

142 Pat Robertson, *Evangelical Christians Support Israel* - The Herzliya Conference, Dec. 18, 2003.

143 Chapter 12 Endnotes- Prophetic Signs of Perilous Times Darrell G. Young, http://www.focusonjerusalem.com/periloustimesshallcome.html

144 Patrick J. Buchanan, The Death of the West (New York, NY: Thomas Dunne Books, 2002, 28).

145 How Porn is Strangling Men Across the Nation, Charisma Magazine, February 2016, p.35.

146 Ibid.

147 Dan Stolebarger, The Piece Process - http://www.khouse.org/articles/2011/1006

148 Sarah Fowler, *Abortion is Leading Cause of Death*, 10-23-2013, http://flfamily.org.

149 Grant R. Jeffrey, *Final Warning*, (Eugene: Harvest House Publishers, 1999). 281.

150 Pat Robertson, *What's the Fastest Growing Criminal Industry Today?* 700 Club, 7-25-2012.

151 http://www.sentencingproject.org/template/page.cfm?id=107

152 *2002 Guinness Book of World Records, p. 111*

153 Liz Sly, "*Al-Qaeda Disavows Any Ties with Radical Islamist ISIS Group in Syria, Iraq*, Washington Post, Feb. 3:2013.

154 Jay Sekulow, *Rise of ISIS*, Howard Books, A Division of Simon & Schuster, New York, 2015) 7.

155 Janine Di Giovanni and Conor Gaffey – The Exodus – Christians Fleeing the Middle East http://www.newsweek.com/2015/04/03/new-exodus-christians-flee-isis-middle-east-316785.html

156 Engun Mehmet and Emir Fethi Caner, *Unveiling Islam* (Grand Rapids, Kregel Pub.), 15, 16.

〉 Chapter 13 Endnotes - Prophetic Signs in the Heavens

157 John MacArthur, Author and General Editor, The MacArthur Study Bible, Revised and Updated Edi-

tion, Nashville, Thomas Nelson Pub., 1997, 18.

158 Perry Stone, Three Religions that Believe the Earth will Shake in the End Time. (Voice of Evangelism, March- April 2010), p. 21.

159 Ibid.

160 Ibid.

161 Joel Richardson said on Sid Roth TV Show

162 http://beforeitsnews.com/prophecy/2015/06/the-bethlehem-star-is-returning-today-june-30th-2015-2470466.html

163   http://www.prophecynewswatch.com

164 David Lev, Lunar Eclipse on Shabbat Will Be Visible from Israel http://www.israelnationalnews.com/News/News.aspx/150530#.VbMVpZt0xD8

165 Mark Biltz, Blood Moons, WND Books, Washington, D.C. 2014, 31.

166 Ibid.

167 John Hagee, Four Blood Moons, Worthy Publishing, Brentwood, TN, 2013, 224.

168 http://corsicaministries.org/meaning-mystery-four-blood-moons

❯ Chapter 14 Endnotes – Compare Christianity, Judaism and Islam

169 John Hagee, *The Battle for Jerusalem* (Nashville: Thomas Nelson Pub. 2001), 35.

170 Ibid.

171 http: www.ask.com/world-view/leader-islam-53c1843c20577f17

172 Professor Moshe Sharon in a speech presented at International Christian Embassy in Jerusalem: *Understanding the Language of Islam* (Moaz Israel Report, February 2002), 5.

173 John Hagee, *Jerusalem Countdown, A Warning to the World*, (Lake Mary: Front Line, 2006), 35.

174 Ibid.

175 *Iran leader's messianic s mission*; http://wind.com/news/article.

176 Professor Moshe Sharon's Speech, 6.

177 Jeffery L. Sheler, *Hell Hath No Fury*, U.S. News and World Report article, January 31, 2000), 48.

178 Lisa Miller, *Why We Need Heaven*, Article in Newsweek Magazine, Aug. 12, 2002), 48.

179 Grant Jeffrey, *Heaven, the Mystery of Angels*, (Toronto: Frontier Research Pub., 1996), 95.

180 Ibid.

❯ Chapter 15 Endnotes – God's Prophetic Time Table

181 http://www.raystedman.org/old-testament/daniel/gods-countdown

182 Grant R. Jeffrey, Final *Warning, Economic Collapse and the Coming World Government* (Toronto: Frontier Research), 13.

183 http://www.raystedman.org/old-testament/daniel/gods-countdown

184 Dr. Mike Evans, The Prince of Peace vs. the Prince Who is to Come – Friends of Zion, December 2013 Magazine, p. 19.

185 Hal Lindsey, *Planet Earth, The Final Chapter* (Beverly Hills: Western Front LTD. 1998) 77-80.

186 Sir Robert Anderson, *The Coming Prince*, Kregel Publications, Grand Rapids, 1984, 67, 68.

187 David Jeremiah with C.C. Carlson, *The Handwriting on the Wall, Secrets from the Prophecies of Daniel*, (Dallas: Word Publishing, 1991), 186.

❯ Chapter 16 Endnotes– Pre-Tribulation Rapture: Fact or Fallacy

188 Writers of the Early Church Fathers – The Didache –110 A.D. http://www.freeworldfilmworks.com/when-chap05.pdf

189 Ibid.

190 Ibid.

191 Dr. William R. Crews, *Will the Church Pass Through the Tribulation?* www.theawakeninghour.org

192 George Eldon Ladd, *The Blessed Hope* (Grand Rapids, William Eerdmans Pub. Co., 1956) 62.

193 Ibid.

194 David R. Reagan, *The Lamplighter Magazine*, Vol. XXVIII, March -April, 2007, p. 17.

195 Thompson Chain Reference Bible, J.B. Kirkbride Bible Co., Indianapolis, Indiana, 1964.

196 *William J. Cadigan, CNN – Christian Persecution Reached Record High in 2015- http://www.cnn. com/2016/01/17/world/christian-persecution-2015/index.html*

197 Ibid.

198 Engun Mehmet and Emir Fethi Caner, *Unveiling Islam* (Grand Rapids, Kregel Publications), 15- 16.

199 Bob Unruh, World Net Daily.com, May 31, 2007.

200 Mark Finley, *Revelation's Predictions for a New Millennium*, Fallbrook, Hart Books, 2000), 111

201 Ibid.

202 http://www.tedmontgomery.com/bblovrvw/Rapture/ruth.html

203 Jonathan Cahn, *How America Can Avoid Calamity*, Charisma Magazine – May 2015, 41. http://www. charismanews.com/opinion/49503-jonathan-cahn-how-america-can-avoid-calamity.

> Chapter 17 Endnotes– The Antichrist and False Prophet

204 Arthur W. Pink – Results of the Redeemer's Reign – Internet Software

205 Pat Robertson, Spirit Filled Bible, 2001.

206 Arthur W. Pink, *The Antichrist*, Internet Software, p.18.

207 Pat Robertson, Spiritual Answers to Hard Questions – Spirit Filled Bible, 2001.

208 David R. Reagan, The Symbol 666 - http://www.lamblion.com/articles/articles_revelation14.php

209 Ibid.

210 Ibid.

211 Paul Crouch, *Shadow of the Apocalypse* (New York: Berkley Books, 2004), 101.

212 Ibid, 216.

213 Ibid, 216.

214 http://www.ask.com/history/countries-were-roman-empire-bb0b32370f9fe987

> Chapter 18 Endnotes- Four Horsemen of the Apocalypse

215 Jack E. Hayford, *E Quake* (Nashville, Thomas Nelson Publishers, 1999) 170.

216 Warren W. Wiersbe, Be Victorious, David C. Cook Publishers, 1985, 79.

217 Joel K. Bourne, Jr. *Our Hot and Hungry World Could Face A Perpetual Food Crises*, National Geographic, June, 2009, p. 38.

218 Irvin Baxter, *Behold, A Pale Horse*, (Endtime Magazine, Jan. Feb. 2000), 8.

219 Ibid., 8

220 Warren Wiersbe, p. 81.

221 Liz Sly, "*Al-Qaeda Disavows Any Ties with Radical Islamist ISIS Group in Syria, Iraq*, Washington Post, Feb. 3, 2013.

222 Jay Sekulow, *Rise of ISIS*, Howard Books, A Division of Simon & Schuster, New York, 2015), p 8.

223 http://www.inquisitr.com/2566962/isis-headquarters-in-iraq-destroyed-just-hours-after-paris-terror-ist-attack-250-militants-killed.

224 Wiersbe, p. 81.

> Chapter 20 Endnotes – Importance of the Resurrection

225 George Eldon Ladd, The Blessed Hope (Grand Rapids: Wm. B. Eerdman Pub., 1956), 80.

226 2 Corinthians 5:1-10 TLB

227 Hank Hanegraff, *Resurrection* (Nashville: Word Publisher, 2000) 87.

> Chapter 21 Endnotes – Glorious Return of the Messiah Grant R. Jeffrey, Triumphant Return, (Toronto: Frontier Research Pub., 2001) p. 202.

228 David Jeremiah, *Jesus' Final Warning* (Nashville, TN: Word Pub., 1999) pp. 81-82.

229 Arthur W. Pink, *The Redeemer's Return* (Swengel, PA; Bible Truth Depot, 1918), 386-387.
230 Jeffrey, 10
231 Lydia Prince, Appointment in Jerusalem, Old Tappen, NJ: Chosen Books with Derek Prince, 184.
232 Ibid., 185f
233 John Hagee, *His Glory Revealed*, (Nashville: Thomas Nelson Publishers, 1999), 18, 19.
234 Ibid.
235 Ibid.
236 Pink, 385

› Chapter 22 Endnotes - Thousand Years of Peace

237 Dr. David Jeremiah, *Escape the Coming Night*, Vol. 4 (San Diego: Turning Point, 1994), 47.
238 Arthur W. Pink, and Luther C. Peak, *The Golden Age: A Treatise on the One Thousand Year Reign of Christ on Earth* (Dallas: The Evangelist Press, 1960), 16.
239 Jeremiah, 47
240 Ibid. 47.
241 Arthur W. Pink, and Luther C. Peak, *The Golden Age: A Treatise on the One Thousand Year Reign of Christ on Earth* (Dallas: The Evangelist Press, 1960), 381.

› Chapter 23 Endnotes - New Jerusalem, City of God

242 Warren W. Wiersbe, *Be Victorious*, David C. Cook, Colorado Springs, 1985, 179.
243 J. Vernon McGee, *Thru the Bible with J. Vernon McKee*, Vol. 5, Pasadena: Thru the Bible Radio 1983, 1070.
244 Barclay, William, *The Revelation of John,* Daily Study Bible Series, Vol. 2, Westminster Press, Philadelphia, PA, p. 214-215.
245 McGee, 1071.
246 Ibid. 1071.
247 Ibid. 1071.
248 Ibid. 1072.
249 Randy Alcorn, *HEAVEN* (Carol Stream, IL; Tyndale House Publishers, Inc., 2004, 78.

› Chapter 24 - Final Judgment

250 Randy Alcorn, *Heaven*: (Carol Stream: Tyndale Pub. 2004), p. xix.
251 Rex Humbard, *Where are the Dead*, (Rex Humbard World Outreach Ministry, 1977), 66.
252 Ibid.
253 Ibid. 67.
254 Nelson Illustrated Bible Software, Thomas Nelson Publishers, 1986.
255 Warren W. Wiersbe, Be Victorious (David C. Cook, Colorado Springs, 1985), 176.
256 Herbert Lockyer, Edited by Herbert Lockyer, Jr. *All about the Second Coming* (Peabody: Hendrickson Pub., 1997), 182-183.
257 Ibid. 183.
258 Warren W. Wiersbe, Be Victorious (David C. Cook, Colorado Springs, 1985), 176.
259 Lockyer, 183.
260 Lockyer, 184.
261 Women's Study Bible, Thomas Nelson, 1995, p. 2080.

› Chapter 25 Endnotes - Horrows of Eternal Hell

262 Randy Alcorn, *Heaven* (Carol Stream: Tyndale House Publishers, Inc., 2004), 28.
263 Mark Rutland, *What Can We Know About Hell*? Charisma Magazine, June 1993, p. 21.
264 Ibid.
265 Jeffery L. Sheler, *Hell Hath No Fury*, U. S. News and World Report, Jan. 31, 2000, 48.
266 Ibid.
267 Rex Humbard, *Where are the Dead*? (Akron: Rex Humbard Outreach Ministry, 1977), 40.

268 John MacArthur, http://www.biblebb.com/files/mac/sg2304.htm.

269 Ibid.

270 Robert Morris, Gateway Church, Sermon on Hell

> Chapter 26 Endnotes - Wonders of Heaven

271 Randy Alcorn, *Heaven,* (Carol Stream, Tyndale House Publishers, Inc., 2004), 27.

272 Address by Billy Graham in Moscow, 1982.

273 Alcorn, 27.

274 D.L. Moody, http://users.belgacom.net/gc674645/prose/heavquot.htm

275 Alcorn, 78.